A PRACTICAL CASEBOOK OF
TIME-LIMITED PSYCHOANALYTIC WORK

Modern Kleinian Therapy is a model of effective psychoanalytic work that offers relief to deep internal conflicts by establishing and maintaining analytic contact, and beginning to unravel, modify and heal turbulent and torn minds. This book defines Modern Kleinian Therapy as a modality for treating severely affected patients in a fairly traditional psychoanalytic manner, even when the environment or frequency of sessions is compromised.

Chapter by chapter, the book provides detailed clinical material to illustrate the complex dynamics that unfold when working with more closed off patients, and each case report shows the often limited clinical situations that the contemporary analyst must contend with. The book's detailed material serves to emphasize the nature of psychoanalytic work with individuals and couples, who otherwise rarely find their way to healthy attachment or reciprocal whole object relational harmony. Included in the book:

- technical and theoretical methods of Modern Kleinian Therapy
- psychoanalytic treatments to modify internal object relational conflicts
- the Modern Kleinian Therapy approach to couples treatment
- the value of analytic contact.

A Practical Casebook of Time-Limited Psychoanalytic Work: A Modern Kleinian Approach introduces new aspects of Kleinian work and offers a contemporary view on Kleinian techniques and concepts. It will be valuable reading for psychotherapists, mental health workers and psychoanalytic therapists.

Robert Waska is a graduate of the Institute for Psychoanalytic Studies, an International Psychoanalytical Association affiliate organization. He runs a psychoanalytic practice for individuals and couples in San Francisco and Marin County, California, USA.

A PRACTICAL CASEBOOK OF TIME-LIMITED PSYCHOANALYTIC WORK

A Modern Kleinian approach

Robert Waska

Routledge
Taylor & Francis Group

LONDON AND NEW YORK

First published 2013
by Routledge
27 Church Road, Hove, East Sussex, BN3 2FA

Simultaneously published in the USA and Canada
by Routledge
711 Third Avenue, New York, NY 10017

Routledge is an imprint of the Taylor & Francis Group, an informa business

© 2013 Robert Waska

British Library Cataloguing in Publication Data
A catalogue record for this book is available from the British Library

Library of Congress Cataloguing in Publication Data
Waska, Robert T.
A practical casebook for time-limited psychoanalytic work : a modern
Kleinian approach / Robert Waska.
pages cm
Includes bibliographical references.
1. Brief psychotherapy--Handbooks, manuals, etc. 2. Psychoanalysis--
Handbooks, manuals, etc. 3. Klein, Melanie. I. Title.
RC480.55.W38 2013
616.89'17--dc23
2012043935

ISBN: 978-0-415-81745-5 (hbk)
ISBN: 978-0-415-81746-2 (pbk)
ISBN: 978-0-203-38316-2 (ebk)

Typeset in Garamond
by Saxon Graphics Ltd, Derby

CONTENTS

PREFACE

Modern Kleinian Therapy is a contemporary hybrid of classical Kleinian psychoanalytic technique and a clinical approach to working with the more disturbed or complicated patient in a private practice setting under less than optimal conditions. Modern Kleinian Therapy uses a psychoanalytic focus to understand and work with both internal resistances and external roadblocks to psychological integration. External obstacles include various restrictions from insurance companies and third party agencies involved in the treatment; limited numbers of sessions available and/or a enforced termination date; a more severe or complex diagnosis; and, most often, a reduced frequency.

In the outpatient setting, most psychoanalysts and psychotherapists in 2012 are rarely seeing patients 4–5 times a week on the couch. It is much more common to be seeing individuals 1–2 times a week or couples 1–2 times a week (Cherry et al 2004; Waska 2005). Typically, our patients have been in a marked state of distress for quite some time before entering treatment and often have some current external crisis going on. The treatment profile is often quite messy from the start, with optimal frequency usually unavailable. There is immediate acting out in various degrees and forms, creating a lack of stability in the overall therapeutic frame, psychological states of mind that are fragmented and fragile, and the severe or exclusive use of splitting and projective identification in the transference. The external crisis or chronic external troubles these patients bring with them create realistic obstacles to much needed deeper exploration but also serve as challenging defensive retreats for the patients to find refuge and control in when they are reluctant to join the analyst in looking at their lives in a deeper or broader manner.

Clinically, we see many patients who tend to quickly subsume us and whatever we do or say into their pathological organization (Spillius 1988) with its familiar cast of internal characters. Modern Kleinian Therapy focuses on the interpretation of this particular transference process by investigating the unconscious phantasy conflicts at play and highlighting the more direct moment-to-moment transference usually mobilized by projective identification dynamics. Bion's (1962a) ideas regarding the interpersonal aspects of projective identification, the idea of projective identification as the foundation of most transference states (Waska 2010a, 2010b, 2010c), and the concept of projective identification as the first line of defense against psychic loss (Waska 2002, 2010d), difference, or separation all form the theoretical base of my clinical approach. Taking theory into the clinical realm, I find interpreting the how and the why of the patient's phantasy conflicts in the here and now combined with linkage to original infantile experiences to be the best approach with such patients under these more limiting clinical situations.

In doing so, the main thrust of the analyst's observations and interpretations remains focused on the patient's efforts to disrupt the establishment of analytic contact (Waska 2007). We strive to move the patient into a new experience of clarity, vulnerability, reflection, independence, change, and choice. Analytic contact is defined as sustained periods of mutual existence between self and object not excessively colored by destructive aggression or destructive defense. These are moments between patient and analyst when the elements of love, hate, and knowledge as well as the life and death instincts are in "good enough" balance as to not fuel, enhance, or validate the patient's internal conflicts and phantasies in those very realms. These are new moments of contact between self and other, either in the mind of the patient or in the actual interpersonal realm between patient and analyst. Internal dynamics surrounding giving, taking, and learning as well as the parallel phantasies of being given to, having to relinquish, and being known are all elements that are usually severely out of psychic balance with these more challenging patients. Analytic contact is the moment in which analyst and patient achieve some degree of peace, stability, or integration in these areas.

So, analytic contact is the term for our constant quest or invitation to each patient for the found, allowed, and cultivated experiences that are new or less contaminated by the fossils of past internal drama, danger, and desire. These moments, in turn, provide for a chance of more lasting change, life, and difference or at least a consideration that these elements are possible and not poison. Paranoid (Klein 1946) and depressive (Klein 1935, 1940) anxieties tend to be stirred up as the patient's safe and controlled psychic equilibrium (Feldman and Spillius 1989) comes into question. Acting out, abrupt termination, intense resistance, and excessive reliance on projective identification are common and create easy blind spots and patterns of enactment for the analyst.

While there have been many compelling texts that demonstrate the theoretical and clinical aspects of Kleinian psychoanalysis with patients attending 5–6 times a week, there is almost no literature on the application of the regular Kleinian technique to difficult and disturbed patients only able or willing to attend once or twice a week (Waska 2006, 2011b). I will demonstrate with clinical material how there is no real need to modify the technique. However, in low frequency cases, certain aspects of pathology, of transference, and of defense become highlighted and heightened so certain aspects of technique must also be highlighted.

The Modern Kleinian Therapy approach is a clinical model of here-and-now, moment-to-moment focus on transference, counter-transference, and unconscious phantasy to assist difficult patients in low frequency therapy to notice, accept, understand, and resolve their unconscious self and object conflict states. Projective identification is often the cornerstone of the more complex transference state (Waska 2004) and therefore is the central target of therapeutic intervention and interpretation.

A good deal of patients being seen in today's private practice settings are mired in the primitive zone of paranoid and narcissistic functioning without access to the internal vision of a pleasurable object to merge with without catastrophe. These are patients who are using vigorous levels of defense against the more erotic, pleasurable, and connective elements of relationship just as they are massively defending against the fears of conflict, aggression, and growth. And, this is a state of psychic conflict so intense it may in some cases create psychic deficit.

While Modern Kleinian Therapy is fundamentally no different from the practice of Kleinian psychoanalysis, due to the limitations of reduced frequency, more severe pathology, and external blocks such as health insurance limitations and personal financial limitations, a greater flexibility is required in the overall treatment setting. Also, there is a greater need to notice the ongoing and immediate impact of unconscious phantasy, internal conflict, and transference that occurs in the analytic relationship. Careful monitoring of the counter-transference for the presence of projective identification based communication is an important Modern Kleinian Therapy technique. The importance of combining interpretations of current here-and-now transference and phantasy with occasional genetic links as a therapeutic hybrid approach is also a modification of sorts unique to Modern Kleinian Therapy. However, this is more a question of emphasis than a new or radical theoretical shift or unique technique.

Due to the specific pathology and conflict state these hard to reach and slow to thaw patients usually exist within, many cases fail, others prematurely end, and others terminate with only partial resolution. And, they often do not have the resources or motivation to attend 5-times-a-week psychoanalysis. However, I think these patients are helped in ways far superior to simple suggestion provided by behavioral therapy or counseling. So, the way of judging success is also something to consider.

Because of the lower frequency of treatment, many might call my model psychoanalytic psychotherapy. So, from that perspective, my approach is not radically new when you consider the vast offerings of psychoanalytic psychotherapy that exist today. Indeed, many psychoanalytic institutes do far more training in this area and have far more candidates for that than their training of classic, on the couch, 5–6-times-a-week psychoanalysis. Many articles, workshops, books, and classes have been available for many years now by well-known psychoanalysts who all advocate this low frequency approach.

Unfortunately, for many decades and still continuing, there has been a great deal of political and theoretical debate in the field of psychoanalysis about the differences between psychoanalysis, psychoanalytic psychotherapy, and supportive therapy. To this day, the debate is usually but wrongly simplified to defining everything as either "proper" psychoanalysis, watered down psychoanalysis combined with supportive techniques, or suggestive/supportive therapy.

There is the smaller group who see a place for psychoanalysis being practiced at a reduced frequency with or without the couch and it still being considered psychoanalysis. This was the stance of Merton Gill (1994) in his last book on the subject. I agree with this view. However, I am unique in practicing a Kleinian model from this theoretical vantage point and hence it is called Modern Kleinian Therapy. I use the word therapy to avoid the ongoing debate about analysis versus psychotherapy.

Modern Kleinian Therapy involves the establishment and maintenance of "analytic contact" (Waska 2007). This includes constantly looking for how both the analyst and the patient may try to deny, delay, decay, or destroy the intimacy, truthfulness, and vulnerability that analytic work creates, demands, and discovers.

Overall, I believe good, sound Kleinian psychoanalytic technique, as practiced both by classical Kleinians such as Hanna Segal and refined by contemporary Kleinians such as Betty Joseph and Michael Feldman, is transferable to low frequency cases, to couples therapy, and to work with more disturbed borderline, narcissistic, and psychotic patients.

Modern Kleinian Therapy is about working in this deep analytic fashion with the less than ideal patient population we all encounter these days. While the therapeutic result is often more messy, more complex, and prone to more enactments by the analyst, the work is still possible and often successful and transformative.

The counter-transference is more complicated and the patients often end treatment abruptly or prematurely with some remaining symptoms and conflicts. However, a great deal of change can be created for the external symptom profile the patient suffers with as well as a modest or sometimes profound change of his or her more fundamental internal psychic structure and the profound conflicts that exist within.

ACKNOWLEDGEMENTS

This book is only possible because of the special and privileged relationships I have with my patients. While every patient resists revealing and sharing him or herself in the unique space of the psychoanalytic setting, all patients do eventually reveal and express at least a small portion of what has previously been hidden, held hostage, or controlled. To let oneself, even for a moment, slip out of the emotional darkness and risk encountering the reality of the self, the other, and the world at large is an act of psychological bravery. So, I thank all my patients for the chance to be a part of that.

My wife, Elizabeth, is always beside me in my endeavors. I thank her for the consistent support and encouragement she so predictably offers. Emotionally, she is my coauthor.

Finally, I want to acknowledge *Other/Wise*, the Online Journal of the International Forum of Psychoanalytic Education for allowing me to reprint material in Chapter 1, the *Psychoanalytic Social Work* journal for allowing me to reprint the material in Chapter 5, the *International Forum of Psychoanalysis* for allowing me to reprint material in Chapter 6, the *Scandinavian Psychoanalytic Review* for allowing me to reprint material in Chapter 9, and the *American Journal of Psychotherapy* for allowing me to reprint material in Chapter 10.

Waska, R (2010) 'Stumbling Along in the Counter-Transference: Following Up Enactments with Balanced Therapeutic Interpretations'. *Psychoanalytic Social Work*, 17(2): 99–115.

Waska, R (2011) 'Catching my Balance in the Countertransference: Difficult Moments with Patients in Psychoanalytic Treatment'. *International Forum of Psychoanalysis*, 20(3): 167-175.

Waska, R (2011) 'The Limits of Our Value and the Value of Our Limits: Looking at What We Can Offer the More Turbulent Patient and Why That May Be Enough'. *Scandinavian Psychoanalytic Review*, 34(2): 77–85.

Waska, R (2012) 'Barely Here to Begin With and Not-So-Goodbyes: Keeping the Faith When Working with Turbulent Patients'. *American Journal of Psychotherapy*, 66(1): 23–44.

Waska, R (2012) 'Modern Kleinian Therapy and the Initial Psychoanalytic Interaction'. *Other/Wise, the Online Journal of the International Forum for Psychoanalytic Education*, Fall, Volume 8.

Waska, R (2012) 'How the Analytic Process is Captured and Absorbed into the Familiar, the Feared, and the Desired'. *Psychoanalytic/Review*, 99:5, 717–741.

INTRODUCTION

The start of a psychoanalytic treatment can be quite varied depending on the nature of the patient's phantasies, internal conflicts, their resulting transference and projective identification process, and the impact of these factors on the analyst's counter-transference. Chapter 1 presents the first twelve sessions of a Modern Kleinian Therapy treatment process. This material will show the reader how the unfolding transference and counter-transference are understood, and how important it is clinically to deal with the patient's phantasies and anxieties as soon as possible through the mode of interpretation, analytic observation, and containment. This extensive case report demonstrates the Modern Kleinian technique of working with difficult cases in whatever setting, frequency, and situation they present.

Chapter 2 continues to illustrate the Modern Kleinian Therapy approach by following one case of weekly treatment with a patient suffering from a chronic sense of abandonment as well as a drinking problem. Modern Kleinian Therapy is shown to encompass the essential elements of contemporary Kleinian psychoanalysis with accommodation for the additional transference and counter-transference difficulties presented by infrequent sessions and lack of analytic couch. The material shows how the same focus on unconscious phantasy and internal object relational conflict can produce the same integration and psychological healing as a more frequent and intensive treatment.

Melanie Klein concentrated her psychoanalytic theory and clinical focus on the intense unconscious object relational struggles that begin in childhood and spread throughout the adult's internal and external life experiences. As Salzberger-Wittenberg (1970) notes, these deeply rooted conflicts with love, hate, and knowledge lead to either hopeful or frightening phantasies that create a vicious cycle of seeking out, expecting, or demanding the very thing we fear or avoiding the very thing we desire. These are either paranoid-schizoid (Klein 1946) or depressive (Klein 1935, 1940) patterns of perceiving the self and object. Chapter 2 follows the details of a Modern Kleinian Therapy treatment with a patient who felt trapped by the helpless, hopeless, and guilt ridden elements of a severe depressive state that led to destructive acting out including fits of rage, desperation, and alcoholic drinking.

1

The patient dreaded the idea of being left alone and of feeling not wanted, but also felt extremely anxious about leaving the object alone without enough love and attention. Grotstein (2009) notes how through projective identification, the infant or child puts his own pain, despair, and rage of being neglected into the object and then either has to rescue, avoid, or placate that bad object. This was a primary internal conflict for my patient that in turn came alive in the transference and counter-transference. The initial twenty sessions of weekly Modern Kleinian Therapy are described in great detail to show the effectiveness of this approach and its capacity to provide deep and important structural change.

In Chapter 3, the initial therapeutic encounter is examined once again to outline the technical and theoretical methods of Modern Kleinian Therapy; a psychoanalytic treatment modality for patients attending once or twice a week with or without use of the analytic couch. The case material demonstrates how this Kleinian method is identical to a more typical 4–5 times weekly psychoanalysis. However, because the transference and counter-transference will be more difficult and complex due to the reduced frequency, sharper scrutiny of elements such as phantasy, defense, here-and-now transference interaction, projective identification, and enactments is necessary. The value placed on the working through of transference and phantasy is the same but often requires more rigorous examination because the transference in low frequency treatments is much harder to locate and utilize.

The case material in Chapter 3 follows one patient who struggled with paranoid-schizoid pathology that left him in a precarious position at work, home, school, and in the world at large. He suffered the lasting internal and external effects of a traumatic childhood and resurrected these conflicts in his adult life through intense projective processes. While the period of treatment examined was brief and only the initial phase of therapeutic action, the material nevertheless establishes how analytic contact was made in moment-to-moment clinical interactions and how the patient's unconscious conflicts were worked with to provide the start of a gradual shift in how he perceived and related to himself and others.

Chapter 4 continues to examine the Modern Kleinian Therapy approach by examining a couples treatment process in close detail. In particular, this chapter follows the slippery and complicated climate that exists in the early phase of work with turbulent, hard to reach, and emotionally combative couples. It is not unusual for these reactive and difficult cases to abort or terminate abruptly. So, the cases presented in this chapter did in fact come to an early, sudden, and negative outcome. However, some progress was made along the way and analytic contact was established in random moments before being eroded and lost. Striving to establish analytic contact is part of a constant dual track in practicing intensive analytic work. While attempting to help the patient, we must always be struggling to accept the many failures and almost but not quite outcomes that come with the territory of standing in the trenches with people at their most vulnerable and most chaotic internal moments.

In Chapter 5, the case material allows the reader to become familiar with the many clinical situations in psychoanalytic treatment that create counter-transference pulls or invitations on the analyst to participate in enactments of varying degrees. In these projective identification based transferences, the patient is often successful in drawing the analyst into archaic object relational patterns of acting out. During these moments, the analyst must struggle to find a way to stay therapeutically balanced. The urge to rush to judgment with punitive, seductive, rejecting, controlling, or manipulative comments rationalized as interpretations must be managed. If these unavoidable counter-transference enactments are isolated and studied, they can provide useful information about the patient's internal struggles. They show the way to making more helpful and more therapeutic interpretations.

In Chapter 6, the author uses case material to explore psychoanalytic treatments in which troubled patients are helped to access, understand, and modify their internal object relational conflicts. However, due to the extensive and chronic nature of their struggles with love, hate, and knowledge, these patients often abort treatment early on or exit after a lengthy stay in a manner that speaks to their remaining repetitive pathology. These common situations are easily dismissed as failed analytic treatments, unfinished or unrealized cases, or devalued as "only psychotherapy". However, the author argues that the contemporary psychoanalyst encounters many such cases of rigid, turbulent, and slow to thaw individuals who show considerable intrapsychic progress paralleled by external improvements after either a short stay or a long period of analytic work. However, these same patients also tend to leave abruptly or simply fade away without a sense of great accomplishment or a marked transition into a new way of being. Rather than see this as a failure, the author seeks to understand these particular cases as inevitable works in progress that show transformation but also remain in partial embrace with the old, the familiar, and the destructive.

As Aronson and Scharfman (1992) and others have noted, today's psychoanalyst does much more psychotherapy than psychoanalysis. Modern Kleinian Therapy is founded upon the clinical tenant that the psychoanalytic procedure can be the same and offer the same benefit, regardless of frequency, diagnosis, or duration of sessions. The goal remains the establishment of analytic contact (Waska 2007, 2011a, 2011b). But, the reality of psychoanalytic practice today is that most patients are seen once a week or as couples (Carey 2002).

So, Chapter 7 will examine the Modern Kleinian Therapy approach to couples treatment and in particular the slippery and complicated climate that exists in the early phase of work with turbulent, hard to reach, and chaotic couples. It is not unusual for these reactive and difficult cases to abort or terminate abruptly. Therefore, one case will be presented that did come to an early, sudden, and negative outcome. However, some progress was made along the way and analytic contact was established in random moments before being eroded and lost.

In Chapter 8, the psychoanalytic approach of Modern Kleinian Therapy continues to be illustrated with extensive case material. In addition, the idea of sustained or embedded enactments is introduced. While much has been written recently about enactments, from both Kleinian and other viewpoints, enactments are usually conceptualized as brief, transitory, or fleeting. And, for the most part, they are thought of as intense moments in which the analyst slips into counter-transference acting out that is at a later time noticed, understood, and used as helpful information about the patient's object relational struggles.

Embedded enactments are more enduring and ongoing psychological dynamics between patient and analyst. They come out of a specific transference profile that the analyst becomes ensnared in. The embedded enactment is at its core the patient's essential unconscious phantasy regarding self and other that becomes played out through excessive reliance on projective identification. The analyst must continuously interpret this transference pattern, but this task can be very problematic and confusing as the embedded enactment process usually occurs at the same time as the interpretation takes place. Unlike fleeting or momentary enactments where the analyst can step back and reflect and at a later time make a helpful interpretation, these are strong projective identification mechanisms that pull the analyst into sustained states of mind and the counter-transference acting out is ongoing. And, this cobweb of psychic and interpersonal interaction is not halted or radically reduced when accurate and useful interpretations about the patient's transference are made. Rather, it is a long, strenuous, and recycling process of shaving down the projective pathology over time as the enactment process slowly declines and the patient slowly allows new thoughts and feelings to exist within a formally fixed and unyielding mental system.

If the analyst can find a way to not act out too severely and can be alert enough to this embedded mutuality to keep interpreting it even under the counter-transference sense of failure or impatience, a gradual reduction of the patient's anxiety and core pathology will result in parallel to a reduction of the analyst's acting out. It is a strenuous process for the analyst as he or she is subjected to a "here we go again" experience throughout the treatment. But, instead, the analyst must hold back from feeling like a failure or from forcing rapid fire "hurry up and change" confrontations into the patient. Instead, the analyst must realize there is a need for this mutual playing out of core unconscious conflicts in the transference/counter-transference as the interpretive work goes on. With that realization or insight on the analyst's side, there can be a hope of purpose, not just an aimless repetition of pathology. The analyst can be of help in a long and dark night that will eventually find the light of day.

One extensive case that was rocky, unconventional, and difficult will be used to illustrate both the Modern Kleinian Therapy method and the complicated and confusing periods of transference that create, compromise, and maintain the thorny and unshakable nature of enactment that occurs in these "embedded" situations of projective identification based conflict.

Chapters 9 and 10 continue this examination of analytic work with patients who are slower to emotionally thaw. While some patients are unable or unwilling to step into the difficult and uncharted explorations that psychoanalytic work entails, the author shows how the effort to establish analytic contact with each individual can pay off and provide a level of valuable support, containment, and growth for many patients. Such patients may display great resistance to the challenge of psychoanalytic treatment, subtly herding or coaxing the analyst through projective identification processes to succumb to specific counter-transference acting out. These may be motivated by a desire to master and learn, a need to communicate and relate, or more evacuative, predatory, or destructive urges.

These turbulent patients often leave treatment under very abrupt and unprocessed circumstances. It is suddenly all over and that is that. This is usually a continuation of their remaining pathology and conflictual phantasies that have played out in the transference throughout the length of the analytic process. The analyst cannot always prevent this. Rather than see it as a complete failure, we can try to maintain ourselves within the depressive position to realize we are being used as a provisional therapeutic and psychological placeholder or temporary container for the patient. This is a model of grieving in which we acknowledge and accept what we cannot have, what we are not, and what should be but is not. Struggling with these issues in the counter-transference is critical for our ability to help such patients since these are exactly the issues they cannot bear at this point in their lives. If we cannot bear them, the patient has no hope of ever surviving them.

In Chapter 11, the author presents material from two Modern Kleinian Therapy treatments in which there were only brief and ultimately unsustainable moments of analytic contact. The first case, of a couple, was chaotic, brief, and explosive with the case terminating unfavorably early on. The second case of an individual was much more successful but also ended abruptly, with acting out a noticeable aspect of the transference. The two cases are presented to showcase the often fragile, confusing, and slippery relationships patients bring to us and engage us within.

Issues of perverse use of the analyst container, resistance to the grief and loss of giving up the projections evacuated into the analyst, and no longer relying on manic independence or parasitic dependence are all issues that bring up unbearable anxiety over separation, individuation, trust, and control. Without the willingness to re-own toxic projections and gradually serve as one's own personal container, there is a quick possession and rejection of the container analyst in these difficult and sometimes impossible treatment situations.

While not often written about, the author believes these types of clinical disappointments, modest victories, and unsurprising failures are common in day-to-day private practice. Practicing from a Modern Kleinian Therapy perspective, the author shares these rocky moments as a way to learn about the delicate and formidable work the contemporary analyst faces when faced with the more overwhelming and resistant aspects of projective identification.

In their transference efforts to maintain psychic equilibrium (Joseph 1989), some patients will do their best to convert us into familiar, dreaded, or desired internal objects that they then react to or relate to. The interpersonal, interactional, and intrapsychic pull for the absorption and utilization of the analyst into a predesigned and pathologically limited figure creates counter-transference struggles and phases of enactment that can go unnoticed, denied, or justified. Even when we maintain our analytic balance, the patient can manipulate, mishear, and transform our words, actions, and intentions into very specific archaic objects or part objects.

In Chapter 12, case material is used to illustrate the way in which patients attempt to turn the analytic process and the therapeutic relationship into an acting out of wished for or painfully familiar self and object interactions. This method of subsuming the analytic method can be quite subtle or it can be very obvious but still extremely difficult to shift, interpret, or recover from. Indeed, the analyst can easily be drawn into this perversion of analytic procedure and end up participating in various enactments.

In Chapter 13, the author uses case material to show how in working with patients from a Modern Kleinian Therapy perspective, the analyst does his best to concentrate on the elements of transference and counter-transference as well as how these two dynamics are being shaped by the patient's reliance on projective identification. Especially with the harder to reach, more turbulent patient who suffers from either more paranoid or more primitive depressive conflicts, there will be ongoing intrapsychic and interpersonal cycles of invitation, enlistment, and psychological kidnap that may create enactments from the analyst that parallel acting out by the patient. In this complicated push/pull relational chaos, the patient will be systematically giving aspects of their mind to the analyst in forceful or loving ways. In that process, the analyst will feel depleted or changed in a variety of ways. This "give & take" or "eject & replace" cycle of transference and counter-transference is best understood as the outcome of excessive projective identification mechanisms.

1

MODERN KLEINIAN THERAPY AND THE INITIAL PSYCHOANALYTIC INTERACTION

Most of the patients receiving psychological treatment from practitioners trained in psychoanalysis are seen once or twice a week, have limited resources, and suffer significant emotional distress (Spivak 2011; Waska 2005, 2006, 2011a, 2011b). This chapter will follow the initial twelve visits with one such patient seen in a private practice setting. He was provided a psychoanalytic treatment process that is meant to be helpful to patients with severe paranoid-schizoid (Klein 1946) or depressive (Klein 1935, 1940) disturbances who are limited by choice or circumstance to only attending once or twice a week. Modern Kleinian Therapy is an effective therapeutic process for such situations and can provide important and lasting psychic change (Waska 2010a, 2010b, 2010c, 2010d).

Modern Kleinian Therapy is a therapeutic approach designed to establish analytic contact (Waska 2007) with patients who are struggling with ongoing internal conflicts of a more primitive nature and who equate change or growth with damage and danger to self and object (Waska 2006). Therefore, they live within a state of perpetual distress, anxiety, paranoia, guilt, or loss. Normally, the term therapy or psychotherapy indicates a diluted form of psychoanalysis, a supportive method, or a deliberate manipulation of the transference. The procedure outlined and illustrated in this chapter is not diluted, singularly supportive, or manipulative. Indeed, it is a psychoanalytic treatment that aims at working with the patient's unconscious conflicts, their object relational phantasies, and their transference perspective.

As such, the technique of Modern Kleinian Therapy is no different whether practiced once a week or five times a week. The infrequent visits can and do create more difficult transference and counter-transference situations and the patient's defensive system and pathological organizations (Steiner 1987) or retreats (Steiner 1990, 1993) as well as core issues of loss that are defended against with pathological levels of projective identification (Waska 2002, 2004) are more entrenched and difficult to unravel. However, it is still an effective, robust, and productive way of potentially transforming formally unreachable individuals and offering them a new and dramatically different way of living.

Modern Kleinian Therapy is a psychoanalytic method of treatment based on the work of the contemporary Kleinians of London (Schafer 1994). It is a therapeutic system that integrates the work of Kernberg's TFP (Transference Focused Psychotherapy; Clarkin, Yeomans, and Kernberg 1999, 2006), the CCRT (Core Conflictual Relationship Theme) method of Luborsky (1984), earlier work of Waska (2005, 2006), some ideas from Sandler (1976), and a mixture of flexible technique principles from a wide variety of analytic thinkers such as Merton Gill (1994), Searles (1986), and others. The moment-to-moment focus on the total transference situation (Joseph 1985), and similar work by Segal (1962, 1974, 1975, 1977a, 1977b, 1993, 1997b, 1981), Britton (2004, 2008), Spillius (1983, 1992, 1993, 2007), Steiner (1979, 1984, 1987, 1992, 1994, 1996), and Feldman (1994, 2004, 2009), is adapted towards a continuous effort to establish analytic contact (Waska 2007) regardless of frequency or diagnosis.

One guiding principle is to use the healing aspects of new knowledge about self and other gained from analytic observations (Waska 2012) and interpretations to bring about insight and foster psychic change and growth. This is similar in practice to work by Clarkin, Yeomans, and Kernberg (1999, 2006), Luborsky (1984), and others who focus on the here-and-now transference and core phantasy conflicts of the patient's dynamic unconscious world. Modern Kleinian Therapy helps neurotic, borderline, narcissistic, and psychotic patients to engage in a restorative therapeutic process geared towards examining and shifting fundamental object relational conflicts.

Again, I deliberately do not call this approach a psychoanalytic psychotherapy but rather a psychoanalytic method and a psychoanalytic treatment because the vast majority of authors who write about and advocate psychoanalytic psychotherapy describe a deliberate watering down of traditional psychoanalytic technique, a reduction of interpretation regarding the transference and defense systems, and an increase in supportive and behavioral interventions that utilize manipulation of the transference instead of interpretation. I think this is a mistake with all patients if we are really trying to offer them the greatest degree of change and psychological growth. But, to not utilize the primary tools and potential of the analytic method with the more disturbed patient can be even more of a clinical failure in not offering what might be most needed.

CASE OF Y

The Initial Session #1

Y struck me as a very intelligent young man with great curiosity about himself as well as the genuine desire to change and to find satisfaction in his life. At the same time, I felt cautious and suspicious when he talked about his issues in a fuzzy, grandiose manner with excessive remarks about "spirituality and the essence of inner meaning, fulfillment of the heart, and true emotional resolution". It sounded like something he had read in a self-help book and a way to avoid sharing his real self and his actual feelings with me. I made that interpretation and Y seemed interested. Indeed, he had attended many such workshops and programs over the years but never had been involved in any psychotherapy or psychoanalysis.

The more we talked, the more I felt he was both articulate and insightful yet out of touch with reality. In other words, I thought that Y's grandiose, paranoid, and possibly delusional way of relating to me was buffered by a partial anchoring into a more intellectual, sincere, and eloquent manner of relating. As a result, I felt uneasy about whom he was, what he was really all about, and how he was really going to utilize me, depend on me, or possibly discard me. It appeared we would have a rocky ride in and out of grounded reality and possibly a relationship that would contract and expand in tricky or unexpected ways.

Y talked at great length about the "dynamic involvement" he found in the human potential workshops he had attended and the "interesting historical lineage" of the New Age church he had recently converted to. According to Y, this church advocated strict or fundamentalist rules of behavior about routine confession, no sex before marriage, and regular prayer combined with a Buddhist mentality. Y seemed to be very drawn to the punitive aspects as well as the rigid structure. He talked at length about how he felt spiritually drawn to the church, how he had a spiritual awakening recently when he heard the choir singing. He fell to the ground crying and thought he could see the image of his dead mother at the altar. He told me he had met a member who had his mother's name and who introduced him to the head priest who also had a sister with his mother's name. Y felt it "was destiny" and how it must be "a special spiritual path that had brought him closer to being able to finally find his mother again". This sounded similar to his description of the time at a Zen retreat he "knew he was Jesus and obviously had special mystical powers".

When I noted that he seemed to like the rules and structure of the church but that organized way of living was quite opposed to the way he had been in the last three years, Y told me, "I love the structure. I need structure. When I picture the ultimate way of feeling at peace, I have the vision of being in my mother's arms". I said, "So, you feel the structure of the church is much like the security and structure of being loved and back in your mother's arms". He said, "Yes. Even better would be to be back in her womb. That would be the ultimate structure!" In the counter-transference, my mental image was of something so wonderful and cozy but then suddenly too tight, confining, and restrictive. Y's psychotic desire to reenter his mother gave me some ideas about how he might want to possess me, abort me, and establish an "ultimate fusion" state with me, to avoid differentiation and loss. These were provisional ideas based in my counter-transference feelings at this early point in the treatment.

9

Over the last three years, Y had traveled around the world in an aimless and desperate attempt to escape from his inner demons. At the same time, he felt it was a "wonderful quest in many ways, finding a spiritual path and many deep spiritual revelations along the way". Over the course of our first two sessions, I learned how Y had grown up in a family of four brothers, two younger than him. Y's mother died of cancer when he was three years old and his father remarried a few years later. Y told me he realized a few years ago that his lifelong unhappiness and sense of fragmentation comes from the loss of his mother at this sensitive young age. He believes this early loss has brought about his mental breakdown he says he had three years ago.

Y's older brother has some type of psychotic condition and has been in and out of mental institutions. He has been given various anti-psychotic medications and mood stabilizers that Y says he has tried himself in an effort to "find some calm and clarity during the rough times".

I interpreted that perhaps he identified with his brother and sought out the same kind of help with the medications. Here, I introduced an idea about him somehow seeing himself as his sick brother and needing the same treatment. I was not sure about anything else regarding his brother but I felt it important to comment on this sense of sameness. It was useful to see how concrete Y was in his reply. He said, "I just thought his meds would help me with my moods and depression because my brother suffers with them as well. But, they did not help and I think they screw up your brain anyway so I am glad I stopped taking them".

So, I kept my idea of him wanting to be the same and losing his identity in the process as a question mark. I knew he could be correct in diagnosing himself as suffering the same illness as his brother but the way he described it had a feeling of a more blurred attempt at fitting into his brother, a way he seemed to desire fusion or sameness. This was all in the tone and manner in which he conveyed the story to me. Y went on to elaborate how the "main and most devastating problem in my life is the death of my mother. She died of cancer when I was three and I finally realized a few years ago how much that has affected me. That is the central core of all my issues. I must find her and reconnect that spiritual bond and find that missing part in me". He went on to tell me of his "mental breakdown" three or four years ago and his "voyage ever since to free myself".

Y told me he smokes pot every day to calm down and to find some peace of mind. Y also drinks heavily when he cannot find enough pot. When we were discussing his long time addiction to pot and how he uses it or alcohol to "self medicate", Y casually mentioned an incident the prior week.

He told me that he had moved into the city about two months ago and had quickly found a job in a small grocery store. His job was to stock the shelves. Y said he hated it because it was boring and when he was done for the day, it was a long walk to the bus stop. But, he kept at it for about three weeks. Then, one day at work he decided to consume a "pot brownie" and when he started to feel really high, he went to his manager and told him that he was now too high to work and wanted to see if he could leave early. The manager promptly fired him.

I asked Y what he had expected would happen. Y said he was not too surprised but he "always hopes that people can maybe see the real truth and find a way to have a connection that transcends the weight of rules and convention". I said, "You seem to be hoping for a pure, honest, and all accepting connection, perhaps the sort of thing you feel you lost out with your mother dying". Y said, "Exactly!" I added, "It also seems to be a way that you sabotaged yourself and got fired. You could have hung in there and not told your boss or you could have elected to not get high. But, you took away something you had created in your life".

Y said, "I do that over and over and over. I tend to achieve something and then give up on it or screw it up somehow. I have done that with girlfriends and plenty of jobs". So, we discussed the elements of this pattern and how he seemed to be happy and proud of himself but then turn away from himself and let go of that positive element to create a negative. Here, I was thinking about the clinical manifestations of the life and death instincts and the destructive conflicts that can occur in that phantasy realm (Steiner 2004; Rosenfeld 1971; Grotstein 1985). I also wondered to myself how long it might be before he took what we will build together and try to kill it off as well.

I noticed Y had a pen and pad on which he was taking periodic notes. When I made an interpretation, he wrote it down. He asked if we would be working psychoanalytically. I said he probably knew I was an analyst. He said he did and wondered where I was trained. I paused and said I was trained in the city but wondered what exactly he wanted to know. He wrote something down again. I asked him what he was writing and what exactly he was trying to find out about me. Y said he had written down what I said about trying to search for the perfect bond and structure with his mother and how somehow it always collapsing without him being able to sustain it. He said he was also writing down where I was trained so he could look it up.

I said, "It seems you want to know me and own me in some way that also makes it hard for you to be here right now. By trying to pin down everything on paper, you are not getting to know me right now". Y said, "I am just a curious person and I want to know what type of treatment I am having and a little about the person I am supposed to trust in that treatment".

So, for now, Y kept us at that concrete distance but based on my counter-transference, it seemed that internally he was fishing around to know me, possess me, and get inside me. I thought this might be part of what I would term the extraction process of pathological projective identification in which the subject attempts to hijack or acquire certain aspects of the object to call their own. It becomes an emotional theft based in envy, intense anxiety over not knowing, and not having control of the internal environment. I thought he might feel so weak or vulnerable about wanting to know and having to find out through an ongoing relationship that he was trying to hijack it immediately.

Session #2

When I went to the waiting room to find Y for his second session, I found him standing there with his bicycle. He said he did not want to leave it on the street and have it stolen so he wondered if he could leave it in the waiting room. I had several thoughts about this. While there was no one else out there, it is interesting that Y did not think of how his bicycle would impact the next patient or how he might be impacted by them. I think he felt it was *his* waiting room and it felt safe to leave the bicycle there.

I was worried that someone would come into the waiting room and steal the bike so I suggested he leave it in the hallway by my office door. But, either way, I felt he was moving in. This sensation was confirmed when he entered my office and took out his cell phone and a charger and said, "Can I plug this in somewhere?" I had two feelings about this. The first feeling was that I had no choice. I had to either say yes or I would be telling him no in a very rejecting way, telling him that there was no room for him in my home.

The second feeling was that Y was indeed moving in. So, I said, "Looks like you are moving in! I wonder if you have decided you can trust me. But, with such a fast move in, I wonder if you will be able to stay for a while?" I said this based on the feeling that this was an impulsive move into me and could easily be followed by an impulsive retreat. Y confirmed my interpretation when he said, "I have always had a hard time with commitment. I have a pattern of really getting into something and then it all falls apart. I give up on it".

I asked, "Do you give up or do you choose to retreat and pull out?" Here, I was seeing if Y was able to consider himself as an active player in his life or just a passive observer. I wondered if he was caught in a more persecutory vision of himself or knew he was participating in what happened around him. Y said, "It feels like I just give up. I go into the job or relationship with a lot of hope and excitement. It works out and I am happy for a while. I am very successful at most of the jobs I take on and I have been very connected with a number of women. But, at some point, I feel it is almost going too well and I give up and stop trying. I think I can't handle it and so I sort of fade away".

I said, "I wonder if something about being successful, happy, or close makes you anxious and then you have to fail. Almost punishing yourself or running away from something positive". Here, I was interpreting a possible fear of success, a dread of closeness, and a reaction to having dove too deep into the object or situation. Y said, "I think that could be. I tend to fail at commitment".

So, after only seeing Y for two visits, it is unclear what his struggles are and how the treatment will unfold. However, by adhering to a Modern Kleinian Therapy approach, I was able to make a few interpretations and help Y open up in certain ways. This has started a therapeutic process in which we have already established a degree of analytic contact, exploring and examining his internal world and the various unconscious phantasies and conflicts he is suffering with.

In the counter-transference, I notice that my feelings and thoughts sometimes parallel his description of himself and his emotional patterns. Specifically, I notice myself liking him as a person, trusting him, and wanting to engage in a working relationship. However, at the same time, I have an uneasy feeling, a slight distrust, and see him as more disturbed than he appears and possibly ready to terminate at any moment. So, I am keeping this counter-transference impression in mind as we proceed. I think it may help me understand him more and find my way as we continue our analytic journey.

For Y, he was still splitting his objects into ideal, all good, but unobtainable pieces as well as into omnipotent, all bad and hateful pieces. Y seemed to be lost in the quest and search for this mythical perfect object as a way to avoid facing the grief and rage he felt over the aspects of his lost object he resented and pined over. Thus, he lives in a psychotic world full of incredible possibilities and constant failure.

Session #7

I had seen Y for six sessions when he canceled the next two and went out of town. He left for several weeks on a "wonderful business opportunity to provide some professional consulting and to begin to put together a potentially vast corporate investment". When he returned from a rather disastrous financial experience of high expectations and low results, we continued to investigate what was fueling such internal and external instability.

When Y walked into my office after this disappointing trip, he said, "Hello Doctor. Did you forget me?" I let him settle in, thought about what he said, and listened a bit more. After hearing some details about his trip, I said, "I think you are not sure who is feeling what or who is doing what to whom sometimes. You took off and left our regular meetings. But, now, you are worried I have forgotten you. It seemed like *you* might have forgotten us the way you just sort of slipped out of town". I wondered if he was feeling guilty for forgetting about me and now was trying to flip it around to feel better. Y replied, "No. I think I am afraid that you are angry with me for canceling the two sessions and that you might not want to see me anymore". I said, "you are anxious that our bond is very precarious and that you could ruin it very easily. It is hard to trust that I could care for you and not just abandon you if there is some friction or if you need to be somewhere besides here". He said, "I was worried that you felt I blew you off so you closed the door and just gave away my time to someone else. I am glad to hear we are ok".

13

I thought to myself that Y had indeed "blown me off" and that this was part of his entitled, challenging transference in which he did as he pleased but then dreaded the fallout.

In this seventh session and into the eighth, we continued exploring his desire to find some sense of peace and understanding about the loss of his mother and to understand how that might still be driving the direction of his life and creating the aimless and empty feeling he was plagued with. However, much of how Y spoke to me and much of how he thought about himself was distorted and filtered through a very intellectualized, manic effort to feel in charge, in control, and forever hopeful.

Y tried to feel successful about how he was doing in life, whether it was about the emotional issues we were exploring, his housing situation, his finances, or his relationships. But, the sad truth was that Y was in the middle of a collapse in all these areas. He was trying to better himself but also was in denial about the more destructive ways he thought about and related both to himself and to others. He felt entitled and spoke of "not caring about doing much because it didn't hold enough meaning for me" and "not really wanting to work at something I don't like because I don't want to be bothered". Y told me of a "wonderful, tight bond with my roommates and the million dollar deals they were putting together" while he was actually being told to move out because his roommates were sick of his pot smoking and lack of employment.

In reality, Y was now on food stamps and barely able to find money to take the bus to see me. I understood these psychotic distortions in a number of ways, but primarily interpreted his precocious mourning (Feldman and Paola 1994) in which his desire for his idealized mother and their wonderful union felt beyond the ordinary grip of everyday life and created a constant conflict with reality. This caused him intense envy and anxiety. As a result, he was constantly fleeing emotionally from the overwhelming loss that reality brought him face to face with. He was always juggling his fragile quest for unavailable entitlement with his reach for illusive grandiosity. All this was tempered in some respect by his use of intellect and his talents and skills that seemed to have gotten him by, just barely, until now. However, his envy for the unreachable ideal self and other/mother put him at a distance from reality and from building any creative or emotionally profitable support system that would anchor him into everyday life.

Session #9

During the ninth session, Y told me that he had been to the psychiatrist as suggested by his social worker and was told he was probably bipolar with some psychotic or manic traits and had been given an anti-psychotic medication and an anti-anxiety medication. Y told me he was planning on not taking them because he "preferred natural remedies and didn't really think he needed them". Y said, "The psychiatrist thought I was manic and said the medications would help with that. But, I think that how I am right now is just fine. And, if I am manic right now, then I think it is ok because I am not being destructive in any way. In fact, I am being extremely productive. I read a 600 page Russian novel in the last week. And, since I saw you last, I have stopped smoking pot altogether. Now, I work out every day at the gym and I do yoga by myself. I am praying and singing at church and feel great about life. Things are alright with my life and I don't think I have any real problems right now".

I said, "You seem to want to convince me of how wonderful you are doing and how carefree your life is. Since you are telling me today that you are broke, barely have enough for bus fare, are on food stamps, and are soon to be homeless because your roommates are kicking you out, I think it must be very painful to be more in touch with yourself and the lost and scared feelings that are probably there. I am glad to hear that you are not smoking pot and that you are working out now. But, I think you are quick to try and hide from the difficulties that are inside of you which leave you feeling alone and searching for mother".

Here, I was interpreting his manic stance in the way Rosenfeld (1971) has noted that narcissistic defenses guard against the threat of separateness and the resulting loss and mourning of what could have been and will never be. I was interpreting it both from a genetic perspective as well as a here-and-now transference comment. Steiner (2011a) has noted that certain patients will utilize projective identification to prevent any sense of loss or separation from their hoped for ideal object. A manic, narcissistic stance is developed to ward off the recognition of both bad and good elements that reside in both self and object. Y would not allow for these aspects of himself or his internal world and demanded excellence and bliss with no limits or restrictions.

Y said, "I am trying to realize she is no longer around and that I can never find her. She is gone. But, I have her inside of me!" I said, "I agree. But, there is something a little too quick about all this progress. I am concerned you are trying hard to feel better by ignoring some of the hardships in your life, and that could backfire".

Here, I was interpreting his reluctance to face the ongoing experiences of loss in his internal and external life. He used a manic defense against the mourning of his ideal object as well as the ideal vision he had of himself. Finally, I was interpreting how Y wanted to appear a certain superior and controlled way with me, not ever wanting me to notice the tattered and torn painful little boy that embodied his current existence.

Y said, "I know what you mean. When I went out of town, I thought I was going to make some real money. I was asked by an old friend to come down and consult for his small company. My job was to set up the structure for the people he would hire next year. I did a whole lot of work over the week for him, but in the process we ended up having some of the same old fights we have had in the past. I realized I had made a mistake in judgment and that he was still the same very disturbed person I wrote off last year. I woke up the next day and told him I was leaving and that he owed me $500. He said he wasn't going to pay me anything. I didn't have any money at that point, so I asked him for the bus fare back. He refused. I had to use the last money I had in the world for a bus ticket back to the city, and when I got here two days ago, I had twenty nine dollars to my name. I am glad I secured food stamps. Now, I am hoping to sleep at the church. But, if I end up on the streets, so be it. I always bounce back and that is what life is about, these golden opportunities!"

I said, "You are feeling very upset over the loss of your mother and in the process you have never found yourself. That conflict and struggle seems to keep getting played out in a lot of your relationships and in how you try and avoid any pain or unhappiness". Y said, "I have felt left behind by my mother for so many years. It is a great sadness that has taken over my life and left me terribly lost and alone. I have lived a lifetime of emptiness. But, now I am trying to find a new way of being and a new way of feeling. I want to take care of myself and respect the talents that I have. Coming here, going to church, and working out are some of the ways I believe I can accept her loss and continue to live my life".

I said, "I think you are right. We have to keep exploring the mixture of feelings that keeps you on this zigzag pattern of come and go, commitment and disengagement with yourself, with me, with relationships, and with life. That way of wanting to be engaged and then disengaging happens here between us, and you have pointed out how it has happened many times over with girlfriends and jobs and friends. You must feel quite pulled at times to want to be with someone and then suddenly not so comfortable with that contact and have to pull away. It is a confusing way of being with others but also a jumbled way of being with yourself". Y said, "That is a good word to describe how I feel some of the time, jumbled".

Session #10

Y began the tenth session by telling me about his favorite movie, a tale in which there is a poor, ignored man who is actually a genius and is able to show up the head of his company with his incredible intellectual powers but never "becomes a victim of the corporate mentality". He does what he wants and lives his life the way he wants, never letting himself be "controlled or taken over by the edicts of society". I interpreted, "You seem to be feeling like you are that genius, fighting and winning against all the controlling authorities around you. You maybe even feel proud and superior in some ways".

Y said, "Well, I actually do. I have always felt that I know much more than most people and have an edge on others in many ways. I think I have a great deal of creativity and special ways of thinking about things that put me above the herd, not just a follower". I said, "From what I remember of the movie, the person you are seeing as a hero is also a very sad character who sabotages himself over and over and ends up quite alone. Maybe you have the same sort of struggle with wanting to feel so strong and smart but always having to fight the system so in the end you end up feeling little and lost".

Y said, "I do feel that way. But, I also have a hard time figuring out why it would do me any good to be a part of what looks like a broken system. Instead of doing God's work, people are just out for themselves and racing after power and money. I don't see the point". I said, "With me and with yourself, you seem to get stuck between these two black or white choices, to join the devil or fight against him. Maybe, we can sort out some other options, some middle ground". Y nodded and said, "I am up for that!"

Session #11

Not surprisingly, this brief phase of curiosity and reduction in anxiety, manic rebellion, and resistance was short lived. In the next session, Y came in and said he had spent the night in a homeless shelter and that "at first it was a frightening and humbling experience. I felt out of control. But, then it occurred to me that I don't need a home. No one does. We are all part of God's home and that in many ways being homeless would help to teach me what I need to learn".

I said, "I think it is hard for you to be vulnerable with me and to face those frightening feelings of being out of control. It is easier to try and see it as a golden opportunity you are in charge of". Y said, "No. I feel great. I don't need to have to claim anything as mine. That is a big problem in the world. Everyone is too scared to see that they have nothing except the love of God. We have to learn to be happy with that and not be chasing so much more all the time".

I said, "You have been chasing something your whole life. You want to find peace of mind and a sense of being loved instead of feeling lost and forgotten. But, you don't want to depend on me or anyone or anything, maybe for fear of being let down again". Y said, "That goes right back to my mother. I felt completely torn away from her and I have been searching for her ever since. But, I know that already! I want to know what you are going to do to help me with all of this. What exactly are you thinking about regarding my diagnosis and how you will be treating me? And, how long do you think it will take? I am not sure this is even the right type of treatment for me or the most effective solution. I have heard of quite a few other treatments that might be better!"

In the counter-transference, I felt challenged, attacked, devalued, and ready to be discarded. I interpreted, "You are making me useless and pointless by demanding that I help you after barely just meeting you. If I can't solve it and fix it right away, there is something better somewhere else. This is the way you have been living life and in the process never giving yourself a chance. You are always pulling the plug on yourself as well. You are so busy wanting the magical reunion with your mother instantly that you are not giving us a chance to see what is really bothering you and to build a solution together. You don't like the idea of needing me, of having to take some time to invest in yourself, and of not knowing or having it all immediately. That must be very hard to tolerate. But, we must try so we can get to the other side". Y did not say much. It was the end of the session and he left.

Session #12

In this next session, Y seemed quite agitated and manic. He was irritated and spoke of many situations in which he was unhappy or angry. He talked about "being sick and tired of how people like to dominate each other and how he will never allow that into his life". Y insisted he "will always choose the road of freedom and self-expression over being dominated and categorized". Y had many examples of how "culture encourages domination" and how the "class system has brainwashed people into accepting this power imbalance". He told me that "having me be on this couch is an example of that. You just want to feel impressive, lording over me like some kind of fucking authority figure. I don't accept that. I would rather find someone who understands me and realizes that under God, we are all equal and should always relate to each other as equals".

I said, "It is interesting to notice how out of all the possible ways of experiencing being here with me, you end up feeling dominated. Some people might feel freed up or given a special opportunity to relax and simply express whatever they wish at whatever pace they choose. But, you quickly push us into the box of jailor and prisoner, dominated and dominating. Perhaps it is uncomfortable to allow for something else".

Y said, "I do go there very quickly. I don't know why. But, I see what you mean. I just don't like being told what to do. I never have. I feel I have the right to do what I wish and no one should tell me otherwise. This is God's earth and it doesn't belong to anyone". I said, "You want me to see you as this special person with special rights and who is above the rest. I wonder if you feel weak or like a failure in some way so you have to fight hard to look the opposite?"

Y replied, "I do feel incredibly weak and like someone who has never found the answers. I have spent my life looking but I have yet to find them". I said, "That sounds sad and a bit scary. A small boy lost in the world with no mother, no answers, and no direction". Y began to weep.

After a few minutes, he went back to his more entitled, manic stance. He told me about how he had gone to church and started singing in the middle of the service, feeling "connected with God and in touch with the universe". When the priest asked him to stop, Y asked why and the priest said it was just not something that they wanted because there was a service going on and that should be respected. Y became angry and told him that "this is God's church and you can't tell me to do anything!" The priest told Y that he needed to respect the rules of the church to which Y yelled at him, "I will never come here again! I will find a church that allows me to worship like I want to. You don't have the right to prevent me from praying in the fashion I need to or want to!"

I said, "You seem to not want to respect the church or the priest's property and regulations. You are trying to impose your wants and ways on other people. It seems you are in fact the one doing the dominating. It seems like it makes you very angry to encounter limits or to be told no". Y said, "I don't want any limits. I will do what I want or go elsewhere if I can't. No one is going to put limits on me".

I said, "Maybe, you are furious and very hurt about the limits that you felt when your mother died. Now, you are taking that out on me, the church, the priest, and the world". Y said, "I am very angry and hurt about my mother". At this point, he pulled out a book that he had borrowed from the local library. It was about the effects of death on young children. He started to read passages to me about the devastating effects of a parent's death on a young child. I said, "You really identify with that. You still feel completely lost, still very sad and angry. I think you feel very much entitled to do as you please now so as to maybe finally get to be special. You want to be special now because you feel you lost out on a mother who could treat you special". Y said, "I think you are reading my mind, Doc!"

As he was reading the library book, I noticed how many of the passages were underlined. I asked, "Did you underline the passages?" Y said yes. I said, "Maybe that is another example of how you want to feel special and above all the ways of the world, over death and disappointment. The book is not your property, it belongs to the library. But, you ignored that and decided to treat it as if it is your book without regard to the library or the next person who wants to read it. And now, you have pulled me into being a lecturing or dominating authority telling you off. So, I think you really want the right to be special so you don't have to feel so unspecial and unimportant".

Y yelled, "That is bullshit! This book belongs to no one. This is God's book! I don't care and I will do what I want! I am trying to learn something from this book and if I want to underline it I should be able to!" I said, "I think you feel, deep inside, that either you are special and entitled or small and meaningless. You feel you have to grab what you want or you will have nothing". Y said, "Well, that is true. I don't want to miss the bus in life. I want to find out what is wrong with me and put my life together!" I said, "It is hard for you to find a peaceful place to fit into life when you are either feeling dominated or when you are dominating others like the church, the library book, or wanting me to fix you in a handful of sessions. You need to allow for some disappointment and delay in order to get what you want, but I can see how hard that is. You don't want the pain of that limit". Y said, "It is very hard".

Session #13

In the next session, Y seemed a bit calmer and less angry. However, he told me about how he was "now focused on finding the answers to his problems, moving ahead in life, and putting things in perspective and in the past". He said this in a pressured and rushed way that felt like he was impatient and somewhat demanding. He went on to talk about how he "wants to know how I see him and what I think his problems really are". He said, "What is your assessment of me, Doc? What do you think is going on and how can we change things so I can move into a more holistic way of living and find a more complete way of seeing life or reaching my goals!?"

This struck me as not only rushed and demanding but also part of a globalized, generalized way he would sweep his hand over the world and come up with grand and entitled slogans that sounded great but were really so intellectualized and far reaching that they were out of touch with reality and certainly out of touch with us in the moment. So, I interpreted, "You seem to be jumping away from your feelings and the problems we are working on together and suddenly going to this more global vision of how you will find the answers and finally live your life. But, in the process, you are more and more out of touch with yourself. What we are doing here today in this room seems more and more useless and meaningless. I think your desire for something very special and big gets in the way of what you actually have now or what you are actually achieving right now".

Here, I was interpreting his devaluation and attack on our life together and how he was replacing us with a demanding search for the ideal. Y said, "I see what you mean. I gave a lot of thought to what we talked about last time and I think we are learning things. I just want to find my way and start to live life". I said, "You have put your life on hold trying to find your mother or at least trying to find the feeling of being with a perfect loving mother".

Y said, "I have. I try and go after other things but I always get detoured back to trying to find what is missing in me". He paused and went on, "But, I just want to know what you will be doing for me and how we will be proceeding. I want to know that we are making progress". I replied, "You do not want to have anyone say no to you or put limits on you. You want what you want when you want it. By not accepting that you can't have it all or that it might take some time to get what you want, you are missing out on the good work we have done and the good direction we are headed in".

Y nodded and smiled. The session was over. When I went out through the waiting room some ten minutes later to get something from my car, Y was sitting in the waiting room. He was reading one of the waiting room magazines and said, "Doc, can I borrow this magazine and bring it back next time?" I replied, "No. It is the office's magazine and needs to stay here on the property. But, I think you are testing out what we talked about today". He laughed and said, "Oh no! You are right. Sorry". This unconscious way of seeing the world as a place where he can receive everything he wants when he wants it with any push back is experienced as a gross rejection and outrageous restriction continues to be a major factor in his internal life but one we are working on.

The following week, I came out to the waiting room to find that Y had unplugged the lamp in order to plug in his mobile phone. I said, "Did you unplug the lamp?" He said yes. I said, "Plug it back in". I was aware of the irritation and the forceful authority he engendered in me as part of the projective identification process that is so much a part of his object relational conflicts and his transference struggle. He was able to tolerate me being a roadblock to his maternal utopia and said, "Ok".

Another example of this was when Y came into a recent session, the twentieth visit, and said, "I hope you brought your cell phone charger today. I want to use it to plug in my iPod". I responded to his entitled and bullying way of being by interpreting, "No. I will not give you the charger. There are limits. You are often testing the limits with me and others and never want to be denied. But, we must look at what it means to feel disappointed and not have everything or everyone care for you right away". Y was angry and told me I was a "shitty person". He was upset and agitated but we were able to go on to a discussion about how difficult it is for Y to feel special and loved without having to constantly grab for what he wants and feel entitled to it.

No doubt, we will continue to navigate and explore those moments of friction, demand, and disappointment and gradually explore a way to replace them with some hope, acceptance, and healthy mourning.

Discussion

To summarize briefly the Modern Kleinian Therapy approach, it is a style most characterized by Betty Joseph's (1985, 1987, 1988, 1989) way of working in the moment, examining the here-and-now interaction between patient and analyst, both intrapsychically and interpersonally. I apply this focused intrapsychic and interpersonal style of working to individual patients or couples who are suffering with significant psychological disturbance often seen only once or twice a week.

This reduction in frequency reflects the current state of practice in most analysts' offices in which patients are unable either financially or practically to attend more often or are unwilling emotionally. However, they still are looking for psychological assistance and we can still offer them significant help. The reduction in frequency naturally brings about some degree of difficulty in the overall treatment process. The transference will be harder to find, engage, and interpret and the patient's pathological defensive systems and psychic retreats will be harder to work with. Acting out is often more severe and difficult to contain and analyze. Counter-transference can also be more tricky and enactments more probable. However, we must work with what we have and the Modern Kleinian method uses the containing and reparative aspects both of analytic observation (Waska 2012) and of analytic interpretation to help the patient restore and renew their internal knowledge of self and object, free from his or her more destructive phantasy view of the past. This enables the patient to cope better with reality and to begin to unravel and untangle their unconscious conflicts with love and hate, life and death, knowledge and the unknown.

This process is what I term the establishment and maintenance of analytic contact (Waska 2007); a therapeutic process that is at the foundation of any true and lasting working through procedure. The case of Y, a very difficult to reach and hard to thaw patient, allows the reader to really see the in-the-moment, step by step way the Modern Kleinian Therapy approach actually works right from the beginning of the treatment process. The working through of the total transference and complete counter-transference (Waska 2010a, 2010b, 2010c), in which therapeutic success and insight and psychological transformation can take place, is still the cornerstone of the treatment, along with the inevitable failure, resistance, and acting out (Rosenfeld 1979, 1987) that takes place in all therapeutic endeavors.

2

ONCE A WEEK FREQUENCY WITH MODERN KLEINIAN THERAPY

Most patients seen by psychoanalysts choose to attend once or twice a week and may or may not use the analytic couch. Often, these are individuals suffering from long-term personality conditions with severe internal conflicts in the realm of either paranoid-schizoid (Klein 1946) or depressive (Klein 1935, 1940) phantasy. Modern Kleinian Therapy is a hybrid of the elements that comprise contemporary Kleinian psychoanalysis. The technical approach is the same but the analyst is aware of the increased resistance and counter-transference strain that occur with a reduction in frequency.

The ongoing task for the analyst in either treatment environment is to establish and maintain sufficient analytic contact (Waska 2007, 2010a, 2010b) or potential space (Winnicott 1968). As Spivak (2011) notes, the analyst must resist internal pressures to foreclose that space. These pressures to give in, give up, support, enlighten, fix, attack, or judge are all projective identification based invitations towards enactments in the realm of love, hate, and the desire to gain or avoid new knowledge of self and other.

With less frequent meetings and with patients who are more disturbed, there is an increase in the tension between new possibilities of relating to self and object and pathological retreats (Steiner 1993) into familiar states of psychic equilibrium (Joseph 1989). It is more difficult for the analyst to translate the patient's unconscious communications and transference motivation because it is much more of a moving target. Also, it is more complicated to consistently act as the analyst/mother who tolerates the patient/infant's unbearable anxieties and slowly return them in a loving and caring manner (Bion 1962a). While our patients consciously want us to help them detoxify their psychological landscape, they unconsciously create a detour and work against our attempts to make their cast of internal characters more friendly and bearable (Sandler 1984). This is all the more so with hard to thaw patients attending only once or twice a week.

Modern Kleinian Therapy is a therapeutic approach no different from standard Kleinian psychoanalysis but with a greater emphasis, by necessity, on the technical issues of transference, interpretation, analytic observation

(Waska 2012), projective identification (Waska 2004), acting out, the complete counter-transference (Waska 2010c, 2011a, 2011b), and the here and now. The genetic history of a patient's interpersonal and psychological troubles is important but only as far as understanding how the past lives on in the present. These refinements and areas of concentration make for a clinical strategy much more in line with the types of complications we find in treating the borderline, narcissistic, and psychotic patients so often seen in private practice settings (Waska 2005, 2006).

CASE OF DAN

Session #1

Dan was an ex-college football player who had injured his shoulder two years ago and could no longer play professionally. He had originally wanted to be in the professional leagues and thought he was good enough to try out for them, but also wondered about the intensity of the lifestyle and the often short lived career path of such athletes. Now, after the injury, he worked as an electrician and enjoyed the job. He thought of one day "becoming his own boss and building up a small business that gave the client good work for fair pay and provided a sincere and honest service to homeowners and business people". Dan was a large man who looked like a football player but also presented himself as a very friendly and polite man. I have seen him for twenty sessions in psychoanalytic treatment, from a Modern Kleinian approach, once and sometimes twice a week.

Originally, Dan came to see me because he was feeling "down in the dumps nearly every day and could not get certain thoughts out of his mind". He avoided telling me the details of these obsessive thoughts for the first session and concentrated instead on telling me a bit about his family and his current life situation. He said he had been raised in a "very loving family and his mother really emphasized the importance of being nice to others and having others think well of you". He told me how he has been dating his current girlfriend for a year now and they now live together. Dan said he "is definitely in love with her and can see getting married and maybe even having kids". He told me he was disappointed when the very week he moved in with his girlfriend she had to travel for work and was away for that whole week. Dan told me he "felt lonely and isolated and even a bit irritated that she chooses to go out of town the very week I moved in".

I said, "You felt sort of rejected or like she deliberately left you right when you needed her?" Dan said, "Well, I understand she couldn't help it. She told me so. But, yes. I did feel a bit left in the dust". I noted to myself how this seemed to be a significant struggle or conflict for Dan.

Session #2

During the second session, Dan told me how six years ago he had left a bar where he and all his friends had been drinking. He noticed a person on a motorcycle pull out of the parking lot and dared him to race. So, at 1 am on a dark night, Dan was driving at speeds above 100 mph with the motorcycle ahead of him. When they approached a sharp turn in the road, the motorcycle went out of control and hit a tree. When Dan pulled over, he could immediately tell that it was a good friend of his. Apparently, Dan's friend had just bought the motorcycle, so Dan had not realized it was him. Frightened by the accident and realizing he would be arrested by the police for drunk driving, he sped off into the night. The next day he heard that his friend had died at the scene.

It was six months before Dan told anyone. He finally broke down and told the brother of his dead friend. The brother understood and they kept it a secret. Dan has told his current girlfriend and now he told me. We spend the next few sessions going over in detail the events and his thoughts and feelings about them, not only back then but through the years and into the present. Dan is very guilt ridden and he was obviously still very traumatized by this awful event. Even though he knew intellectually that he was not to blame and there was no way for him to have known it was his friend on the motorcycle, Dan still feels "deeply devastated by that event and how I feel I was somehow responsible for it". I thought that Dan was possibly suffering from some degree of post-traumatic stress disorder from this incident. But, I also considered it a sort of screen event by which he organized his inner life and projected his internal conflicts onto. So, I kept an eye out for other ways he might feel responsible for bad things or for hurting others.

Sessions #3–4

Alerted to how Dan described his drinking at this accident as so "much a usual state of affairs", I asked Dan more about his drinking patterns. It turned out that he "usually ended up quite drunk most weekends and it wasn't uncommon to put away two six packs of beer and a few shots on any given night with the boys". Dan told me it "was just the way he socialized and that since he was a young teen he and his friends focused everything around drinking". He said, "we have fun spending the day in the bar and end up drunk. It is what we do". I asked him if perhaps he noticed any problems with this way of living. Dan told me that he did find himself "in quite a few fights and I have driven drunk more times than I would like to admit".

Dan continued to describe how heavy drinking was really the only social outlet he had except football. He loved football and was obviously very skilled at it. He had spent most of his time practicing and playing football since he was in high school. All the rest of his time, except for school work, was taken up drinking with his friends, mostly at bars. I was astonished at how much

Dan said he could drink in any given setting. However, almost all his drinking took place on the weekends or holidays. I noted that he never felt the need to drink much during the week. And, if he had a big football game on the weekends, he would not drink at all. So, I interpreted that his drinking seemed linked to feeling he should fit in with his friends and follow their footsteps or he might feel anxious and not liked or included. Dan agreed and said he felt enormous pressure from himself but also from his friends to be a "part of the club" even though he "has sort of grown out of being in fist fights and having no memory of what he did or said over the weekend". Dan was surprised when I said he had an alcohol problem but seemed to understand and agree when I pointed out the possible psychological reasons. He was glad to be understood from a psychoanalytic perspective about his more unconscious motives and conflicts.

When I said he seemed to feel left out or inferior to his friends and that alcohol was a way of coping with these feelings, Dan elaborated. He told me that when he spends time with his friends, or friends of his girlfriend, he often "feels they are better educated and have better careers, so they must think of me as a lower or even pathetic person who is just a working class guy. I am an electrician and they are managers at big high tech companies". I interpreted that he drank to avoid those awful feelings of rejection and failure. Dan agreed and gave me some examples of when he had done just that.

I noticed how in the counter-transference, I felt like coming to his rescue by reminding him what a skilled athlete and trained electrician he was. I considered those feelings to be based on his projective identification fueled transference in which he hoped I would rescue him like he tries to rescue others. So, I interpreted that instead of rescuing himself with confidence, reassurance, self-pride, and a sense of mature equality, he wished for me or someone to be there for him while he languished all alone, depressed and hopeless. I would have to prop him up and reassure him he was important and had strong qualities that defined him as equal or even better in some cases. Dan understood and told me it "made sense" but that it "also made him nervous to think of acting different that way".

Sessions #5–9

We focused on his drinking for the next few sessions and looked at how he might start to decrease the drinking and avoid the times and places where he seemed at risk for becoming drunk. In addition, I looked at the transference situation for more insight into his phantasy conflicts and as a result we worked on his feelings of inferiority and his desires to be rescued without having to define himself or see himself as deserving more.

I had already noticed in the counter-transference how Dan seemed delicate and insecure. I had noted that while he was a 200 pound, 6 ft 6 in football player who was now a construction worker and electrician who often got into drunken brawls, I never felt intimidated or uneasy with him. In fact, he seemed more like an anxious, big, passive puppy dog. I felt Dan tried to be polite, nice, and do what he thought a good patient does.

When I made these interpretations, Dan was surprised to hear that he appeared that way to me but quickly agreed that he liked it when "everyone was getting along" and that he "wanted to be thought of in a good way". I interpreted that he may feel anxious that I, all his friends, and his girlfriend were thinly attached to him and it would not, in his mind, take much to tear us away. I interpreted that being a nice guy who makes sure to fit in and please all of us was a way to control this threat. This was an analytic observation (Waska 2012) of how he viewed his objects and how he treated them. Analytic observations often are helpful to offer before introducing an interpretation of unconscious motive.

In telling me about his dislike for getting drunk all the time, Dan told me he was sick of being hung-over. "But, the worst thing about it seems to be how I end up feeling much more paranoid or insecure about things when I am drinking". I asked for details.

Dan gradually shared various stories with me about how when drinking, he felt very "paranoid" and "fragile", "similar to when I am sober and my girlfriend travels, but much worse". He told me his girlfriend travels a great deal for work and when she is away, he finds himself lonely and missing her. Then, he may sometimes start to worry about whether she is cheating on him. If he drinks, Dan told me he then takes any comment he hears about her going out to dinner with coworkers or how she went to a bar to unwind after a busy work day with other coworkers to mean that she "probably ended up drinking, partying, and hooking up with some local guy".

Dan has voiced these concerns to her before and she has assured him she is "in it for the long haul and is totally committed to him". But, Dan says he still cannot stop thinking and worrying about it. I reminded Dan that while we work on solving the core problem behind these worries, he is also noticing how much worse it is if he is drinking. Therefore, it was crucial we also focus on the reduction of his drinking.

Dan told me of how he and his girlfriend had gone out to a bar to drink with friends. A male friend of his girlfriend showed up and the two of them spent a good deal of time talking and laughing. While Dan was at the bar ordering drinks, he noticed they were sitting fairly close to each other and were laughing and smiling. He said, "He seemed to have sat down next to her closer than the regular distance most people choose. It didn't look right".

I said, "So, you started to feel like he was moving in on her?" Dan said, "Right. I started to feel uncomfortable and what really didn't feel good was that she didn't seem to be uneasy about it. I started to feel very worked up about it. Normally, something like this would have resulted in my starting a fight and maybe getting thrown out of the bar or having the police called in. But, after we have been talking about how I get insecure and start to imagine all these things especially when I drink, I managed to walk outside and have a smoke. I tried to cool off. But, after a while, I could still see them there having a good time and I couldn't take it. I told my girlfriend I needed to go home and that I had too much to drink. She wanted me to stay but after we talked for a bit, she could see how upset I was and agreed to go home with me. So, in the end it worked out as far as me avoiding a fight or some kind of disaster. But, I still don't like how I got so close to the edge".

I said, "Well, the first thing seems to be that you drank too much alcohol. You were drunk or on your way to being drunk. And, you were in a bar, which makes it very hard to work on your alcohol problem. But, you are right in that there is something about these situations that makes you start to feel very jealous and worried, like you will be abandoned. We are working on that but since it only gets much worse when you drink, you need to not drink while we figure it out".

Dan agreed that he needed to reduce his drinking and somehow avoid the bar scene. We started to talk more about how to do that and what it meant to him to try to do so. In the meantime, I continued to interpret his sense of the object as only temporarily, thinly attached to him, easily pulled towards a better more enticing object, and leaving him as if he was meaningless.

A week later, Dan told me about the "disaster that happened when he and his girlfriend went out of town to a weekend rock concert". Apparently, they drank all day the first day and listened to music. They were "drunk by noon" on the second day and somehow started talking about each other's dating history. Dan asked her how many men she had slept with prior to him and when he heard her answer he was shocked. He told her, "I hope I am the last guy in that record setting list!" She took great offense to his comment and slapped him hard in the face. He got angry and called her a whore and stormed off. Later, she tried to call him but he had lost his phone and traveled back home without her. When they sobered up the next day, they made up.

I interpreted that not only was it obvious he had a drinking problem but he seemed to have started or at least contributed to creating a discussion that only fueled his insecurities. He seemed to want to find evidence of possible rejection or abandonment lurking as well as always wanting reassurance against it. This was an interpretation of his projective identification dynamic in which he was putting his vision of a turncoat object onto her and then reacting to it, but also demanding she assure him otherwise.

So, Dan seemed to split his objects into a rejecting and hurtful one that neglected his needy, vulnerable self and an object that could potentially soothe, reassure, and heal his tender anxieties and sense of helplessness.

Dan agreed but said, "Why would I do that and why do I feel this way?" I said, "That is what we are working on. The outer layer of working on it is to stop the drinking because it really fuels this fear. But, the inner layer is much more muddy and hard to understand so we must slowly try to explore it together as we have been".

These issues emerged in the transference when Dan called me at the last minute before one session to say he was held up at work and couldn't make it. When I saw him the next time, he immediately said, "Doc, I am so sorry. I really am. I didn't mean to put you out. I wanted to be here. I really did. But, my boss had a real backup on the big job we are doing right now. I don't think it will happen again. So, again, I am very sorry. I did not forget or anything. It was out of my control".

Noticing the anxious way Dan tried hard to repair what he seemed to think was a dangerous rupture in our connection, I made an interpretation of that phantasy. I said, "I think you are worried you have broken our connection. It seems you are anxious to assure me that you are not hurting me on purpose and that you are still loyal and want us to be ok. But, it sounds like that is based on some frightening feelings about how you really messed us up and ruined our connection. Now, you are feeling a bit insecure and not sure if we are still attached or still ok".

Dan replied, "I do feel that way. I just want to make sure you understand that it wasn't anything I did on purpose and that I do want to be here". The more we explored these anxieties and reparative attempts, this depressive emergency to make reparation as soon as possible, we ended up discussing how he was trying to make sure I did not end up feeling as abandoned or jealous and rejected as he often did with his girlfriend.

In other words, using my counter-transference as a guide, I realized he was picturing me as suffering in the same insecure and abandoned manner he had been describing about himself when his girlfriend goes traveling. So, through projective identification, his transference was to a weak, hurt, and lost object that had been cast aside for a better, more important object, and now he wanted to save me, heal me, and rebuild me. I made all these interpretations and Dan seemed to be able to take them in, feel less anxious, and begin to use this new knowledge to reconsider his image of self and other.

These discussions also led to a similar insight in the next session about how he was treating two coworkers. Dan was telling me about how he makes a point of always offering two coworkers a ride home after work. He told me he "felt sorry for them as they work a hard long day and then don't have a car to get home with, so they have to take the bus. It seems unfair that they have another hour before the day is done and their time is not their own. I have a car and I felt it was only friendly to tell them I would make sure to give them a ride at the end of every day". Now, to "make sure" to "be nice" meant Dan went an hour out of his way every day to do this. Thus, his time was now no longer "his own".

I interpreted that Dan forced a sad and lonely picture onto them, whether it was true or not. He insisted, in his mind, to have them be helpless, sad, and lonely little boys who were forced to take the bus home, and he was determined to rescue them. From what I could gather in his description, the two had told Dan they were fine but after Dan kept insisting, given Dan outranked them at work, they agreed. I said they might think it was strange that he insisted in going an hour out of his way and insisted on dropping them off at their homes instead of letting them live their own lives.

In other words, I interpreted the controlling and forceful aspect of his alleged rescue. With his forceful projective identification dynamic, he made them out to be pitiful figures in need of rescue. I also interpreted that he may have made me into one of those sad faces when he had to cancel our session and then he had to find a way to make it up to me.

The more we worked on his unconscious phantasies and conflict state, in the transference as well as in his extra transference references, the more we had a handle on what his drinking was about. Dan told me he "thinks others really want him to join in drinking and if he doesn't, he feels he will hurt their feelings and not be respecting them". He told me he "feels he will not fit in and will be seen as an outsider, not understood or liked by others". Here, I was able to interpret his intense desire to be liked in a certain way, thus controlling his objects and shaping them into a particular type of judge and jury.

Dan told me he "has always tried to focus on how he looks in the eyes of others and tries to make sure he is always doing whatever would make others see him in a positive light". I interpreted that he is being controlling and is forcing me and others into the role of an object that wants only specific behavior and that other behavior is not allowed. I must want to see him in only one way and that I would never accept, understand, or be pleased with him in any other way. So, I said he is worried I would be angry at him for being late when he was kept back at the job where his boss wanted him to continue finishing the big job. But, he never considered I could be understanding and even proud of him being asked to stay late because he is thought of so highly by his boss and does such a great job.

Dan was very surprised to hear this and said, "Wow! I never thought of it that way, that you or anyone could see me in a good way if I am doing my own thing". I said, "That probably includes never picturing others respecting you and looking up to you for choosing to not drink and to do something instead of hanging out at the bar getting into fights".

Here, we were starting to make significant progress in working with his core ways of viewing self and object and the manner in which he controlled others internally. His projective identification system was fixed and rigid, not allowing for a widening of self-definition and an expansion of how others might love him or accept him.

Sessions #10–20

During the time between sessions ten and fifteen, the elements of his insecurity with his girlfriend and with me seemed to begin to crystallize a bit. Through his talking about various incidents with his girlfriend, I started to have a sense about him as a very sensitive boy who felt left out and alone very easily. Dan began to talk about his upbringing and his family. In doing so, he revealed two aspects of himself that seemed to be replayed over and over. While he said he had a close relationship with his father through playing games and sports, Dan told me he "had a very close tie with his mother growing up". He told me that he was always by her side and felt very loved and understood by her at all times. "I was never out of her sight and whenever I could, I was sitting right next to her. We were very close".

Over the course of several sessions, Dan mentioned in passing that he "really missed his family and found himself crying when he heard about his sister giving birth to her first child and he was not there to celebrate with her". He told me "how depressing it is to realize he isn't able to be with his mother for her birthday" or how "he wants to be able to spend all the holidays with his family but is very sad when holidays come and go without that traditional family gathering".

Indeed, what alerted me to Dan's sense of emotional collapse when he felt out of touch with those he loved and needed was a particular incident in which he was at home with his girlfriend. She was packing for yet another business trip and Dan was looking out the window. He had been drinking that day so was already feeling emotional. He said, "I looked out the window to the park across the street and saw a few families having a picnic in the sunshine. I broke down in tears as I thought how great it would be if that was my family but instead they are so far away and it will be so long before I see them". Shortly after, Dan went over to this girlfriend who was packing her suitcase and started yelling at her for "leaving him and planning to probably sleep around with whoever she finds on this trip". They started fighting. He called her a slut and left.

When he came to see me the next day, he was devastated by his behavior and wanted help in "not ever acting that way again". I impressed on him that there were two issues we had to continue working on. One was his drinking. I said I thought his sensitivity to feeling abandoned and without his special objects was magnified by drinking and we would have a much easier time working on these matters if he was not exacerbating the problem by becoming so much more sensitive when drunk. Overall, at this point, Dan was doing better with drinking. The day in question he had drank a total of five drinks over the course of the day, which was less than the ten or more he would have usually consumed.

I said, "The most important issue we are dealing with is how quickly you feel left out or unimportant and then you get very sad and angry about it. I think you were already feeling in despair about not being with your family and feeling like they were suffering and you were suffering. It was an easy extension to feel your girlfriend was now leaving you alone on purpose and wanting someone else more than wanting you. You don't like to have to tolerate being without your mother, your family, your girlfriend, or me.

Unless it is your call and you feel in control, it seems you decide we are deliberately making you suffer or that you are deliberately hurting someone".

Dan said, "I really do feel that way. I never thought about how my feelings for my family are involved but now that you bring it up, I realize that might be the case much of the time. I am always missing my family and even though I call them and plan on visiting them, I often feel it is just not fair that I can't be with them. Each special event that happens, I feel cheated if I am not there fully being a part of it. Like you said, I don't like the idea that I have to be without them, just like I don't like the idea that my girlfriend has to leave me so often". So, here, we were starting to find some more internal aspects of Dan's experience of abandonment and his sense of easily hurting others just as he felt easily hurt by the other's absence.

During the course of our work together in sessions 15–20, much more was revealed and worked on. Once again, because of a work issue, Dan was unable to make one of his appointments. When he came in the next time, he said, "I am so sorry! I really hope you will accept my apology. Like I said in my message, the boss asked me at the last moment to stay longer and I was in a real pickle because I know how he is trying to finish the job by this crazy deadline so I didn't want to let him down. Also, as winter starts, work will be slowing down and I want him to remember that I am the one he can count on and willing to go the extra mile. But, I wanted to make my session with you and I was kind of irritated that he would wait till the last moment to tell me to stay so I couldn't find a way to reschedule or move things around. So, I am truly sorry and hope you will understand. I know this is your business and I want to respect it but I tried to sneak out after he told me to stay and I couldn't. He stayed around and was watching everything. So, like I said, I am sorry and I hope we are ok".

I said, "You are worried you have hurt me and injured our bond together. You must feel like you are really in the middle and caught by trying to please your boss on one hand and me on the other. To make sure you were getting what you want must seem almost out of the question without ending up hurting someone else. You are not sure if I am ok and if we will survive these bumps in the road where you decide to do something for yourself or someone else instead of strictly pleasing me".

Dan said, "I do feel that. That is the way I feel a good deal of the time. I just want us to be ok and to not have these patches of friction". I said, "You are worried we can't find our way through them. You have been pretty upset when your girlfriend goes away or doesn't seem to treat you as number one. Maybe, you are worried I will feel like you do and think you are not making me number one". Here, I was interpreting his projective identification based transference. Dan agreed and said, "It is always like that!", showing how he felt a victim to his own pathological organization.

As Feldman (2009) notes, the analyst is constantly trying to find out, through interpretation of the transference, the sort of unconscious object he represents to the patient. For Dan, I seemed to be a fragile, hollow object that was easily hurt, damaged, or angered by his less than perfect behavior. If he acted on his own behalf, he felt he was shorting me and being selfish. As Feldman (2009) recommends, I had to resist the projective identification based counter-transference pull to reassure him and forgive him immediately, preventing or erasing conflict before we had to notice it. This technical approach is also what Steiner (2011a) suggests, citing the importance to notice the projective identification seduction to react in particular ways and instead to try to learn from these unconscious communications, to contain them (Bion 1962a), and to ultimately find a way to interpret them.

In response to my interpretation, Dan continued, "I try and make sure everyone in my life is respected and that I treat all of you as important and with priority. But things like the work situation get in the way and I end up anxious and uncertain about what will happen. You mentioned my girlfriend. That whole thing came up again over the weekend. She was going out of town again and I tried my best to keep it together. But, something happened. I had saved up and bought her this really nice necklace last month, right after we had that really big fight. I had told her that it was symbolic of how much I love her and how much I want a future with her. She said she really liked it. But, after she went on her business trip, I noticed that she had left it behind in the apartment. I got really mad and thought that after all the time and effort I put into getting that for her and how much I try and do for her, she would dare to leave it behind. Then, after I had driven her to the airport on my time off, she expected me to pick her up. When I was ten minutes late, she called and sounded irritated and asked me where I was. I couldn't believe that she was taking me for granted especially when I was doing so much for her. Anyway, we got into a bit of a fight and I brought up the necklace and she told me that she hadn't forgotten it but that it was so precious and important to her that she didn't want to risk losing it on her trip so she left it home for safety. I was stunned and apologized".

I said, "First of all, were you drinking?" Dan said, "I had only had two beers that day and I haven't had more than 2–3 beers in any given day for a couple of weeks now. I am really getting that under control". I said, "Well, I hope that you are doing that for yourself and not to please me since that is a pattern we see so often. But, it is very fortunate you were not drunk because before this type of situation would have ended up in a severe fight with disastrous results. Besides the drinking, it seems you want so much to be a good caretaker for all of us and never let us down. But, deep down, you also get hurt when you don't feel appreciated. I have noticed you want me to realize how hard you try to be here on time and for me to know how hard you are trying to be a good patient and do what's right".

Dan said, "I have always done that. When I was a little boy, I always tried my best to take care of my mother and to do the right thing. She was always depressed and I always tried to make her feel better or at least not do anything that would cause her to feel worse. She spent her life trying to please others and make me happy but never seemed happy herself. She sacrificed everything for me and just wanted to make sure I was ok. I remember being a child and noticing how she never bought herself anything much and how she made do day to day with only the basics, never anything too frivolous or special, nothing fancy. I learned how to be that way from her. I made sure to make do myself. I tried to be fine with whatever I had. I remember how all the other kids used to get a new bicycle every Christmas. It wasn't because they needed one, the one they had was still fine. So, it was an extravagant purchase that they didn't need. When it came Christmas time, I told my mother I didn't want a new bicycle because mine was fine. I only asked for one when mine was worn out or broken. I did the same with toys and clothes".

Listening to this, I thought these were depressive phantasies of a beloved object who was broken and weak. Therefore, Dan made sure to never have more than his depressed mother, never expressing any need or desire that might hurt his suffering object. I thought this was the same type of transference phantasy he was demonstrating with me in many of our sessions.

I interpreted that Dan wanted to make his unhappy and depressed mother better and he tried to never be a burden on her or to take up more space than her with his excitement or desires. So, even though all the kids loved their toys and new bikes, he tried to convince himself he was fine without. I told him that he seemed to believe that by staying in the trenches with his mother he could make her feel better instead of feeling like he had abandoned her or betrayed her by wanting his own life full of possibilities and desire. He said, "That is how I felt. She seemed so sad and I didn't want to make it worse. I didn't want her to have to worry about buying me toys and everything when she rarely treated herself to anything".

I said, "You feel guilty about wanting more and paying attention to yourself instead of her". Dan said, "Most definitely". I interpreted, "It seems like you see me as needing that kind of special attention and that you could hurt me very easily as well by not making it to the session or being late. You are not sure I am strong enough to survive your mistakes or your just being yourself". Dan replied, "I just don't want to disappoint you. I like to have everyone happy".

I said, "But you feel to do that you have to sacrifice what you want. There is never room for both of us to have what we need. One person wins and the other loses". Dan says, "I have grown up being used to that. I can take it. If the other person needs something, I am willing to step aside". I said, "But, your drinking and your frantic panic with your girlfriend suggest that you end up very lonely and wondering when it will be your turn". Dan paused and nodded yes.

As Spillius (1993) notes, if the young child engages in envious attacks on the goodness of the object, there can be a premature development of guilt before the individual can tolerate such a state, leading to a confusion between depressive guilt and paranoid-schizoid anxiety. My patient Dan seemed to feel both a precocious obligation to serve and care for his depressed mother but also resentment over her inability to enjoy anything and her inability to give very little to him. He seems to have felt the parent and child relationship was reversed, she took and he gave. Now, the conflict over this state of internal affairs came alive in the transference as well as in his relationship to those important figures in his life. His deepest wish and fear had to do with wanting his own life but also wanting to never disturb or damage the life of the other. He could not yet figure out how to coexist with his objects without emotional bloodshed. However, we were making progress using the elements of Modern Kleinian Therapy, including examination of the transference, counter-transference, projective identification, phantasy, and the nature of the here and now, in the moment establishment or disconnection of analytic contact.

A few hours before the next session, Dan left me a message asking if we were indeed meeting or not. He said he was a bit confused as we were not going to meet the following week due to a holiday. I returned his message and reminded him that we were indeed meeting that day as scheduled. When he arrived, he told me that his job was still on "critical overdrive with everyone working crazy hours on the big project and his boss still expecting everyone to work overtime". In the past, Dan had tried to please his boss by saying yes to staying and then feeling very guilty and scared of how he had injured or enraged me. We had explored how he often puts himself in the middle that way and ends up with nothing for himself and only partly satisfying his objects. Indeed, when he had said no to his boss in the past so he could please me, he felt sure that "his boss had put a black mark next to his name" and Dan felt he had "let him down when he really needed me".

This time was the same in some ways and different in others. On one hand, Dan was still concerned about causing conflict and distress in others. He told me he "knew his boss was probably going to ask him to stay late but he really wanted to come and see me. But, he also didn't want to take that stance with his boss if it turned out we weren't even meeting". I interpreted, "You finally wanted to see me because you wanted to instead of coming to see me in order to keep me happy. But, you didn't want to shoot off your big cannon on the wrong day". Dan laughed and said, "Exactly". "So", I said, "you wanted to check if it was worth it to risk confronting the boss with your own wants and needs. You want to see me today to please yourself".

Dan said, "Yes. I told him I had to leave and he looked at me and said, 'Really?' I had to look at him and said, 'Yes, I have an appointment'. Then, he said ok. At first he looked a bit bent out of shape but then I think he was ok with it". I said, "You had to stand up to him twice in a row and express your wants and where you draw the line. At first you thought you hurt him and he was going to be angry or resentful. But, then, you felt it would be ok. He survived you growing up and leaving the nest for the day". Dan said, "I wanted to see you today especially since we won't meet next week. I have a few things to talk about".

Dan went on to talk about being invited out to an all-day drinking party and how he was able to say no even though some of his friends were cajoling him to reconsider. I interpreted that it was another story of him deciding he wanted something that was different from the other person's desires but he stood up for himself and felt like everyone survived at the end of the day. This was my continuing to interpret his successful struggle with the anxieties of depressive conflicts and phantasies.

I also did not have the impression Dan was trying to gift me or impress me with these stories. So, I also commented that he seemed to have made those decisions because he felt right about it and was now sharing his own personal victory with me instead of trying to do what he thinks I told him to do and trying to please me by reporting his adherence to my suggestion. Instead, he was feeling like a man, noticing himself growing up and still able to feel close to his objects and trust that they were all still intact, content, and full. He had not drained us and we did not need replenishing. He could pay more attention to tending his own garden and allow us to tend ours without anxiety or guilt.

As a result of this very short period of psychoanalytic work, Dan had markedly reduced his drinking and was exploring and shifting his internal object relational conflicts. There is a great deal of work ahead, but we have made a remarkable start by working in the transference and paying close attention to his phantasies and core conflicts. These are clinical examples of the benefits of Modern Kleinian Therapy.

3

PARANOIA AND THE OBJECT
OF DREAD

During a 2011 workshop, the prominent Kleinian analyst Michael Feldman was discussing the importance of the here-and-now transference, the interpretation of the past as lived out in the present, the predictability of enactment in the counter-transference, and how close examination of mutual acting out can help further our understanding of the patient's projective identification efforts. These elements of technique make up the Modern Kleinian approach to psychoanalytic treatment. Responding to an audience member's question about how these ways of practicing are applicable to all diagnostic levels or if they are helpful to patients only attending once or twice a week, Feldman was very clear in his response. He said that the Kleinian method, especially the way the contemporary Kleinians of London (Schafer 1997) practice, is meant to be a process of one human being willing to take on, take in, and attempt to understand another human being's most volatile, difficult, and confusing internal states. That person attempts to make sense of those projective communications without playing them out in the same repetitive and destructive manner the other is so familiar with and prone to reducing things to. Then, in a series of ongoing trial and error interactions, the analyst offers interpretations and observations of how the patient is living out his or her life within the relationship to the analyst to see if there is a way to find alternatives, change, and healing for what has been a confining and predictable pattern of anxiety, guilt, rage, loss, and fragmentation.

Feldman stated that this process is not limited by diagnosis or frequency, only the willingness both of analyst and of patient to proceed into what can be both an exciting and restorative experience as well as a terrifying, stagnant, or chaotic situation.

In this chapter, the author takes up this idea of psychoanalysis and offers the model of Modern Kleinian Therapy as the treatment vehicle Feldman was describing. While frequency is different and the couch is not always used, the procedure is the same as what is commonly recognized as Kleinian psychoanalytic treatment. The transference is harder to locate, frame, and engage with and the counter-transference is trickier to recognize, manage, and utilize. But, the essential path to insight and change remains the same, with resolution to internal object relational conflict being the goal.

CASE OF DENNIS

Dennis came to see me for help with "the crap at work that keeps getting worse. They just want to fool with me, making things hard because they need to feel powerful". This paranoid phantasy of a power struggle was the way Dennis related to me for the first several sessions. What I mean by this is that he made sure to have us focus on this tale of power abuse at work and how he was being manipulated by his boss but in doing so he also was managing to manipulate us. I felt I had to go along with his paranoid tale. My sense was I could not question his belief in any way and all other areas of his internal and external life were off bounds.

In this manner, his initial complaints were acted out in the transference with him as the one needing to feel powerful. I felt both controlled and intimidated but also felt Dennis was fragile, extremely anxious, and needed to have things be restricted or reduced to this story of accusation and blame. I gradually tested the waters to see if he could tolerate any view but his own and if I was allowed to challenge his story or even ask questions. To do this, I noticed that, in the counter-transference, I felt I had to be brave and risk making him angry or worse.

Dennis had worked at a furniture company for several years and described himself as a "very loyal and trustworthy person, a real hard worker". He described the company as "a good place that feels like family". Hearing this, I immediately wondered how his internal family experience was being played out and how I might end up a part of that. I interpreted, "when you say it feels like a family, from your description of all the problems, it sounds like a very frustrating or dysfunctional family". Dennis said, "Well, it is nothing like some crazy families. But, my manager is definitely a bad part of the family. I enjoy the customers and most of the rest of the staff. But, this one manager thinks it is fun to mess with me and try and show off who is in power. But, I am not about to take it. I will fight back if I have to". The last part of "I will fight back if I have to" seemed like an angry, cornered animal, growling and baring its teeth.

While I was open to the idea that his manager might indeed actually be out to get him, I was considering his anxious and paranoid story to be more of a displacement for internal struggles and possible transference issues. This acknowledgement of his external reality along with a strong focus on what unconscious phantasy that story might be representing is in line with what Grotstein (2009) has noted as the distinction between psychotherapy and psychoanalysis, with psychoanalysis placing the emphasis on the internal phantasy state. Modern Kleinian Therapy is a method of treatment identical in technical process as 4–5-times-a-week analysis. However, the reduced frequency makes these external layers a thicker smoke screen that is more confusing or difficult to work with and easier to become aligned with in various enactments that steer the two parties away from the central internal conflict.

Dennis was an angry looking and muscular young man with a combination of an off putting grimace and a disturbing faraway gaze in his eyes. He also had dark circles around his eyes that marked his bleak, depressed, and tired feelings. I believe what I am describing were outwardly physical manifestations of his internal state of anger, anxiety, paranoia, and hopelessness. Indeed, Dennis told me he was currently "in trouble" at work for not listening to his manager, for talking back, and for intimidating some of the other workers. Over the course of a few sessions, Dennis told me of how he really enjoyed the company and was actively trying to be promoted to a new position, but felt his current manager "had it out for him and wanted to mess with him".

In the counter-transference, I thought Dennis wanted me to side with him against the bad persecutory manager and see how mistreated and misunderstood he was. But, I also felt that was my only choice and if I tried to suggest that he indeed did look angry and might actually be in a power struggle with others, I would get into trouble or worse. I found myself worrying about my safety and wondering if he might "go crazy and lose it". I tried to sort out if this was my accurate assessment of reality or perhaps a part of some projective identification based transference that was occurring.

After a while of considering these thoughts and feelings, I realized Dennis was making me feel powerless and he was becoming the cruel manager that I had to either fight against or to give in to. So, I interpreted that perhaps he sometimes did come off angry and sometimes wanted his way with the manager, customers, and me. And, that he might be trying to assert control in those ways so as to avoid feeling completely controlled and pushed around.

Dennis said he "knows he can be that way" but then said, "I can't help it. Maybe he gets under my skin like that because I don't like anyone thinking they can push everyone around and mess with you just for the sake of it. Sometimes, he reminds me of my father, a person who likes to make other people suffer and to make sure everyone knows he is the most powerful. I hate that. It makes me sick. I want to do a good job and be liked but I guess I am not about to take any crap. Maybe, that is what gets me into trouble. I will talk back. Others won't but I will. I don't care. I will not allow that kind of behavior even if it is my superior. I don't want to have to be silent and take whatever is happening".

I said that it all sounded very ominous and scary the way he described it. I wondered if he ended up feeling like there was something very personal going on that somehow reminded him of something in the past or someone else. Given that he mentioned his father, I asked if that sense of being pushed around could be something with his father. As a result of these questions, we spent the next few sessions exploring his childhood and the continuing problems with his father and his family. This was a slow and difficult interaction in which Dennis did not trust me fully and felt very uncertain and uncomfortable revealing himself. But, it seemed that by containing my counter-transference of wanting to push back or retreat from his initial paranoid power struggle transference, it enabled Dennis to open up a wider scope of therapeutic engagement.

Dennis began to share an extremely painful and traumatic childhood history that still plagues him externally and internally. He shared this with me over the course of several sessions in a disorganized, jerky, and confusing manner. I made the interpretation that he was reluctant, scared, and broken up inside so he was very cautious and only put out certain pieces at a time. This interpretation of his transference caution seemed to reduce his anxiety and Dennis began to tell me more about the frightening experiences he had as a child.

He told me of how his father was an angry unpredictable man who "could get really out of control". I said, "It sounds very scary. Can you give me some examples?" Dennis told me how his father "ran the house with an iron fist" and how his mother "did her best to stay out of the way". He told me, "No one ever got in my father's way. There was no telling what he was capable of. What we got on a daily basis was bad enough. It was always a big mistake to say no to him or to do anything he didn't like". I said, "It definitely sounds like he had a terrible temper. It also sounds like he beat you". Dennis said, "Yes. All the time. There was way too many times to count". Telling me these painful stories left Dennis visibly shaken, anxious, and unsure of our relationship. He was obviously still suffering greatly.

He dropped a few clues along the way that made it obvious there was more to the story than just the history of violence. While it was bad enough to hear that he had been removed from the home more than once because of his father's violence and how he was told by his mother to lie to the social worker about the violence, I could tell there was something else that plagued him. He was using phrases like "the other stuff", "the thing everyone could find out about", and the "secrets that we had". I told him I thought there was something else even more disturbing that he was unsure of telling me about.

Gradually, with my questions and supportive interpretations about how worried he seemed of my possible lack of understanding or my judgment, Dennis started to reveal his feelings in the transference. He said, "You could start to see me in a different way. You could assume things that are not true". I asked him what he meant. Dennis said, "You could easily decide I am just like that, you could put me in that category. People like to think what they think and there is never any way to disprove it".

I said, "You are really worried I will start to judge you and not like you if you are more open with me. I wonder if you think I won't understand and just presume things instead of listen to you and try to understand what you are going through". He said, "People like to say that and sometimes they do listen but people are people. They just go with what they think. I know it's weird but I wonder if you already think that and if you have already thought I am like that". I said, "You are very uncomfortable giving us a chance and risking letting me know you. But, if you are not as quick to decide I am just like all the rest for a moment, maybe we can be different and work together on this".

After a moment of silence, Dennis seemed to relax and said, "Things were happening all along that I just didn't know about. Now, people probably wonder and maybe you do too. They wonder just how could I not know what was happening all around me. I think about it all the time and try and sort out when and how and I just never can make sense of it. But, now people can look at me and I think they see it. Or, if they know my last name they could know and then they just follow what you read about or see on TV". I said, "What happened that still haunts you so much?" In this halting, frightened, and disorganized way, Dennis gradually told me about the rest of his childhood trauma that still extends into his adult life.

Besides the ongoing violence from his father, when Dennis was eight years old, his father was sent to prison for molesting Dennis's sister. Apparently, the sexual abuse had been going on for years. His father spent several years in prison but somehow was able to come home for visits. These visits were memories of incredible tension, fights, violence, and anxiety for Dennis. When his father finally was released he came home and lived there for several years before Dennis's mother divorced him. The entire family and extended family was torn apart by the news of the molestation. Everyone took sides and reacted in different ways. Dennis told me this was yet another part of the stress and that "everyone assumed something about everyone".

Over the course of several sessions, I finally was able to understand what Dennis meant about me immediately thinking something about him. It emerged, in an anxious, paranoid, and disorganized manner. But, he finally explained what he was dreading. Basically, Dennis believed that I or anyone else who was interacting with him could somehow detect that he was the son of a child molester. In talking with him, he said he knew this seemed "outlandish and kind of crazy", but he also believed it and feared it. He was sure that with this sort of mind reading, I would see him as a deviant. He was convinced that he would be guilty by association in the eyes of others. Besides this idea of mind reading, he was sure that as soon as others knew his last name, they would look him up on the Internet and find out his father was a convicted sex offender and then think that "the apple doesn't fall far from the tree".

Dennis told me, "I know that especially you, as a professional, would try to be neutral and unbiased but you are still human. Everyone, as soon as they realize, makes assumptions. They have heard from books or television how when someone is abused or is related to someone who is abusing, they grow up to be one too. So, I try and not think about it but I can see it in your eyes and everyone else I talk to. You can't help but think I might be like that too. At first, when I meet someone, I can feel ok or more at ease. But, if we or anyone start to talk and get along, I know it won't be long before they could look me up and then it's all over. I have this curse on me and no one will ever believe me if I say no. There is always going to be that lingering doubt in your mind".

I said, "So, while you want to trust me and depend on me for help, you can't help but think I will betray you by thinking of you as a replica of your father. I won't give you a chance. I will just assume you are as bad as he is". Dennis said, "Yes".

Over the next month or two, we focused on this terrible source of anxiety. There were various levels of his phantasy. In interpreting his transference, we slowly explored how he may focus on the dread of being the same in my mind so as to avoid realizing he is separate and different. In other words, I interpreted that he may feel so overwhelmed by the idea that his father is not remotely like him and is such a gruesome and frightening "not me" character in Dennis's mind that he would rather feel they are the same. I suggested that this unconscious fusion defense may also provide him some perverse phantasy of closeness to his father that the terrible violence and sexual abuse in his family probably prevented. I also interpreted that he would rather think I was judging him as a potential molester then to have to be vulnerable to not knowing how I felt about him. He was scared to risk gradually finding out how I felt about him as our relationship developed. While his reaction to my comments were halting and he found my interpretations emotionally painful, these interpretive directions seemed to help Dennis slowly feel more secure, safe, and stable.

From the very beginning of his analytic treatment, I noticed how Dennis would talk over me or even talk louder than me when I spoke up. He would effectively drown me out. In general, he left me no real opening or opportunity to join in, contribute, or comment on what he was saying. I was forced to be the audience for his nervous, stuttering, and choppy tale of paranoia and darkness. I eventually would get my comments or interpretations in and he did hear them because he acknowledged them by simply saying yes. But, I still felt bulldozed, ignored, and overpowered.

For quite some time, I did not say anything about this, as I felt it served a specific defensive function. As Rosenfeld (1987) and Joseph (1987) have noted, our patients utilize projective identification for a variety of unconscious reasons that often overlap. So, in the beginning, my counter-transference was intense and I felt like fighting back for my verbal space by telling Dennis to be quiet and let me talk. But, I decided that at that point in the total transference situation (Joseph 1985), in order to maintain his sense of internal equilibrium (Joseph 1989), Dennis needed to fill the room with himself, keep me at a distance, and show me that he held the power. So, I let him continue as is until a point in the treatment a few weeks later when I thought his projective process shifted within the transference and his talking over me seemed to serve a different function.

At first, I thought it was a defensive stance against the threat of massive intrusion and psychic takeover, a parallel to his childhood experiences and his current adult anxieties and phantasies. But, after a while, I felt the flavor or tone behind his verbal bulldozer shifted to something more pushy, aggressive, and tyrannical. I began to feel irritated and useless. I thought that Dennis was now giving me a taste of his own phantasy state of when he faced off with his persecutory and dominating objects. In other words, he was now the abusive bully and I was the victim instead of his initial worry that I would bully him followed by his desperate attempts to protect himself with nonstop words.

So, at one point, I said, "You are not letting me talk. Whenever I try and say something you talk louder and talk over me. I think you are wanting me to stand up to you, demand my equal time, and not let you bully me like you feel your father does". Dennis replied, "Sorry. I just have so much to say. I want to be able to say everything and we don't have much time". I said, "In your efforts to unburden yourself and say everything, you are making yourself all alone and preventing us from having a back and forth team effort. Maybe you are so used to feeling alone against all these terrible feelings that you push me away and make it a solitary affair. You might be uncomfortable trusting me to work side by side with you".

Dennis replied, "It is very hard to trust anyone. I am sure everyone will start to see me as the same as him". I said, "So, you think by not letting me in, by talking over me and preventing me from seeing inside of you, I won't think you are a horrible person. But, who you really are and what you need gets lost in the process".

After this exploration, Dennis sometimes still filled the room with his words. But, more and more, he allowed us to be two people talking with each other. And, when he did talk over me, he now made a more elaborative acknowledgement of what I said instead of seeming to completely ignore it.

A couple of weeks later, Dennis's initial paranoia about his work manager controlling him and humiliating him resurfaced in a very similar phantasy about his teacher. Dennis was attending night school and doing quite well, even though he was always nervous about his performance. We had explored his anxieties about being with his classmates over the course of five or six sessions. In that time, we discussed how Dennis felt both above his classmates and beneath them. Dennis told me they all seemed "prone to being elitist, cliquish, and are obviously able to study as much as they want because they don't have to hold down a job as well as go to school". He did not want to "waste his time trying to get to know them as they weren't really his type and they didn't really have much in common".

On the other hand, Dennis told me that he felt he was "not as smart as some of them and that he was reluctant to open up to anyone at school because they could easily find out about him". This meant he thought they would immediately know his father was a convicted sex offender and assume he was one too.

After working with these anxieties for a while, Dennis felt better but then his concerns shifted to his teacher. He told me that while he had been doing fine at the start of his class, his teacher "seemed to have changed" and "now had a darker attitude and didn't seem interested in helping the students as much". I immediately wondered about his transference fears and asked him if we were perhaps drifting apart somehow. He was quick to reassure me that "even though he sometimes worries I think he is warped or sick, overall he is more comfortable and ok".

I believed that Dennis was indeed more comfortable but continued to be sensitive to any transference anxiety regarding my betrayal or change. However, I also considered my suspicious, vigilant, and worried counter-transference about his possible transference to be a projective identification based experience in which he had located his paranoia state into me.

Dennis told me that his teacher "used to be a nice guy who graded fairly and explained everything carefully so the students could easily understand". Now, Dennis felt this man had started to "act strange, make unpredictable decisions about grading, provided no help at all, and seemed to have it out for him". Dennis felt the teacher was now "making sure he would fail" because the teacher thought "I was only partly interested in the class since I have to work full time. He wants me to be completely dedicated to his class or else".

When I asked if he had considered tutors since he was falling behind in his grades and the school did provide tutors, Dennis told me, "The tutors see me coming and don't want anything to do with me. They like to help the smarter students who are more on their level. I can tell they just look down on me".

Again, I addressed the possible transference. Also, I tried to explore his reluctance to see me or anyone else as either able to help him or willing to help him. I said, "I think you want to come here and share all these terrible anxieties and confusions with me. Also, I think you want to seek help from the tutors to find some answers for your problems. But, then you start to doubt if we really care about you or are we just judging you, seeing you as a misfit, and a duplicate of your father. Then, you decide you don't need anyone who would look down on you and not understand you. But, that leaves you all alone and fighting off the world. Let's look at why you need to box us up like that".

At first, Dennis told me that "people are just like that. They can't help it. I know you are a professional so you try to not be that way. In the end people are people. They can't help it. They are always like that". However, the more I talked with Dennis about these projections and this uncertain and cautious transference state, the more he "could see how he was making it hard to get help" and how "it might be ok to keep trying to trust" me. He said that in the end he was only worried about the tutors but I took his comments to reveal his ongoing struggles, conflicts, hopes, and fears about our relationship as well.

Indeed, during this time, he canceled a number of sessions saying it was mostly due to so much school work he had to study for and sometimes because of a work scheduling problem. When he showed up, I told him, "I think you are afraid of what I think and what you will end up talking about. So, even though you want to be here, you end up nervous and unsure".

Dennis replied, "I couldn't make it because of all the extra time I had to spend in the library studying. But, I know what you mean. I get unsure about everything".

Over the course of the short time we have been meeting, I have noticed myself caught up at times in the feeling of not trusting him, being afraid of him, and not feeling like I can rely on him for a consistent or predictable relationship. I understand this to be the result of ongoing projective identification conflicts he brings into the transference that in turn create these specific counter-transference experiences.

An example occurred around the twenty-seventh session. Dennis called to cancel a session and did not say anything about seeing me the following week. I felt a sense of dread, wondering if this was the time honored method of cutting off treatment that so many borderline patients use. I left a message wondering if he would like to reschedule for another time that week or to just meet at the usual time the following week. When he did not return that call, I again started feeling uneasy. I wondered if he was ok but mostly I felt he had decided I was a bad object and had discarded me.

Over the course of two weeks, I left four phone messages, wondering if things were ok and asking him to call. I told him I assumed we would meet at our normal time but would appreciate a call anyway. During the whole time, I worked more and more with my counter-transference state of feeling rejected and strangely treated. I tried hard to hold onto the idea that there was a possibility of instead of the typical borderline exit without words or thought, I might be experiencing something else with a more paranoid but non-borderline flavor. I thought of Dennis as possibly being higher functioning, with some guilt as well as some psychotic features. I thought I should not write him off as quickly as just another one of the aborted treatment experiences I have had over the years. I thought I should give him a chance.

I noticed myself in this back and forth place and embraced it, thinking he might need me to contain myself and to hang in there and to trust him instead of quickly judging him, which was his transference fear. So, I did. The day before our next scheduled appointment, I still had not heard from Dennis and thought this might be the end.

But, then he called. Dennis said he "really wanted to come in and see me and was sorry he had missed the previous session". He said "things had gotten pretty bad with my mother-in-law in the hospital after a terrible car accident. Of course, there is no one I can really turn to with my father and me not on speaking terms and my mother barely able to manage her own life. I really need to talk. I look forward to seeing you".

When Dennis came in for the next session, he started off paying me for the missed sessions and the current one. When he realized he had to give me more than needed due to having no change, he offered to give me even more to "cover the next visit". Given his missing of the last two weeks, the look on his face, and how he seemed quite anxious and possibly remorseful, I interpreted, "Maybe you are trying to pay me off so I am not hurt or angry. You probably feel guilty about not showing up for a while".

Dennis said, "Exactly! I hope you can understand and not feel angry or think I was trying to not be here". I asked why he did not return any of my calls. Dennis told me, "I was totally shut down. I couldn't function. I have been really depressed and shut down. Everything seems to be falling apart". I asked for details and he told me his mother-in-law was taken to the hospital and was on life support with the situation "looking grim". He went on to describe how he is very close to his mother-in-law and is "terrified should anything happen to her". He said that situation combined with the ongoing strain with his father and the "predictable backstabbing and complete disconnection in my family leaves me feeling really alone and sad. There is nothing but this sense of everyone always being pulled apart and never together. My mother-in-law was one person I could count on and respect and now it is unclear if she will be ok!"

After we talked about these difficult events for a while, Dennis brought up how he was "so thankful that school was over for the holidays because school would have been too much to handle on top of everything else". I asked him how he had done in the class where he felt the teacher was against him. Dennis told me he had dropped out of the class "since it was clear he was against me and I had no way out but to withdraw and take it over with someone else". Dennis felt ok about his decision but told me he was really worried about the next class he was scheduled to take. He explained that this one would be a pivotal class to determine if he could be placed on the list for an important internship.

Dennis said, "You know what that means! Everyone will be out to win and will be trying to push me out. I don't know if I will survive it. No one will trust anyone. There is one goal and everyone will do anything to get there. It will be cut throat. I think I am at a disadvantage already because most people in the class will already have some experience in the field and will use that against me. I hope I don't have to withdraw from that class; that would completely destroy my career plans!" I interpreted, "Maybe you are feeling so eager to get the internship and so competitive that you assume everyone else will be too and want to run you over. But, maybe it is your own competitive feelings that scare you. This is a very important goal for you and you are worried about not reaching it but then blaming it on others. Maybe we need to look at your own anxiety about passing the class and the anxiety about finally moving towards something special in your life".

Dennis replied, "I know I am being really paranoid. I need help with that. I notice myself getting really paranoid about all sorts of little things lately.

46

I don't want to start thinking the teacher is out to get me or that the other students are against me. But, lately I find myself getting more paranoid". Initially, I thought this was a good sign in that Dennis seemed to be reflecting on his inner process and noticing the way he was distorting his objects. However, this moment of reality grounding was fleeting.

Dennis continued, "I know that no one will see me as a friend because there are only a few slots for the internship and everyone wants it. So, that makes me the enemy. I will be treated as such and the only thing I can do is fight for my place in the class. But, if everyone is against me I don't feel like I have much of a chance. I hope the teacher doesn't turn on me as well!" Here, Dennis returned to the very concrete paranoid experience of being on his own against others who would turn on him and hurt him to have their way.

We continue to meet once a week and explore this internal chaos and dread. We have met for a total of thirty sessions now. Dennis wants to continue, wanting to make his way through the darkness and searching for a bit of hope or at least "a way to not always have to think about how my father's footprint defines my life".

Discussion

Rosenfeld (1987) has clarified the variety of motives involved in projective identification including communication, defense, attack, control, and fusion. The more anxious or more disturbed patient will overutilize projective methods to the point of internal emptiness and collapse. Dennis was constantly trying to find and control the unpredictable and persecutory object. He was projecting his own sense of self as damaged and suspicious as well as his own judgment or desire for control into the object and then feeling targeted for suspicion. He also wanted someone to agree with him and side with his vision of the world and was not sure about trusting me when I provided alternative ideas or disagreed with his views of the object or himself.

So, I think Dennis was often in a storm of projective identification based confusion in which he was reaching out for help and trying to communicate his isolation and desire for change. But, he was also attacking his objects with accusation and mistrust, trying to overpower them, devalue them, and fuse with a betraying and predatory object as a way to avoid the sorrow, loss, and anxiety that a good object evoked.

As Steiner (2011b) notes, the object is sometimes concretely and ominously incorporated and identified with. This tends to be in instances where separation and individuation are denied or avoided. This prevents healthy mourning and integration and serves as a pathological defense or psychological foxhole (Waska 2010a, 2010b, 2010c) against the most difficult stage of loss and grieving, the final facing of the reality of the loss. This is the acceptance that the loved object, the pined or wished for good object is no longer available or, in Dennis's case, was possibly never available to begin with.

With excessive reliance on projective identification, Dennis was able to deny this reality and the reality of separateness. By seeing himself as the evil extension of his molesting father, he could still have emotional contact with his father in phantasy, even if it meant a persecutory and shameful dread of how others would react.

Markman (2010) has pointed out how in the Kleinian approach, especially as practiced by Michael Feldman, the analyst needs to be aware of and tolerate the need of the patient to locate the analyst within a particular area of their mind and within a specific object relational phantasy. Many other contemporary Kleinian analysts agree with this way of thinking about close process transformative and dynamic work with phantasy and transference. In this way, Modern Kleinian Therapy is a psychoanalytic method of treatment based on the work of the contemporary Kleinians of London (Schafer 1997).

As mentioned in Chapters 1 and 2, this is a therapeutic system that also integrates the work of Kernberg's Transference Focused Psychotherapy (Clarkin, Yeomans, and Kernberg 1999, 2006), the CCRT method of Luborsky (1984), earlier work of Waska (2005, 2006), some ideas from Sandler (1976), and a mixture of flexible technical principles from a wide variety of analytic thinkers such as Merton Gill (1994), Searles (1986), and others. The moment-to-moment focus on the total transference situation (Joseph 1985), the classical Kleinian approach of Hanna Segal (1962, 1974, 1975, 1977a, 1977b, 1993, 1997a, 1981), as well as the work of Britton (2004, 2008), Spillius (1983, 1992, 1993, 2007), Steiner (1979, 1984, 1987, 1992, 1994, 1996), and Feldman (1994, 2004, 2009) are all adapted towards the continuous clinical effort to establish analytic contact (Waska 2007) regardless of frequency or diagnosis.

Feldman (2009) has written about the counter-transference tension to reassure the patient we are not the person or place they project onto us. With Dennis, I noticed a regular pull to reassure him I was not feeling repulsed by him, not seeing him as a probable molester, and not rejecting him before ever getting to know him. Instead, I had to stay within the transference and counter-transference matrix, enduring this pressure and tension of his persecutory and primitive depressive phantasies and try to speak to him about his default distrust of me and others. This is in line with Feldman's view of the transference always being about a particular type of object relational state and the various conflicts between love, hate, and knowledge always being a part of the unconscious relational tension.

The Modern Kleinian Therapy approach is in line with Betty Joseph's (1989) view of the communicative effects and efforts of projective identification and the projective impact on the analyst in the counter-transference as both being central in informing the analyst on how to make immediate, here-and-now analytic observations (Waska 2012) and interpretations (Aguayo 2011).

While this method of working analytically with low frequency patients also uses Joseph's idea of the present always being a reflection of the past, thus leading to the bulk of interpretations being made about the present, the Modern Kleinian approach also values Hanna Segal's (1962, 1974, 1981) view of the present always rediscovering the past and the role of phantasy as two critical areas of therapeutic focus. This, in turn, leads to interpretations about the past and about unconscious phantasy and conflict as well as the here-and-now. The importance of these two Kleinian perspectives as curative and clinical crucial in the working through process has been discussed by Blass (2011) as in opposition or at least in contrast to each other. Instead of being viewed as in conflict with each other, in the Modern Kleinian Therapy method these two approaches are used in conjunction with each other and are found to be very complementary in practice.

4

COUPLES TREATMENT AND THE
QUEST FOR ANALYTIC CONTACT

Melanie Klein's pioneering work with children and adults has expanded
Freud's clinical work and is now the leading worldwide influence in current
psychoanalytic practice. The key Kleinian concepts include the total
transference (Joseph 1985, 1989), projective identification, the importance of
counter-transference, psychic retreats (Steiner 1990, 1993), the container/
contained function (Bion 1959, 1962a, 1962b, 1963), enactment (Steiner
2006), splitting, the paranoid and depressive positions (Klein 1935, 1940,
1946), unconscious phantasy, and the value of interpreting both anxiety and
defense. These components of the Kleinian approach have become so
commonplace in the literature and adopted by so many other schools of
practice it is easy to forget Object Relations theory and technique was Melanie
Klein's discovery.

In broadening Klein's work to match today's clinical climate, I have
developed the use of Kleinian technique in all aspects of clinical practice, with
all patients, in all settings. This includes the psychoanalytic treatment of
couples. I call this approach Modern Kleinian Therapy, with the clinical goal
being the establishment and maintenance of therapeutic "analytic contact"
(Waska 2007, 2010a, 2010b, 2010c, 2011a, 2011b). In this uniquely clinical
focus, the analyst always attempts to engage the patient in an exploration of
their unconscious phantasies, transference patterns, defenses, and their internal
experience of the world. Regardless of frequency, use of couch, length of
treatment, or style of termination, the goal of psychoanalytic treatment
therefore remains the same: the understanding of unconscious phantasy, the
resolution of intrapsychic conflict, and the integration of self↔object
relations, both internally and externally.

Today's contemporary analyst sees many couples, both struggling with
their relational conflicts based in their own individual, unconscious
pathology that join together in rigid and intractable ways. Just as when
treating the individual patient, the Kleinian couple's analyst uses
interpretation as their principal tool with transference, counter-transference,
and projective identification being the three clinical guideposts of those
interpretive efforts. Viewed from the Kleinian perspective, most people in a

relationship, whether a healthy one or not, utilize projective identification as a psychic cornerstone for defense, communication, attachment, learning, loving, and aggression. As such, projective identification constantly shapes and colors both the transference and the counter-transference when couples enter analytic treatment.

By attending to the interpersonal, transactional, and intrapsychic levels of transference and phantasy with consistent here-and-now and in-the-moment interpretation, Modern Kleinian Therapy and the goal of analytic contact can be therapeutically successful with neurotic, borderline, narcissistic, or psychotic patients, whether being seen as individuals, couples, or families and at varied frequencies and duration.

Analytic contact, by definition, strives to illuminate the couple's unconscious object relational world, gradually providing each party and the couple as a unit a way to understand, express, translate, and master their previously unbearable thoughts and feelings. The analyst strives to make analytic contact with the couple's deepest internal experiences. The possible new knowledge gained can bring about learning and change and bring the couple's relationship to its full potential.

Successful analytic contact involves not only psychic change, but a corresponding sense of loss and mourning. So, every moment of analytic contact is both an experience of hope and transformation as well as dread and despair as the couple struggles with change and a new way of being with themselves and each other.

In couples treatment, this can be extra confusing and hard for the analyst to navigate as each party will be experiencing these cycles of hope, anxiety, push back, and risk at different moments and at different intensities. Also, they will have to learn how to successfully establish a mutual level of loss, anxiety, and difference as they give up old ways and try on new methods of being with each other. Successful analytic work always results in a cycle of fearful risk taking, hasty retreats, retaliatory attacks, anxious detours, and attempts to shift the treatment into something less than analytic, something less painful.

The Kleinian couple's analyst interprets these reactions to the precarious journey of growth to each party as well as to the couple as a way of steering the treatment back to something more analytic, something that contains more meaningful contact between each party, between the couple and the analyst, and the back and forth within each party's own unconscious object relational world. The interpretive support that we give our patients includes the inherent vow that we will help them survive this painful contact and walk with them into the unknown where we will all search for answers, truth, and change.

During the initial phase of working with a couple from the Kleinian perspective, the quest for analyst contact can be chaotic, choppy, and difficult. The acting out from either or both parties is significant, often pulling the analyst into a variety of enactments. Concrete, non-symbolic thinking can rule the sessions, reducing much of the interaction to debates about situational nuts and bolts or a he said she said scenario.

If the couple, as a unit and as individuals, can be contained and if their ongoing use of projective identification and splitting can be understood and interpreted properly, there will be a gradual reduction in the anxiety and fragmented quality of the relational atmosphere. This ushers in the mid phase of Kleinian couples treatment, in which there can be more of a clarity and focus on the nature of unconscious phantasy and conflict as it pertains to each party and to the couple.

One aspect of this mid phase is the possibility of both parties benefiting from the witnessing process of couples treatment. I have defined this concept (Waska 2010a) as the chance for each party to observe the other party being open, vulnerable, and expressive of their inner conflicts, desires, and fears without the usual inflammatory results or perhaps for the first time ever. This, at its optimal, gives the observing party a new insight, respect, and compassion for the other party and perhaps helps them take the same risk of sharing themselves without the usual defensive reactions or withholding patterns. Now, it is also common, especially in the early or mid phase of analytic couples treatment, for the witnessing aspect of the treatment to provoke paranoia, jealousy, envy, anxiety, or overwhelming guilt. These reactions can then generate more acting out and attacks between the couple or from the couple at the analyst. However, I believe the witnessing aspect of couples therapy is unavoidable given one party is watching and listening to the other party talk to the analyst in an open way about themselves at some point in the treatment. So, rather than see this as a liability, much like counter-transference was initially seen as a liability decades ago, the analyst can use it as a valuable technical tool in assisting the couple to exercise a healthy, compassionate version of projective identification in which each party can start to imagine what the other is going through and as a result consider where they are coming from and the more core struggles that each is encountering instead of a more combative focus on external factors and old wounds posted on an emotional tally sheet.

The later phase of analyst couples treatment is a period of consolidation, integration, and resolution. There is much less acting out but there can be times of regression and a fallback to more familiar older patterns of defense. The witnessing aspect of the treatment is much more a helpful element and both parties are more able and willing to take in the analyst's interpretations. Thinking is much more symbolic and each party as well as the couple as a unit are able to stay within the realm of depressive position functioning for longer periods and see the self and the other as a flawed person worthy of forgiveness, understanding, and love but also capable of bearing anger, disappointment, or envy without completely collapsing or seeking revenge.

Case material from an early phase couples treatment

C and D were two middle-aged gay men who had been together for seven years. Upon the insistence of C, D had to move out of their shared home because C "was sick and tired of his drug use and heavy drinking". While C would not back down on having D move out, he did want to attend couples therapy with the hope of "working on the problems and seeing if things could be turned around". D felt completely "blind-sided and betrayed by C throwing him out without warning" but was amenable yet reluctant to attend couples therapy.

When D said he was "completely surprised that C had a problem with his drug use or drinking let alone wanted him to move out", C said, "Of course you know. I have been telling you I am sick of your using for the last year or two". D said, "What drug use?" This dialogue was the start of countless debates in my office over whether or not drugs and alcohol were a problem in the relationship. Over time, I realized this formed a psychic retreat in which they both did not have to talk with me or each other about their feelings or conflicts. I interpreted this and how they were hiding what each emotionally wanted and what each might be emotionally missing. So, I gradually began interpreting the defensive denial D had and the ongoing anger and blame C had by which they both escaped facing the more painful aspects of their troubled relationship.

For the first few weeks, C seemed to be the more responsible, mature one in the couple and acted like a focused, sincere person as opposed to D who seemed flamboyant, scattered, and volatile. C was usually silent unless addressed and then he would articulate his comments carefully. D was usually talking a great deal, mostly in a very defensive, choppy, and self-centered manner. Essentially, it looked like C was more of a masochistic neurotic while D was more of a hysterical borderline with a drug problem. One of the times when D told me he thought I was "always focusing on him as the problem child", I told him that "with all his talking, denying, and current drug use he was looking like the problem child". I went on to say that by always talking about himself in the session, he made me focus mostly on him and C got "to hide in the bushes". I suggested that he liked to take up the airspace and liked that attention from me but it was negative attention. I also interpreted that it seemed difficult for him to stop talking about himself and ask C about his feelings and how things were for him, even though C often offered D the floor.

D was able to take these ideas in and in response did ask C to start talking more about himself. Indeed, this led to D explaining that the only times C usually ever said much about his drinking or drug use was when he came home high. Then, C would yell at him and tell him he "was a drug whore and a loser". But, D said, the next day C acted like nothing happened and they went on their merry way. I said that D probably was glad about that on one hand as it took him off the hook and he was not about to bring up his behavior himself. However, I said, D probably wished for C to talk more about himself and open up communication for the two of them.

So, here, I was noting my counter-transference feelings of seeing one of them as sick and one of them as well. This gave me some information as to how they were operating on an unconscious level with each other and with me and how this uneven dynamic was probably a pathological equilibrium in their relationship that caused pain but also provided respite from other psychological conflicts.

I noticed that with D, I was pulled into a debate with him over his lack of sobriety. He would say he was shocked and confused why C had "thrown him out on the streets without warning" and how he would have never done that to C. Of course, C would say in rebuttal that he was not doing drugs and that he had not "thrown him out of the streets" but asked him to leave because of his drug use. D would reply that he did not know what C was talking about. This would push me to point out that D was still doing drugs and drinking and it was a very simple matter of if he was not willing to be sober, C did not want to live with him. But, if he was to be sober, C wanted to continue the relationship. C would nod yes to this but D would say, "You mean to say that is what this is all about? You want me to stop drinking and doing drugs altogether? You signed up for me being someone who enjoys a party when we met, so now you want to say you are surprised?" I would say, "You are not answering his request. Are you willing to be sober and work on the relationship?" D would be silent and then change the topic. This sort of push/pull in the transference would continue until I would say, "I notice we are all making this about the drugs and alcohol. That must be addressed before anything else can really be changed. But, we can work on all of it at the same time. In the meantime, however, the way D is not addressing the sobriety problem makes us in a standoff where nothing gets talked about at all. So, maybe it is safer to argue over drugs and alcohol than talk about the feelings that have been going on for years and are now very raw and in turmoil for the both of you".

So, here, I was addressing the counter-transference enactment I was in, interpreting the mutual defensive transference, and suggesting that through projective identification drugs and alcohol were used as the scapegoat. It was an important and vital problem but one that was being utilized as a detour or convenient hideaway. This line of exploration led to us talking more about how unemotional and unexpressive C usually was. I interpreted that C wanted to blame D more than he wanted to tell me or D about his sorrow of being left to the side while D had an affair of sorts with drugs. I said that C seemed sad that D would rather spend time with his dealer than with C.

C agreed and was able to say that he "never has been able to talk freely about his feelings and had a history of violence in his younger years that he found out in therapy that was a cover up for his emotional problems". So, here, suddenly both parties were able to show some vulnerability and, in doing so, each was able to witness the other being more vulnerable and expressing their deeper selves. This is something they have not been able to do with each other before, so witnessing each other starting to be willing to do so with me is a major step towards finding a hopeful vision of the other as capable and willing to do that with them as well as an incentive for each to consider risking that exposure themselves for their own benefit.

When C was able to begin to be more exposed and start to talk about how hard it was for him to communicate and talk about his needs in general and in particular with D, this witnessing did become too much for D. When one party in couples therapy is exposed to the other party beginning to take this new open and vulnerable role, they may feel scared and defensive about what may be coming their way or about how they will now have to be that way too. So, D started to yell, "See! That is what I mean! You never told me that getting high was an issue for you. You never talk to me about your feelings or anything else. So, after saying nothing for seven years you have the nerve to throw me out of my home!" Of course, now C was feeling attacked and said, "You are crazy! I have told you over and over that I am sick of you coming home drunk and waking me up at 3 am to say something incoherent. You never listened to me because you were too high to hear. I don't want to be with someone who is never around. I am home and you are at your dealer's house. What kind of relationship is that?"

So, here I interpreted to D, "I think you want C to be more vulnerable and talk with you but it seems that when he does it makes you anxious and you start to debate and fight with him. He was starting to talk about missing you and wanting more in the relationship. But, then you started to fight about this and that instead of having to be vulnerable yourself. It must be difficult for you to stop and figure out what your feelings are and share them". This was an interpretation for D. Then, I interpreted to C, "You are fighting and reacting to D now instead of having to continue talking about your sad feelings of being alone at home while he is at the dealer's house. It looks like it is hard for you to tell me or D about wanting to be dependent on him and have him around".

C said, "I don't like to think of myself as dependent. It feels weak and immature". Here, he was revealing his narcissistic shell in which he tried to be independent and strong, never affected by D. C said, "This is true. It is hard for me to talk about these things but I do feel that way. I thought D would know all that by what I usually say". D said, "You have never said anything like this. The only thing you do is yell at me and call me names". They started fighting again for a moment and I told them to stop and said to C, "You want D to dig through all your anger and frustration and find the sadness and loving. But, odds are he won't which just leaves you more angry and lonely. So, you are keeping yourself in control and looking like the mature one but feel very alone and empty".

Then, I interpreted to D, "You keep talking about how C is blaming you and how he threw you out of the house. But, you never take ownership for your drinking and drug use. If you did, then you could also speak up about what you need and want from C emotionally. But, since you are always busy defending your getting high or denying it, you never get to talk about what is missing emotionally in the relationship for you and what you want to give and what you want to receive. Since you don't want to give up your drinking and drugs for a while, you can't ask for anything or receive anything. You are stuck in the same kind of alone and empty place as C. You both are so near each other but never close".

D said, "I miss the person I met seven years ago". For a moment, this was a genuine statement of how he felt and a heartfelt message of what he longed for. It was not long before he added a few accusations and twisted this message into another chapter of the back-and-forth fighting they preferred. But, I interpreted that D was willing to momentarily set aside his problems and his need to have things his way to suddenly speak from the heart. C said, "I remember those days and I would like them back too".

Here, they were both able to step into a new region of vulnerability and open expression, without being overwhelmed by persecutory or depressive anxieties and therefore they both were not relying on excessive defensive strategies that quickly ruled, shaped, and defined the relationship. We were establishing analytic contact and making progress towards new ways of relating.

Discussion

Pick (1992) notes that the early ego processes the world in very black or white terms, easily affected and swayed by moods, needs, impulses, and anxieties. The internal world is full of objects kept in all good or bad categories, highlights of the paranoid-schizoid position (Klein 1946). With integration of pain, disappointment, and loss, the ego can begin to accept that the object they hate, fear, or lose is the same object they love, miss, or need so in this more depressive position (Klein 1935, 1940), they can tolerate, understand, and move past the initial turmoil they are experiencing with the object. In the Kleinian couples approach, the analyst can help the couple reach this more integrated place by making consistent interpretations of conflict, phantasy, and transference.

Pick (1992), elaborating on some of Bion's ideas, has noted that when the patient feels they have finally found a good object they can trust and rely on, they will quickly go about telling the object or analyst how upset they are about not having had what they wanted in the past. In other words, if they can trust the new object, within a positive transference state, then they can feel safe to establish a more negative, yet non-persecutory position in which they can express their loss, anger, and disappointment in their object to that object that they trust to understand, tolerate, and support their feelings.

However, this is a fragile situation prone to easy collapse or break down. At its best, the patient can then go on to express in a fairly integrated fashion, what they miss, what they want, and how they wish for the object to be in the future. This was what I interpreted that C and D were too anxious to do. Instead, this fragile opportunity broke down into more or less their demanding that they have an ideal object to be with that always provided what they wanted and allowed them to do or be however they like. If unavailable, they devalue the object altogether. This splitting kept them away from having to face the pain of what they did not have, what they were not or had not been, and what they wanted and what they would have to become.

Case material from a mid phase couples treatment

S and T have been seeing me in Kleinian psychoanalytic couples therapy for the last three years, two and sometimes three times a week. When they first began, S and T were extremely volatile and turbulent, acting out much of what they felt with hardly any containment, understanding, or even thinking. There were constant verbal fights, screaming matches, and some actual violence on both their parts. They told me "there have been times when we literally came close to killing each other". This dangerous climate was illustrated by one time when they came in and she had some bruises and he had a broken wrist from when they went tumbling down after one heated exchange. So, it took months of my playing analytic referee before we could start to really explore what might be going on inside each of them and between them.

In the last three years, S and T have made enormous progress, but there are times when things slide back to very tense standoffs and escalating accusations. During these moments, S tends to become very agitated and lose his temper, feeling provoked by T and lashing back. T tends to first be very volatile, accusatory, and unable to see herself as contributing to the problem in any manner. Then, she withdraws and will not give any of herself to S for days. A typical scenario is one in which T might say, "So, haven't you gotten around to fixing the gate in the backyard yet?" She often says things with a tinge of aggression, resentment, and demand. Historically, S has not been able to notice this enough to bring it up in a productive manner. Instead, he usually reacts immediately, feeling pushed, blamed, and bullied. He will quickly say something defensive, aggressive, and rebellious. T will take this very personally and lash back or retreat in a passive aggressive manner. I have interpreted these patterns to be one in which T becomes a demanding, restrictive mother and S becomes a spoiled, rebellious little boy. These interpretations have been focused on both parties' transference to each other as well as the couple acting out these dynamics in a mutual transference to me.

With analytic treatment, S and T have been increasingly able to notice these feelings in themselves and notice their urge to react to these sorts of phantasies and role enactments or role responsiveness (Sandler 1976) in the relationship. This provides a moment of reflection and the opportunity to explore, learn, and change rather than confirm their mutual fears and fury. However, their progress is still brittle, new, and prone to collapse. But, the recovery time is also quicker.

As far as their dynamic with me and each other, there was a complicated mixture of unconscious phantasies being played out. For S as an individual, he felt lost in his life, unsatisfied with his career, and often was depressed about "what I am doing with my life". He struggled with a chronic emptiness and lack of purpose. Over time, he was more able to share this with me and T, but T was prone to either try to fix it with some quick advice that S felt was dismissive or she changed the subject into something about herself and her own unhappiness. This often led to S feeling ignored and then the tension would rise and they would suddenly be in a fight. This is an example of the build in predicaments with the concept of witnessing. However, it is not something one can avoid in couples work. Each party is in the room observing and listening to the other party and then reacting or coping with it in a certain way that is often helpful to interpret but also potentially explosive as in this example with S and T.

As far as T's own internal struggles that emerged in the context of the couples work, she is often overwhelmed by her obsessive way of having to control her entire environment by keeping lists, files, and always "thinking things through". This obsessive compulsive pattern that leaves her dwelling on if she turned the lights out or if she received a receipt for her groceries turns out to be part of a very paranoid view of the world in which she "has to look over her shoulder at all times to make sure she protects herself because no one else will and if she gets hurt she has no one to blame but herself". So, she is always on alert and on watch, feeling alone, anxious, and never trusting anyone. The affairs S had only confirm these frightening phantasies about her objects as there to betray her and use her. If I or S tries to talk with her about these dreads and strict views of things, T can quickly feel misunderstood and judged; now confirming her ideas about how people are. Over time, she is a bit more able to take in my transference interpretations and my remarks about this dark world she exists in and she is sometimes able to consider that she may be such a controlling judge of herself and others that she creates a world of dread and chaos.

With S, his own transference to me has been one side of a split. With me, he is the polite, meek, and respectful little boy who looks to me for guidance and answers. But, with T, he, in the same session, may become more the angry and rebellious and impatient little boy who starts screaming and yelling at her. I have interpreted that he is essentially manipulating and controlling me by acting as if all of him is a well behaved little boy and then catapulting his aggression and rage at T. I have said it is very difficult for him to consider that the love and respect he shows me could be also located in T and vice versa. He would have to express his love and his need to be loved along with his anger about not being loved and not wanting to love at the same object. This would be a depressive position way of relating that S is not able to manage yet.

Indeed, I have interpreted to both of them that they make sure at all times to avoid any expression of love, any desire for love, or any hope for love from their minds and hearts. This side of the split is kept hidden and often dismantled and destroyed. There is rarely any reference to love in the sessions, whether about their missing it, feeling it, or wanting it. I interpret that they both would rather get into debates about very concrete and intellectual matters than to admit or show me or each other these much more raw and vulnerable aspects of themselves. Only recently have they been willing to risk some basic steps in that direction.

With T, her transference to me is exactly as it is to S. She is very sensitive to feeling judged or treated poorly and will immediately withdraw and seek revenge through withholding and unavailability. She has told me off and then refused to attend treatment for several weeks on occasion. This is the same as her refusing to return S's phone calls when she feels somehow put down or used. At the same time, she can become very paranoid and aggressive in a flash, yelling at S and immediately linking whatever minor recent disagreement they may have had back to his affair and finding him an "evil soul that should never be trusted" and end up crying about "how foolish it is to have even thought for a moment that he could change". She will find fault in the smallest of things that often is like a match to S's sense of self and he then lashes back as well. However, T has been able to contain some of these feelings and act out less in this primitive manner as we have worked on these issues over time.

Integration and fragile growth

During a recent session in the third year of their analytic couples' therapy, I heard them talking with each other in a back and forth congenial way as I came out to the waiting room. This was quite different from the usual stony silence they have, the tense standoff energy they exhibit, or the disconnected lack of relating that seems to follow them around. So, once in my office, I said, "Looks like you started without me". They both laughed and nodded. I went on to interpret their ability to be connected as two adults who were willing to start a dialogue without an overseer, parent, or referee. Normally, they seemed to be waiting in their respective corners of the ring or cage and then come out to be together in my presence, hoping I will prevent any lethal damage.

S began by saying, "I want to keep talking about something we have been discussing because I think it is important and valuable. But, I am really reluctant because I don't want to lose ground. I feel I have really found a solid good place to be recently and I think it is reasonably strong but I also feel like it is a new place and could easily crumble. So, I want to be careful to not lose it or have it slip away. How we talk about things could do that but I want to make sure it doesn't. In the past, I would never have felt this good place at all.

And, in the past, if I had felt I was on solid ground, I would have to choose to not talk with T at all for fear of losing ground and sliding backwards. But, now, I think I am ready to try it differently. But, I want to know that T is willing to try and maintain this solid place too". T was silent for a while, part of her withholding tactic, but then said, "I guess so. I just want to know what you want to talk about".

So, reluctantly and tentatively, S said, "he had felt very good and happy yesterday when he turned to T and told her that she was his special person". He said, "I felt it, I meant it, and I said it. And, expressing it and sharing it with you felt very good. I thought that was a good moment, an important moment between us and for me. I let myself be open and vulnerable. I wanted to show you my heart". Then S went on to say, "But, now I feel on shaky ground right after I said that to you yesterday, I started to feel on shaky ground. I felt like you immediately wanted to know why I felt you were special. Then, you asked me why, if I really did think you are special, would I have left you for that other girl? Suddenly, it was an interrogation instead of me just saying something loving. Nevertheless, I felt really true and right about what I said and that gave me this feeling of solid ground. I don't want to give that up by being upset with you and ending up in a fight like usual. I want to stay in this place but I don't know if I can and still talk to you right now".

I said to S, "You are not sure which way the conversation will go. You don't know if T will want to engage with you on this solid ground level or if you both will fall down to another more slippery and treacherous place". S said yes and said he wanted both of them to stay on solid ground. I said, "It is new for you to feel you are on your own solid ground and it is also new for both of you to find a piece of solid ground to stand on together". Here, I was pointing to the difficulties they were having as a couple, not just as individuals.

So, S said, "Even though I feel T is putting me down, pushing me, and demanding to know why I think she is special and wanting to crush my good feeling, I am determined to stay on this higher ground. But, I don't know why T has to take this goodness away".

I interpreted, "I think that might be what makes you feel like you are losing that high ground. You seem to feel like she is taking away something that you rarely feel inside yourself and now that you have found it, T is going to devalue it. I also think that on some level, you are upset or angry that you were trying to extend that personal good feeling to something that was a mutual, together good feeling, a new solid high ground you both could live in. You must be disappointed and hurt that she seems to not want that too". S agreed and asked T to talk about how she was feeling or thinking.

Here, I was interpreting not just his internal struggle to obtain a new sense of integration, security, and trust in the object but also his hurt that T did not seem to want to join him in this mutual emotional embrace. This was a brittle depressive moment that S seemed aware of and was dreading how easily it could shift into a persecutory paranoid experience. I emphasized this short lived brittle moment in my interpretation, highlighting this more mature, whole object vision of a bridge between him and her with which they could be together in a sustainable and peaceful manner. S was essentially defending those hopes and felt T might attack them or never accept them.

As soon as T began to talk about her feelings, it was clear she was angry and out to loosen S's solid ground. She demanded to "know what he meant and why he said it". It was clear that S could clearly never answer well enough to satisfy her. She was using questions as a weapon to strike back at him. I made this interpretation and she was silent. This silent treatment in the transference was something I had faced many times over the years with T.

I told T, "You want to make me suffer right now by not giving me anything. I wonder if you are thinking that S isn't allowed to say you are special if he cheats on you and you won't let him love you if he has hurt you". So, first I was interpreting her acting out in the transference to me. Next, I interpreted her transference to him as an eternally betraying object to beware of and to seek revenge from. She was deliberately silent again, refusing to make eye contact with me. S was concerned and curious but this alternated very quickly with him starting to "lose ground" and feel angry and attacked.

I interpreted to S, "I think you are losing that solid ground you spoke of and are starting to feel attacked. Now, you want to attack back. Of course, that will erase that special feeling and bond you were trying to build and enjoy". S said, "I am trying very hard to do it differently". Turning to T, I interpreted, "you are not letting me in and you are refusing to let in any love or attention from S. By slamming the door shut like this, you are turning the hope, love and change I think you experience here into mistrust, pain, and isolation".

As a result of my interpretations, their individual and mutual anxiety decreased and there was less defensiveness. S and T were able to now begin talking with each other about what it meant and what it felt like when S said he loved T and that she was special. For a moment, they seemed to allow a mutual intimacy but it was extremely thin and brittle. As S talked about how what he said was a special message, he said he wondered how T felt about the many times he says he loves her each day when they wake up or when they go to sleep at night.

T was silent for a bit and I could see that she was sliding back into an angry and sealed off position. She told S that "words are useless and empty, action is what matters. I don't care about what you say and unless you show me something different with action I don't think your words mean anything. They are hollow and useless". S said, "So, when I tell you I love you, those words are hollow and useless?" He said this with pain and anger. T nodded yes, in an arrogant and defiant manner. It is common for T to always bring everything back to the time when S cheated on her, regardless of what the issue is. So in this moment she started talking about how he needed to show her action not words and used housework as an example. She said he could do more housework and that would show her how he really feels. But, her feelings of resentment over S never doing enough to help around the house easily and suddenly became linked with the cheating and she started to cry and yell. Suddenly, both cheating and housework ended up as examples in T's mind of betrayal and deliberate injury.

At this point, they were fighting about housework, her lack of a job, his cheating on her, how they can't trust each other, and the lack of hope that anything will ever get better in the marriage. I had to resume my role as psychological referee and container, setting limits and translating what had become a more primitive cycle of acting out.

So, this session is a demonstration of how they have been able to reach a more mature, mutual level of integration in which they can momentarily relate to each other from a more depressive position and begin to build a whole, hopeful and rich unity. But, this new third location in their lives still promptly breaks down under the weight of either or both of them bringing in more destructive and primitive aspects of functioning, the outgrowth of more sinister internal conflicts.

During the next session, they came in and S said he wanted to discuss a recent event. Overall, S is the one who always brings up issues. This is part of both the transference and their own individual levels of growth and progress. In the first year of their Kleinian couples therapy, both S and T were hardly ever able or willing to begin a discussion or dialogue. Instead, much of any communication was built around accusations and defensive rebuttals. Over time, with my consistent containment, limit setting, translation of their projective identification patterns, and interpretation of the core conflicts that maintained their pathological relationship, they were more able to find this relatively new place of peaceful exchange.

Initially in the history of their treatment, S was prone to constantly losing his temper, yelling at T, and ignoring my comments. T was more prone to aggressive silent withholding with me and S, followed by yelling at S and not returning for the next session or two to punish me and S. She would tell T, "This therapy is a waste of time. You never change and I don't like the doctor". Then, S would have to relay this to me in her absence and I would have to explore that transference experience with T when she returned. Now, in the third year, S was more able to contain himself and is more able to identify his thoughts and feelings that he wants to discuss with T without it being part of an attack or lash back for her latest accusation. T is more able to do the same, but overall is less willing to examine herself and her contributions to any problems. Currently, she continues to have these patterns of silent, angry withdrawal followed by angry outbursts.

So, in this session, S said he wanted to bring up "a recent incident that he felt they could both learn from". This way of introducing the topic also showed his progress. S explained to me that he had told T a "funny story the other day. I told her I had put some clothes in the washer, which I rarely do. T usually does the laundry. But, I end up doing some of our clothes about once a week so I was turning some pants inside out before putting them into the washer and I didn't realize it but my wedding ring got pulled off in the process. Later, I put the clothes in the dryer and walked upstairs. I noticed my ring was gone and I freaked out. I was running all over the house and couldn't find it. I was so upset! At that moment in my story, T said, 'So, did you shrink my sweater last week? I noticed my sweater was ruined from being shrunk in the wash. Did you do that?' The way she said it made me very upset and very irritated. I am not sure exactly why but I felt like I wasn't able to continue my funny story till later".

I said, "It sounds like you felt she interrupted your story to turn to her own agenda and in the process accuse you of ruining her sweater". S said, "I didn't think about it that way at first, but that is exactly it. I felt she suddenly ignored me and started to make it all about her story. And, her story sounded like I had done something wrong". I pointed out to T that many times in the past we have explored how she is prone to saying things in a shrill and judgmental manner when they could be discussed in a more neutral back and forth manner. We have also established that sometimes S merely takes whatever she says very personally and out of context, experiencing T as persecutory when she is not. But, we have established that T is often sharp, judgmental, and demanding in a very concrete way and this matches up with S's tendency to take things very personally. This is obviously a recipe for sudden and intense fights.

When T recalled exactly how she had spoken to S, it did indeed sound like she had initiated a sudden, out of the blue attack or judgment. I said this and wondered if when she felt S was being nice and being friendly with his story, she felt off balanced, disturbed, or anxious about his more loving way of relating to her. She said that was true sometimes but she did not think so in this instance. In the counter-transference, I thought to myself that she says that about every example we ever bring up but kept that to myself as something to think about later and possibly learn from.

S said that he was able to explain to T, in that increasingly heated moment, that he felt she had "derailed his funny story". Then, "they talked about it a bit" but that he was still upset about it. Even though they had navigated themselves through this rocky patch, it was very touch and go and they obviously were still not out of the woods. S told me that he had "finally" been able to finish the story. Apparently, as he was running around the house anxiously searching for his ring, he heard an annoying bang, bang, bang coming from downstairs in the washer/dryer room. He was angry that this was distracting him from his search and he said he cursed the noise and angrily stormed downstairs to find out what was making it. It was coming from the dryer and when he opened it up he discovered his wedding ring. We all laughed at this point. I realized this was also a disguised message from S about his marriage and his feelings about it, but I choose to stick with the immediate action in the room as the focus.

In discussing this entire scenario, we went over how they were working and playing together verbally and emotionally when suddenly their mutual harmony was stretched thin. But, somehow, they were able to maintain their emotional balance and regained a mutual understanding. I interpreted that each party was struggling to give to the other, without falling back into previous grievances or visions of persecution that required revenge. I interpreted that they were willing to share with me instead of use me as a parent who could side with their anger against the other. Also, I said they were both willing, for a moment, to put aside their own way of seeing things to try to understand how the other person was feeling and thinking. Here, I was interpreting the healthy, mature aspects of projective identification and the beneficial aspects of the process of witnessing in couples therapy.

In working with S and T, I was using various Kleinian concepts as guideposts to understanding their couple's dynamics as well as their individual conflicts. In examining their gradual progress, both S and T have been able to move away from the more persecutory experiences of the paranoid-schizoid position towards the more whole object experiences of the depressive position. This has provided them a shift from a focus on self-survival to a gradual recognition of dependence on the object, resulting in concern for the object. My elaboration on Steiner's (1992) idea about the initial, more primitive stage of the depressive position is that the first emergence of concern for the object is selfish. In other words, the phantasy is "I need this object so I better make sure to protect it and care for it, otherwise, I will suffer". The more mature stage of the depressive position is when the object is respected for itself as a separate entity that one cares for out of selfless love and respect, realizing there is an important symbiotic relationship present but seeing the object as a lovable entity in its own right.

With S and T, they were often off balance in this realm, teetering between the primitive and the mature aspects of the depressive position. So, T would become furious when she felt her dependence on T because it meant a cruel forced concession of needing a person who has betrayed you and will probably betray you again. She was angry she needed his love and attention, as if this meant he controlled her. She felt vulnerable and used. But, over time in the Kleinian couples treatment, she was able to somewhat tolerate needing him and wishing for his love without as much narcissistic outrage. And, S was more able to see T as someone he genuinely wanted to understand, without simply using her as an object he needed for pleasure and survival and only showing her care so that his needs would be met.

Over time, they shifted from feeling the good object was suddenly replaced by the bad object to more of an integrated but difficult realization that the good object might just be temporarily unavailable and not necessarily replaced by the bad object. This was a shift for both of them from a more troubled marriage mired in the paranoid position to a more gratifying and fulfilling marriage based in depressive functioning.

It is typical to encounter a slippery and rocky therapeutic road when treating couples, especially in the beginning and mid phases of trying to establish analytic contact. Couples usually wait until they have reached severe and often near emotionally fatal points in their relational bond. When they come to our office, it is usually the final and last ditch attempt to save the relationship or to put the last nail in its coffin. So, we expect to meet with very turbulent and volatile individuals and to encounter very destructive and treacherous couples who want help but are also very much in full battle gear.

In the early phase of Kleinian couples treatment, it is common for the analyst to have to contain or even confront and set limits with a couple who uses acting out as their primary mode of relating. This acting out is often mobilized by excessive use of projective identification and splitting. It can interfere with the analyst's neutrality and therapeutic stability, creating intense or confusing counter-transference feelings that can pull the analyst into various enactments. However, this can prove ultimately helpful in understanding the underlying dynamics of the couple if the analyst can carefully monitor and gradually decipher the counter-transference, realizing it transmits valuable information about the couple.

Steiner (1979, 1987, 1994, 2006, 2008) suggests that the analyst looks for the way in which the patient uses the analyst because as clinicians we recognize more clearly in the last few decades how our patients act out their internal conflicts and anxieties in the transference. By projecting parts of themselves and of their internal objects onto the analyst, they act on us and try to recruit us to act out with them.

The Kleinian quest for analytic contact with couples necessitates a sharp and ongoing focus on the underlying presence of projective identification as the central bridge between each party in the couple as well as between the couple and the analyst.

Joseph (1988, 1989) and Waska (2010a, 2010b, 2010c, 2010d) have noted how transference itself is based on projective identification. Parts of the self, phantasies, and internal objects are projected into the analyst and/or the other party of the couple and then the patient then behaves towards the analyst or other party as if this were the truth. With couples, each party of the couple is often engaged with each other and/or the analyst in this manner at the same time. Therefore, analytic couples treatment can be extremely dense, complex, and confusing as there can be multiple transference states whirling about in the room directed at more than one person at a time.

Bion (1962b) and Rosenfeld (1983, 1987, 1990) have described how projective identification is both an attack, a defensive expelling, and a means of communication. The analyst must be able to tune in to the patient enough to decode the nature of the projections and when necessary to be able to contain them before translating them with interpretations. In working with couples, this initial containment may have to go on for a longer period in some cases due to acting out and each party's anxiety level or the mutual persecutory or depressive anxieties of the couple as a unit. In other cases, the nature of the couple's phantasy state or each party's internal conflict might be such that, after the initial containment, the analyst must make a much more rapid interpretation to provide the support and intervention needed right then and there.

Each party of the couple may have projections that exist purely in phantasy, not emotionally affecting the analyst or the other party at all. Other times, one party may have such strong and disruptive phantasies that their projections will affect the interpersonal realm. One party may unconsciously attempt to stimulate and provoke the other party and/or the analyst to behave according to these unconscious expectations. In these ways, the history of the patient's internal object relational world comes alive in the transference that in turn is at the core of the therapeutic goals in Kleinian couples treatment. The task is to identify, claim, tame, and rename or work through this mutual blend of object relational history and conflict in the couple and challenge the ways and reasons it still comes alive, dominating the couple's current reality together.

Joseph (1983, 1988, 1989, 2003) recommends the analyst always focus attention on what is going on in the room, on the nature of what is being lived out, and how we are being pushed or pulled emotionally to experience or behave in various ways. Some couples or one party of the couple will reject any transference interpretations and cling to concrete blame and grievances. They will show great difficulty understanding their relationship to the object, how they impact others, or even the concept of give and take. This would be the party or couple existing more in the paranoid-schizoid state (Klein 1946) and a more narcissistic view of the world. The Kleinian couple's analyst needs to find out how each party uses the analyst and each other, whether inviting us into some sort of repetitive acting out or trying to examine things in a more realistic fashion.

The couple, as a unit, wants to learn and change but naturally ward off new knowledge about themselves as it upsets their psychic equilibrium (Spillius 1988, 1994, 2007). So, in gauging whether we are colluding with this defensive closure or not, O'Shaughnessy (1992) and Spillius (1992) suggest we should notice if our technique wards off rather than permits the entry of what is new and disturbing, and whether the type of interpretive movement by the analyst and emotional movement by the couple is towards or away from "trying to know".

Betty Joseph (1985) has provided the notion of total transference situations and elaborated how they are vital to our understanding of our patient's inner life. I believe this is true with couples as well and the total transference mode couples elicit. This can best be gauged by the analyst noticing how the couple is using the analyst and each other beyond what they are actually saying to each other or to the analyst. In other words, the concrete topic or issue may be a defense against the deeper transference state occurring in the room. Much of our understanding of the transference comes through our understanding of how our patients act on us to feel things for many varied reasons, whether as acting out or veiled communications. Each party of the couple will convey aspects of their inner world that are often beyond the use of words, and will often set into motion various feelings in the analyst's counter-transference.

Joseph (1988, 1989) has noted that counter-transference, like transference itself, was originally seen as an obstacle to the analytic work, but now is considered as an essential tool of the analytic process. Further, the notion of our being used and of something constantly going on, if only we can become aware of it, opens up many other aspects of transference (Sandler 1976). I have offered the concept of the complete counter-transference (Waska 2010a, 2011a, 2011b) to parallel Joseph's (1985) concept of the total transference. In the complete counter-transference, the analyst tries to consider all aspects of their feelings, thoughts, urges, and sensations as part of the unconscious communication that is being directed at him or her from the patient via projective identification. This generates particular states of mind that, if studied, can offer important and otherwise unavailable clues and solutions to the patient's conflicts and internal struggles. This technical approach was illustrated in the case material, showing moments of therapeutic usefulness as well as moments of enactment and counter-transference confusion.

Kleinian couples treatment relies on the core elements of Kleinian psychoanalytic work with individuals. The procedure is both similar and different. The Kleinian approach to couples work respects the need to work with each party at times in a way that is very similar to individual analysis. However, this one-on-one work is done in the context of the other party witnessing the interaction and having the chance to learn from that. Also, the individual focus is done in conjunction with the ongoing quest for analytic contact with the couple as a unit. Indeed, the Kleinian concept of analytic contact makes the direction of analytic couples work always in favor of understanding unconscious conflict, the individual and mutual phantasy world, and the constant role of projective identification in shaping the health or sickness of the couple. Observation and translation of the complex and multiple lines of transference is necessary and interpretation of both the paranoid and depressive aspects of that transference state must be constantly explored.

5

STUMBLING IN THE
COUNTER-TRANSFERENCE

Following up enactments with
balanced therapeutic interpretations

In the course of our work to uncover and work through each patient's unique core pre-oedipal phantasies and the subsequent oedipal elaborations and compromise formations, we discover many obstacles in the way of psychic change (Chessick 1994). While the counter-transference can be a remarkably helpful tool in unearthing and understanding the patient's internal struggle between self and object, the counter-transference can also become part of the overall pathology, playing out a mutual reenactment of archaic object relational conflicts. Newman (1988) discusses how many of our more difficult patients will work to prove their conviction of having no useable or reliable objects. I would add that they may act out their conviction that they are a useless or even dangerous object to others, including the analyst in the transference. Newman (1988) states that these patients will evoke complementary pathological responses from the analyst that serve only to prove their case that object relations must be controlled, avoided, or obliterated for the sake of either self or other. This notion is similar to the clinical observations of Betty Joseph (1989) in which she examines the moment-to-moment invitations and interpersonal as well as unconscious pull for the analyst to shift into certain paranoid or depressive counter-transference states. Of most clinical concern are the situations in which the analyst is temporarily maneuvered by projective identification processes into paranoid-schizoid experiences of counter-transference anxiety, competition, desperation, demand, or aggression that when acted out only serve to validate or intensify the patient's existing paranoid or depressive phantasies regarding love, hate, and knowledge.

At times, our communication about what we see occurring in the patient's transference and in the patient's internal phantasy experience may indeed be a cold splash of honesty and reality to the patient. However, there are some counter-transference moments of acting out in which the analyst uses their interpretive authority to make a cold and cruel slap of honesty and reality. In other words, the message may be meaningful and helpful, but the tone or method of delivery may be a counter-transference acting out of some type of projective identification based transference dynamic being pushed into that clinical moment.

Making sure to link a useful interpretation to our confrontive splash of reality can be what helps us stay in the realm of clinical healing and out of the murky area of disclosure and the hurtful area of acting out. Often within a particular treatment, enactments are unavoidable and we make a rush to judgment in our interpretive efforts. But, by closely monitoring our counter-transference states of mind, we can still sometimes manage to follow it with a therapeutic shift to a more constructive interpretation that can also, sometimes, include a reference to the transference/counter-transference acting out that just occurred.

This is not an all or nothing, anything goes approach. In fact, it is the acknowledgement of the inevitable, universal pull of the transference and the almost predictable counter-transference enactments that follow in almost all treatment settings. However, the analyst can become familiar with the projective identification based transference induced counter-transference state that is unique to each patient and then find his or her analytic footing instead. Then, the particular form and flavor of the transference/counter-transference acting out can serve to provide the ingredients for a valuable and transformative series of interpretations that explore that clinical moment and expand upon it.

Case material:
Normal levels of counter-transference acting out

David had seen me for more than four years following his discharge from the psychiatric hospital he had been taken to for severe depression. He continued on several medications and was part of an ongoing research study group following patients suffering from major depressive episodes.

When I started seeing David, he was dating a woman whom he treated in a rather condescending manner. This was usually triggered by him feeling furious with her emotional troubles impacting their relationship. While she certainly had some severe paranoid and obsessive issues that crippled her functioning, we gradually discovered that these situations brought David back to early states of anger and disappointment with his family of origin. He had spent most of his life resenting his family and feeling like he always had to be the one "to clean up their mess, bail them out, and educate them on the right thing to do". Alcoholism, drug addiction, lack of education, financial problems, and chronic fighting were the norm for his family and David felt he was the only one that had managed to climb out of the fire. So, he looked down on them and resented that he had to care for them and never got the chance to be cared for by them.

In the counter-transference with David, I found myself fluctuating between various complementary and concordant states of mind (Racker 1957). On one hand, I felt I was much like him when I felt numb, bored, cutoff, and not too interested in what he had to say. I was not motivated to be in touch with him emotionally. Externally, this was the result of being bombarded by his extremely sterilized, intellectualized, and stripped down way of non-relating to me and others, usually fortified with countless details about his work day and work projects.

At the same time, I felt David was often judgmental and even arrogant of his friends, family, and girlfriend and I wanted to put him in his place with some form of judgment or criticism. In his transference, I felt David was being cold and aloof to me when he described his dependence on me as "glad to have an additional medical appointment along with my psychiatrist in which I can process the ineffective patterns of thought that lead to my depression".

Other times, I found myself siding with him against his family. I felt outraged at their simple-mindedness and constant parasite-like dependence on David for money and advice. I felt sorry for him when he described his wife's constant controlling ways and her tendency to heckle David about everything and anything. Based on our work together, I told him he probably did feel quite angry and upset over many things which would make anyone depressed but that he felt guilty about it so he was extra depressed.

Overall, this fluctuating counter-transference, a result of identification with his multiple states of conflict embedded within a strong reliance on projective identification, involved a third object. Over and over again, I was feeling either for or against one object and siding with or despising another. So, I was on his side against his girlfriend, feeling in synch with his family against him, or feeling sorry for his girlfriend as a victim just like me to David's cold logic. Thus, there was a constant aggressive struggle in which he was upset with another and I was pulled in to side with either David or the other party.

During periods in which he was acting particularly cutoff from me or intensely attacking his wife or family, I felt pushed to intervene abruptly or call him out on his nasty behavior. So, when he was putting down his girlfriend or family, I felt offended at being the dumping ground for his narcissistic proclamations. I felt he was refusing to look at his part in things or to have any compassion or curiosity about the other person's plight. Initially overcome by this counter-transference tension, a paranoid-schizoid state of anxiety and anger, I was prone to want to lash out and put him down. Sometimes, I did this by saying, "That sounds pretty angry, like you think you are above them or entitled to have what you want when you want it". While what I was saying was accurate and could be fine as an interpretation or confrontation, as soon as I said it I was aware of the slight degree of anger and critical demeaning attitude behind what I said. I was hit by a sense of guilt and remorse, signaling a depressive reaction to my initial attack.

So, I added, "Maybe there is something behind all that anger and aggression. Maybe you are sad that you never had the family you wanted and never have felt that others were there or are there for you. You withdraw because you feel no one is there for you so why bother. So, you are angry and entitled, fed up with others but also very lost and sad that you can't find a way to connect with others".

Here, I managed to regroup in the counter-transference, stepping back from my emersion in David's projective identification process of paranoid and destructive phantasies. I moved into a more alpha function (Bion 1962b) version of containment that enabled me to interpret from a more depressive position perspective. His transference response to all this was somewhat of a parallel to my counter-transference (Racker 1957) in that David first felt guilty. He said, "You are right. I feel bad when I am like that. I shouldn't treat people like that. I just don't know what happens, I feel so upset. I think you are right about missing out on what I always wanted. I look around and everyone else seems to have had a family they could count on and parents who took care of them instead of the other way around. I can see they have their own issues and it's not a personal thing but it is hard to not take it that way". So, here, we were now both functioning in a more mature, depressive manner, trying to understand and bear things that may or may not be in our control.

So, with David and with many other patients, I notice that when I am caught up in the projective identification process and become pulled into a counter-transference interpretive enactment, I am initially making a paranoid-schizoid remark, usually attacking, controlling, or judgmental. At some point, hopefully right away, the intensity of my remark, to me and only on occasion to the conscious reality of the patient, alerts me to my misstep. Then, through a sense of responsibility, intrigue, and guilt, I am able to rebalance myself and try to learn what the counter-transference might be about and how to use it to find meaningful therapeutic direction. At that point, the initial remark that I regret can serve as a productive springboard from which to explore a less rigid and more expansive line of analytic investigation.

Over time, as we worked on David's anger, resentment, and entitled bitterness, my difficult counter-transference states reduced as he felt less and less outrage and grievance. He was able to move from a more paranoid-schizoid (Klein 1946) state of feeling put upon and having to fight back to a place of genuine mourning for a family that never lived up to what he wished for and a painful lack of connection to his parents and siblings. This working through of loss and grief helped David to accept his girlfriend's flaws more so that he could start to talk with her about his feelings rather than act them out in anger. This change led to them discussing issues and negotiating problems so that their relationship shifted to a much more satisfying experience for both. In the transference, David was able to make a gradual transition from his more obsessive, intellectualized, flat, and deadened way of relating to me to a more enlivened and engaging relationship. Over the last year, he focused more on the positive aspects of his life and feeling more competent and hopeful rather than angry and depressed.

71

During the fourth year of his analytic treatment, things were going quite well but much busier and more hectic for David as he and his now wife began preparing for the arrival of their second child. He had been talking about how he might have to "really cut back the time he spends on things other than family". We explored how he had always used work as an obsessive retreat into which he could withdraw, feel in control, and not be bothered by the short comings of all his objects. We also discussed how, just like with the birth of his first child, we would probably have to stop meeting for a while. His desire to work less and spend more time with his family was important as it was external evidence of his new ability to tolerate contact with the good object. Rather than tear down the good object with grievance and resentment, he was able to slowly tolerate the flaws and disappointments of the good object enough to allow himself to love and depend on it without feeling taken advantage of or abandoned. This was a gradual reversal of his enforced splitting (Bion 1962a) and a healthy measure of grieving that allowed him to tolerate and benefit from connection with the good object (Ahumanda 2004).

A few months later, David began missing many of his weekly appointments and leaving messages about being overwhelmed with work projects that needed to be finalized before the birth of his second child, now due in a few weeks. I started thinking that he would probably tell me he was stopping treatment altogether since he would have to take a month off for the birth and then it would take a while for him to catch up at work. Plus, he would be helping out at home after work with his new baby. I thought it would be sad to see him go and that he could still profit from more work but that overall he had made enormous changes and internalized a significantly different image of himself and his objects during the course of our work together.

David arrived for his session and lay down on the analytic couch. He told me he was going to stop coming and said he thinks it "makes sense to stop at this time because of the baby and because of how I am doing overall". But, he added, "I am also worried that you will be hurt by me saying this and I am scared that you will be offended. So, I guess I am wondering if you will approve of what I want to do or not". After I gathered a few details about the manifest reasons he wanted to stop, such as his job pressures, the upcoming birth that very next week, and the expected new level of obligation to family that would take up more of his free time, I made a few interpretations.

I said, "You want me to judge you by approving or not approving, giving me all the power and you having to wait to hear my judgment. You also feel guilty and worried about how I will be, will I end up hurt or angry? Well, I think those are the very themes we have made a great deal of progress on but obviously there are still a few rough edges. So, I think you have made a great deal of very important progress. If you wanted to stay or come back later, I think you would profit from that too. But, if you stop coming now, I will survive and you probably will too. I am happy about your progress and that won't change if you stop".

David said, "I am really glad to hear that I could come back. I wasn't sure. I do think I have made a lot of progress. In fact, my entire life has changed. When I started to see you, I was only dating Sally and I wasn't sure if I could ever commit to getting married let alone put up with her issues. Now, I am married and have two kids! And, my life is really nice. We have a great family and I am not sorry for that choice. I can't believe I used to think that work was more important than her or the family. Now, I can't wait to get off of work and go home to see them. I love them". David began to cry.

After a bit, David went on to say, "As you know, I have always wanted to let my friends know how much they mean to me but I can never find the courage. After we hang out for the day or the weekend, I want to tell them how much they mean to me but I feel so knotted up inside and too scared or nervous to say anything. I feel so bad because then they go away and never know how much I feel for them and how grateful I am to have them as friends. With our work together, I think I have become more able to start doing that, a little. I think it is now much more in reach, a possibility". I replied, "I think you are trying hard to tell me about your feelings for me".

David paused and then started to sob. He said, "Yes. I do feel that and want to tell you how much you have helped me and really showed me how to change my life. Everything in my life is so much better. I can't imagine how shallow and miserable I would still be if I hadn't come here for the last four years. I want to say thank you and tell you that I am really grateful for what you have done for me".

In the counter-transference, I was thinking of how rare it is to have such a successful, ongoing treatment and to hear a patient feel grateful and embrace the changes they worked on. At least in my private practice, it is much more the norm to encounter very difficult or hard to reach patients who terminate abruptly, maintain a generally negative transference throughout the treatment, or simply stop attending without any positive or negative feedback at all. I was reflecting on how this fragmented, choppy, and stormy or sterile profile is common and David's method of ending was so pleasantly different.

After a moment of silence, David said, "I bet you are so happy to have a job like this where you have everyone ending up so happy and grateful. It must be so satisfying to hear people tell you how their lives are improving and how much you have helped them". In the counter-transference, I felt an enormous push to say, "Actually, you have NO idea! Everybody is usually angry and ungrateful. And, I get blamed for their lack of progress". I stopped myself and wondered what that might be about. In other words, I recognized it might be solely something about me that I need to look at and work on or it could be something that was a part of the projective identification based transference David was engaging me with.

I said, "I think you mean we together have hung in there and made the commitment to work on your issues long enough to make some real progress. We hung in there together and started to see the rewards and the value of working out some difficult problems. You can see that and you are telling me that you are grateful for what we have done together". David started to weep again. After a minute, he said through his tears of gratitude, "Yes. That is it. I want to thank you for that. Thank you so much!" I replied, "You are very welcome. I think you have just been telling me your feelings like you have wished you could do with your friends. You are finally being honest about the warmth and love you feel and expressing it directly". David nodded emphatically.

After the session, I reflected on my counter-transference experiences and came to a few insights. I think that my counter-transference reaction of responding to his vision of me as always being surrounded by grateful, tearful patients expressing their deepest heartfelt emotions was too much for me. Through projective identification, I wanted to be like David, defending against closeness, turning away from any meaningful expression and instead focusing on my resentment for others. He had spent many years using his family as an easy target for bitterness and resentment. This allowed him to avoid any feelings of tenderness or gratitude that was part of the conflict and knotted internal bond with them. So, for a moment, I leaned in the direction of focusing on my difficult and nasty patients so I would not have to deal with the painful and exposed feelings of love and dependency that arose from David's comments.

I was not aware of all these details in the clinical moment. All I could make out in the heat of the exchange was my sudden and intense desire to utter these complaints and grievances to David to bulldoze over his vision of me being surrounded by love and gratitude. I simply could tell, from my immediate phantasy state that something was up and I should approach with caution rather than blurt out my feelings or act on what was bubbling up in me. As a result of my quick self-containment, I was able to make an interpretation that was more in synch with his immediate anxiety that he was trying to avoid as well as the desire for attachment and his communication of love and gratitude. So, while not a completely conscious act, my analytic experience of staying more on balance and not acting out even when buffeted by strong desires or fears helped me to speak more to his immediate phantasies than to act out our mutual defenses against them.

Case material: Counter-transference moments of crossing the line and then coming back

Rebecca had been seeing me for about three years, twice a week sitting up, when she began a pattern of "trying to do things for myself and honor what I want". She had enrolled herself into a Salsa dancing class that for Rebecca meant claiming "the right to have fun, enjoy my body, and not judge myself on some exacting level of perfection". She felt good about these new ways of being in her life. She brought several small art projects she had completed in for me to see. This was significant since she had put her artistic side on hold for many years and this was a risk to show me and not be overcome with a feeling of me judging her, her disappointing me, or my not liking her anymore because of her "making it about herself". This last part was an element of the transference we had worked on for years. She often worried that with me and other men she might cause a permanent fracture in the relationship if she showed too much of herself. She thought that it would go better to cater to us and not really ever have a presence. In fact, she would instead try to always give us the limelight and the final say.

For many years, I had struggled in the counter-transference with how agreeable Rebecca could be, giving me the limelight and the role of the leader with final say. I felt I could easily lead her in almost any direction if I wanted to and she would respond with agreement and polite compliance. This was tempting at times as a way to feel in charge as her special guide and be able to control her at will. She evoked these moments in me by her extreme passivity, her idealization of my knowledge and skill, and her waiting to see what I would say or do rather than express herself as feelings and thoughts emerged. Indeed, I interpreted this as her "wait and see, put herself on hold just in case, hope for the best, wait on the sidelines approach to me and to life".

When I noticed myself drawn to becoming her commanding overseer, I stopped short of this projective identification based transference pull to act out her archaic phantasies of how object relations should or must be. Then, I was left with the counter-transference frustration of how much Rebecca seemed to refuse to have a mind of her own (Caper 1997). Interestingly, Rebecca came to me after being in therapy for years with someone whom she said, "had her own agenda, told me about her frustrations with her own daughter's dating problems, and seemed to want me to do and be all that her daughter failed to do and be. I went along with it for a long time and finally was fed up at being completely ignored and having to cater to her. She never seemed to pay attention to my needs. So, I finally quit". We had processed many times how in some ways she pulled for me to be exactly like this last therapist even though she also hoped I would be different and recognize her as an independent and separate person that I respected.

So, part of the work of shifting through Rebecca's transference was confronting Rebecca on the way that while she may want me to encourage her and allow her to have a mind of her own, she simultaneously censors and hides her mind from me. Joseph (2000) points out how some patients use compliance and agreeableness as a massive resistance to exposing their own mind. Bit by bit, Rebecca and I explored and worked through, often in a push/pull manner, the conflicts and fears she had regarding the safety of self and object when it came to allowing herself to think and feel.

So, when I had changed all the art hanging on my office walls and she walked in and looked around, Rebecca had an extremely controlled reaction. First, she said in a very sedate and soft manner, "I see you changed a few things". I said, "Yes. You are not saying what you think about the change". After a minute of looking around, she said, "Well, I notice most of the pieces are horizontal". Over the years, Rebecca had established a pattern of relating to me in this flat, distant, and non-relational manner. In the counter-transference, I was left feeling alone (Schafer 1995), cast aside, and unwelcome. I came to understand that this was a projection of her own feelings of both feeling left out and deliberately staying out of touch so she could avoid rocking the boat and being cast overboard.

I replied, "You seem to be anxious about telling me of your feelings about my office and my new art so you are being extremely diplomatic and safe by sticking with the mechanical angle the pictures are hanging at. To tell me more about how you feel, expressing your mind, must feel dangerous". Rebecca said, "Oh! I see what you mean! Wow! I am doing that. It sounds funny now that I think about what I just said. Yes. I do think I am uncertain about just expressing what I think". I interpreted, "You think I will be unhappy with what you think?" She said, "Not so much that you will be unhappy but that I don't know exactly how you will react. It is more the unknown". I said, "So, it is easier to make it known by controlling it with logic and sterilizing it with diplomatic answers". She nodded yes.

I said, "So, you still haven't told me what you think". Rebecca said, "I kind of like that one. It reminds me of a sunset scene I wanted to paint in my art class. It gives me some ideas". I thought to myself that she now rendered me and the art as non-dangerous so she could use it and take it with her emotionally. In this case, she could use it as an inspiration or internal guide to help with her own art project. So, she was internalizing me and my office in a helpful and safe way instead of an unknown and possibly dangerous way that she had to control, keep out, and neutralize. This pattern of careful avoidance of any mutual interaction with her objects in which she could play an equal and participatory role was a hallmark of her lifelong conflicts and the transference profile.

During the course of her analytic treatment, we had examined this way of being or not being especially in how she picked boyfriends who were selfish, unreliable, and not willing to commit to a long term relationship. But, Rebecca would wait and wait, hoping her object would one day change and decide to want her and love her. She felt that if she curtailed her own expressions of either positive or negative desire, she could keep the object around. By not causing any conflict, maybe the object would notice her and like her. So, she was the passive victim or ignored bystander in most of her relationships, including within the transference in moments such as the one involving the new artwork.

When Rebecca started her analytic treatment, she was grossly overweight and out of shape. During the time we spent together, we addressed how she was so out of touch with herself and chose to tend to the needs of the object so much more than the needs of herself that she neglected her diet, overall health, and sense of self confidence. Indeed, to have a defined healthy lifestyle of diet and exercise was a direct self-expression that Rebecca felt could interfere or endanger her chances of being noticed, accepted, or loved by the object. In fact, she was unconsciously convinced that to have such a self-definition would increase the chances of being passed over for love or outright rejected and punished.

In the last few months of treatment, Rebecca had secured a new base of self-definition by deciding to take up hiking and running as a fun activity for her own enjoyment and as a way to get into shape and lose weight. We had spent a fair amount of time discussing this and examining the fears and joys she had as she carved out this new territory that was exclusively hers. The idea that anything would be safe to claim as hers was a fragile feeling still as it pulled on intense phantasies of conflict, loss, and persecution. Specifically, Rebecca would return to feelings of uncertainty in which she remembered how her father, an angry alcoholic, would "become out of control if I dared to show my face or say what I thought, let alone ask for something". And, Rebecca grew up feeling responsible for her mother's chronic depression and eventual suicide. So, creating a sense of her own self that interacted with others in a truly separate and autonomous manner was dangerous and uncertain in her mind.

While Rebecca's hiking and running regime was going well and she was definitely losing weight and enjoying her new body image, there was a sudden shift one day. Rebecca came in and told me about how she had read about a new type of cellulite removal process that was easier and "not surgical". She spent most of that session and the next one telling me about how she had always been unhappy with her "fat thighs and big butt". Rebecca said that even though she had managed to lose a fair amount of weight, she was never happy with her body and this new process she saw advertised seemed to be the "magical cure without the invasive surgical approach".

As she went on and on about this, I started to feel tense and somewhat irritated, thinking that she was joining the crowds of women signing up for Botox, liposuction, and plastic surgery, all with some form of intellectualization or justification but ending up a plastic replica of some ideal they had demanded of themselves. In the next session, Rebecca told me she had met with the doctor. After an examination, he told her she was not a good candidate for the procedure until she lost some more weight. For a moment, I thought I had misjudged this doctor as another plastic surgeon making money off of gullible women. But, Rebecca then told me that he had recommended she sign up for his "holistic weight loss program for only a few hundred dollars a month".

I was immediately aghast to think that this doctor was now going to make money off of my patient in this way before she started paying for his other treatment. Rebecca told me he sold "special herbs that helped to flush out toxins and scrub out the old and unhealthy flora in the intestinal track". He had gone on to tell her how certain meals can remain "stuck in the intestine for weeks or months essentially rotting and preventing the intake of healthy vitamins". Rebecca said, "So, these toxic particles need to be flushed out with his specially mixed blend of flora scrubbers". Rebecca went on about this with excitement and said she felt lucky to have found this out and was looking forward to using the products and losing all her weight.

Hearing all this, I sat there in shock that Rebecca would be so gullible. I felt she was being ripped off and preyed upon but I also could not believe she was being so ignorant as to go along with it. I felt angry and outraged and compelled to express it. I said, "I find it interesting that you are an engineer with a biology background but you are ignoring the fact that this doctor is telling you things that go against the basic tenants of human biology. So, maybe you want me to know better than you, like you want me to have an opinion on your behalf instead of you realizing what you're getting into yourself". Here, I was starting off with an acting out of my counter-transference, evoked by her projective identification based transference. I regrouped for a moment when I returned with an analytic interpretation regarding how she might be using me to voice an opinion instead of her having to own an uncomfortable feeling and express herself openly. So, I think I was on the right track with that comment but then the counter-transference enactment crept back in and I continued to lecture her.

I said, "There is no such thing as bad flora and certainly nothing that needs scrubbing. When I hear the whole thing, it reminds me of the popular scam in the seventies in which people were told they needed organic enemas or 'colonics' to cleanse their intestines of all the rotting, toxic matter that supposedly interfered with the absorption of positive minerals and vitamins. This is clearly a bogus scam to take your money so I am surprised and interested in what makes you dive into such a thing without giving it much thought?"

I could tell, in the back of my mind, that something was amiss in what I was saying because of how intense I felt about it. I felt I needed to convince her of my point and save her from this stupid waste of money and common sense. After I added a few more negative comments on the new herbal weight loss program, Rebecca told me that I "scared her because I sounded exactly like Ben". This remark was like a splash of water on my face because Ben had been a former boyfriend who strung her along for years, dominating the relationship with his needs and always disappointing Rebecca who stood around waiting for him to propose to her but ended up sad and unhappy after several years of being treated rudely, being ignored and rejected, and possibly being cheated on. Rebecca said, "I hate Ben. This is just like when he would make really strong negative statements about something and that scared me". When I asked for details, it turned out she meant the times when he voiced a very unilateral, strong and sometimes aggressive opinion about something he had heard about not necessarily from Rebecca but just that his way of stating his disagreement was so forceful.

Woken up from my state of counter-transference enactment, I gathered myself from this paranoid-schizoid splitting, devaluation, and control and tried to make a more balanced interpretation based on what seemed like my competitive or defensive attack on an oedipal rival. In other words, I noticed I seemed envious and jealous of her new doctor who had such magical and wonderful solutions for her and how she immediately fell in love with him and his potions. I felt like she had sacrificed her own identity and opinions in the process. So, I said, "You seem to have really fallen in love with this new idea of instant weight loss and in the process given up your own ability to think or decide what is best. It looks like you are blindly falling in love with this idea".

Rebecca replied, "I think I see what you mean. I don't like to admit it but you are right. I want the easy way out to my weight problem and this seemed like a magic fix. I don't have to do anything, exercise more, or anything. I just follow the doctor's advice, pay the money, and take the herbs. So, I guess I just want the easy way out without any work". I said, "But, in the process, you are sacrificing your own identity, your own ability to think, and your own capacity to take control of your body and life. You have turned yourself over to yet another man". Rebecca said, "Oh crap! I see it now. I have done that. It feels so much easier. I want the lazy, quick way and trade my own self over for that but I see how you mean that ultimately it is the same thing I have been doing my whole life. Crap! Why won't you let me do it? You had to call me out on it. I don't want to take ownership of my life and my weight problem. I wanted to hand it over to someone else".

I interpreted, "You are relating to me and others in that way, being dependent and sacrificing yourself in order to get us to take over and give you love and quick fixes, but you lose yourself in the process, waiting for someone else to define you, like with your last therapist, your old boyfriend, and with your parents". This last comment about her parents was based on years of examining the way she felt she had to always wait and see what her parents were up to and never risk expressing herself for fear of making her parents angry and out of control or that her mother might become more depressed or kill herself, which in fact she did.

When Rebecca left at the end of that session, she said, "Wow. That was really intense. I didn't expect all that. You really laid it all out there!" I was left to struggle with a fairly intense counter-transference state of guilt and anxiety. Did I overdo it? Did I express too much? Did I make her angry or depressed? Would she recover from it? I realized I was suddenly in the same place of guilt and fear that she lived in growing up and as an adult. Through projective identification, I was now in her shoes. I had to find a sense of self-security and self-containment in which I could not simply ignore my level of acting out and manically deny its possible effects but also not immerse myself in a torturous self-blaming and persecutory conviction that I had sent her over the edge. I had to feel confident that we were both ok and resilient enough to continue, to be curious, and to find a way to learn and grow from the experience. In other words, I had to believe that this moment might leave us intact or even bring us closer rather that pull us apart or cause a terminal friction.

In the next session, Rebecca began by telling me that what I had said "really made her think and while she was pretty blown away at first" and felt I had "called her out on a few things", she said it "was really new and important". She went on to say that she realized how indeed she was "turning off my common sense and the 2+2 reality that anyone would have seen about the quick fix herbal diet". Rebecca told me, "I felt you really called me out on how I sort of threw myself at the doctor and took whatever he said or sold at face value without questioning it or having my own ideas about whether it was good or bad. In a way, I did want you to make the decisions for me and I guess I was doing that with him too. What really hit me later was how in my wanting a quick fix to my overeating, I was being just like my mother. She had so many emotional problems and needed help, like the help I get here. But, instead she took the quick fix of drugs and drinking and felt she had an instant solution when really she had no solution and was in fact instead being controlled by all the drugs".

After a while of listening to Rebecca, I interpreted that initially she did not like how I "called her out" and wishes I would do the work for her, expressing things that might be controversial or full of conflict so she does not have to look at them. I said, "You don't like it when I call you out but part of you is saying it leaves you with a chance at a new freedom of being more yourself instead of having to simply follow me or him and do as we please".

Rebecca began to cry and said, "I wish someone had called my mother out on her behavior but no one ever did! I had to go along with it and all I wanted was for my father to stand up and tell her to stop taking drugs and be my mother! Instead of paying attention to me and being my mother, all she did was be self-absorbed and take drugs and either ignore me or yell at me. So, I think I was envious that you could so easily call me out when I have such a hard time doing that without feeling like there will be a terrible consequence. At the same time, I really liked having you call me out and make me think of how I was ignoring myself, wanting the quick fix, and letting that doctor tell me what to do with my life. I do need to think for myself more and express myself but I think I want someone else to do that for me".

I interpreted, "You want me or someone to take care of you and love you. But, you think I will only do that if you give up your identity and put yourself on hold until I call the shots". Rebecca said, "I wanted my father to call the shots and make my mother love me. I was a kid and shouldn't have had to tell her that myself, it wasn't my job. But, I was scared if I did she would kill herself. And, she ended up doing that anyway!"

Over the course of the next month, Rebecca brought up numerous examples of situations with men she was dating and situations at work in which she felt she was not getting what she wanted or felt she disagreed with something and then "called the person out". We talked about how she was able to start a reasonable, calm dialogue with the person and discuss the differences she was feeling but the difficult conflict inside herself was that it felt like she was "calling them out" in an aggressive, confrontive way that could cause them to be hurt or push them to hurt her, reject, her, or abandon her. Bit by bit, we worked through these anxieties and the associated fears of giving up her attachment to this less than ideal object and in her mind possibly have nothing ever again. We also explored how the urge to "let her parents have it" and "call them out" was tainting her ability to gauge how she was actually interacting with others.

Contemporary Kleinians try to relate the patient's current internal struggle to early infantile experiences as well as to process them within the immediate moment-to-moment transference situation, clinically known as the total transference situation (Joseph 1985).

During normal development, the infant has both feelings of love and hatred towards the breast and these lead to phantasies of injured, dying, or dead objects as well as angry and retaliatory objects that create an internal world of persecution, despair, and eternal emptiness (Steiner 2004). Klein (1935) has described how identification with these damaged or diseased objects can lead to somatic problems that only begin to shift when depressive phantasies are worked through and sufficient mourning takes place. When I first met with Rebecca, she coughed and wheezed continuously. She sneezed all the time, blaming it on allergies for which she took large amounts of allergy medication. I pointed out to her that usually the points in the session when she began coughing more intensely were the moments when we were discussing something that made her feel more anxious. By the time of the third year in her analysis, she no longer sneezed or wheezed. In the fourth year, she had stopped taking her medications and almost never coughed.

The more Rebecca was able to own and bear her own feelings and thoughts regarding love, hate, and knowledge towards others, the more she was able to acknowledge, understand, and utilize her feelings and thoughts regarding love, hate, and knowledge to care for herself. In other words, as she worked out her conflicts around loving her objects, hating her objects, and wanting to understand them more actively, she was able to permit herself to be loved, draw limits around how she was treated, appreciate learning about her own identity, and come to respect her own desire to be understood by others.

Discussion

The two clinical cases illustrate the common yet difficult nature of working with the counter-transference during the course of psychoanalytic treatment. The nature of the counter-transference is an always present force that constantly, inevitably, and even predictability draws us into very personal forms of acting out to very personal reactions to the transference and projective identification processes so universal in our patient's presentation. These periods of acting out by the analyst can be minor and fleeting or in some cases major and chronic.

At one end of the spectrum, these counter-transference stumbles can be highly useful as a way to truly "taste" the dramatic forces at play in the patient's core phantasies and unconscious conflicts. This in turn can lead us to new insight that can be passed on in the form of helpful interpretations. At the other end of the spectrum, we may be drawn into various enactments that are ongoing and only serve to validate or even intensify the patient's suffering and anxiety.

Contemporary Kleinians (Waska 2010c) provide a clinical approach that acknowledges unavoidable counter-transference enactments that can be studied and utilized in favor of the overall therapeutic work and enable the analyst to make his or her way through difficult impasses to more clinical clarity. Modern Kleinians (Waska 2010c) have shown how projective identification is often the cornerstone to a patient's transference state. As such, there is an ongoing pull at the analyst to embody various aspects of self and/or other from the patient's archaic object relational world.

Throughout most analytic treatments, but especially with those more erratic, entrenched, and disturbed patients struggling with more primitive paranoid or depressive phantasies, the analyst is subjected to constant invitation to be a part of unresolved unconscious tales centered on themes of love, hate, and knowledge. Sometimes, these counter-transference seductions are intense and obvious, other times more subtle and hard to detect. Some counter-transference feelings are more easily detected because they go so against the analyst's own sensibilities. Others are so in line with the analyst's everyday perceptions that they go unnoticed.

Another confusing aspect of successfully monitoring the counter-transference, as evidenced by the two cases presented, is to determine exactly how the patient is using us in the projective identification process at any given moment. We may be enlisted to be the healthy, assertive exploratory mind of the patient so they do not have to think or know. So, we are left with the pleasure and dread of old, current, or new knowledge about them or others. We may be pulled into feeling as persecuted or depressed as the patient does, feeling their guilt and anxiety so the patient feels rid of such elements. We may be molded into a variety of positive or negative figures from the patient's assortment of parental objects, authority figures, lovers, teachers, guides, judges, and prophets. We may find ourselves cast in the role of the third object, an oedipal placeholder in the patient's phantasy of the desired object and the object to compete against, avoid, or give into.

As one can tell, there are countless uses for us in the patient's projective identification endeavors to communicate, attack, resolve, amend, or avoid their core self and any close relational experience with another. All these psychological efforts on the patient's side create an ongoing ever changing matrix of feeling and thought in the analyst, shaping the counter-transference into a rich and dense motif that provides both valuable clues towards a helpful interpretive focus as well as quicksand-like halls of mirrors that blind us, hold us back, and encourage repetitive enactments.

The Kleinian approach provides a helpful therapeutic roadmap to catching ourselves when inevitably pulled into the counter-transference abyss and a way to shift to a more constructive line of interpretive exploration. We can use the counter-transference to enrich our working knowledge of the patients' transference conflicts in the here and now as well as their past object relational struggles. Finding out how and why the patient wants us to be positioned in the counter-transference can show us to "take it personal" in a helpful manner rather than take it in an impersonal or reactive manner.

6

CATCHING MY BALANCE IN THE COUNTER-TRANSFERENCE

Difficult moments with patients in psychoanalytic treatment

It is easy to get caught up in the counter-transference, especially with patients presiding more on the borderline, narcissistic, and paranoid-schizoid (Klein 1946) spectrum but also with those within the more primitive depressive (Klein 1935, 1940) realm. The analyst can easily slip into various modes of enactment. These patterns of acting out are typically evoked by the intrapsychic and interpersonal aspects of the patient's intense reliance on splitting and projective identification mechanisms. While acting out the counter-transference is a universal and unavoidable pitfall to some degree, it is vital for the analyst to find a way to regain his or her analytic balance and reestablish analytic contact (Waska 2007). This is a central therapeutic goal of Modern Kleinian Therapy. Once reconnected in this manner, the analyst can continue to move forward in helping the patient to resolve his or her core conflicts regarding love, hate, and knowledge (Waska 2010b). And, the analyst can then continue interpreting the ways the patient avoids the important and necessary integration of these conflicts (Waska 2006) by projecting unwanted aspects of self and object, avoiding separation, or denying differences between self and other.

To accomplish this, the analyst must find a way to use the initial counter-transference affect or phantasy as a guidepost. This might be a sense of calm, soothing pleasure, intense irritation, a deadened emotional state, or any other irregular state of mind that can help to alert one to the presence of something or someone trying to take up residence in one's mind. Even if it feels good, this counter-transference feeling is an alien presence that is not self. It is something other than self that can be an expansion or decrease of normal aspects of self. The analyst must find a way to make that differentiation between "I" and "I plus". Otherwise the analyst will continue to act out the projection as if it is a part of the normal self and something they will feel justified to try to convince the patient of.

Once aware that projected aspects of someone else's conflicts regarding love, hate, or knowledge are being communicated, smuggled, or forced into one's mind via intrapsychic and interpersonal maneuvers, the analyst can attempt to step back, collect, and contain these pieces and patterns long enough to begin enduring, understanding, and processing them with the eventual hope of interpreting them in some useful manner. This entire process is one in which the analyst gradually shifts from a more imbalanced paranoid-schizoid state or primitive depressive experience to a more mature whole object state of mind in which a therapeutic rather than retaliatory, a collaborative rather collusive, interpretation can be made.

Case material

Abbott has been seeing me for over a year, once a week sitting up. He came in originally to find help in dealing with the breakup of a long distance relationship he had been in for two years. He felt more in love with her than with anyone else he had ever been with but felt she had become cold and distant. Responding to his anxiety of losing her, he became overly controlling when she told him she was going to various parties with her girlfriends. He was jealous and worried and told her not to go. She broke it off for a while. They were ok for a few months but then she seemed more and more shut off for the next year, never initiating any words of affection or talking about their future together. Abbott would tell her he loved her and she would only respond some of the time. He would have to "prompt her" to say "I love you".

He finally confronted her and she admitted she was too busy pursuing her career to be able to commit to the relationship so she thought it best to put it on hold. She also told him she had long standing personal problems regarding commitments so she thought it best to call the whole thing off rather than put him on hold and continue to hurt his feelings. They still stayed in touch with occasional letters and calls so Abbott thought that "maybe one day things would turn around".

We spent about nine months processing the way he put himself on hold, never wanting to either confront her and ask for more or to break it off and give up the chance to be with her. We explored his fear of hurting her feelings, of ending up being totally alone if he broke it off, and "of jumping the gun before she had time to sort things out". Eventually, he realized she was not going to change and seemed too preoccupied with her own problems to be able to engage in a back and forth relationship with him anytime soon. He decided to call it off and was quite depressed for the next few months.

I interpreted how this whole set of dynamics seemed to parallel his difficult childhood. Abbott's mother was never available emotionally because of her severe depression and because of the way Abbott's father would yell at her and generally keep her under his thumb. She was in and out of a local mental institution and slept a great deal when she was home.

Over the course of our work, I suggested that perhaps he felt he had to treat his mother and others, including his girlfriend and myself, in a polite and careful manner to make sure he was not demanding too much or being a bother. He waited in the shadows, hoping for more but not wanting to cause pressure or hurt. Abbott was interested in what I said and thought it was accurate but quickly switched to logic and concrete thinking to say it was only proper to not pressure people and that his mother did the best she could so it would be wrong to expect more.

This theme was repeated in Abbott's relationship with his sister. She always asked him to come over to visit but ended up having him fix up her house, run errands, and work on her computer. She borrowed his car when her car broke down, borrowed money from him when she was short, and so on. He brought this up to me and discussed his irritation, but when I told him he seemed to be sharing the anger that he usually ignores and that he was telling me he wanted some gratitude for his efforts, Abbott quickly retreated into justifications about "she is family, you always help family. It is not about keeping score". I realized that perhaps my interpretation was either too quick, too strong, or simply something I correctly pointed out that Abbott would not permit to exist. He did not want any evidence to leak out about how he was unhappy and wanting more from his objects. In other words, perhaps this was a depressive resistance to the guilt he felt about wanting more from his mother, and now others, than she was willing or able to give him.

In the counter-transference, this left me somewhat frustrated as I thought he was always close to being angry or upset about not being loved enough but would quickly switch to this denial and concrete logic. This was the interpersonal fuel that pushed me to experience what I think he did not want to carry, the more intense feelings of desire, outrage, and assertiveness. I felt he stopped short of telling people, "You need to love me and show that you care. You need to show that you are grateful to have me in your life".

I also interpreted that Abbott played a role in the lopsidedness of his relationship with his sister by never asking her for anything and never depending on her. In fact, Abbott always made a big deal out of being very independent. He "didn't want to feel too reliant" on me, the treatment, or anyone else. He wanted my "help and consultation" but thought it would be "wrong to have to depend on me". We discussed how to need me was too dangerous or wrong and he would be suddenly demanding too much. I suggested that he did not want to lean on me too strongly for fear of hurting me. Abbott would come back with comments like, "Well, it would be nice if you finally just told me the answers and showed me the way, but you obviously won't do that. I have tried to ask you about yourself and you never tell me anything". Here, he seemed to be voicing some irritation or dissatisfaction with me for not providing him enough. I interpreted this and he shrugged it away.

Also, Abbott would always shake my hand at the start of each session but when I tried to explore the meaning of this, he told me it was simply the way he "expressed his pleasure in seeing friends and good acquaintances". Unfortunately, when I tried to engage him about the meaning of his behavior and how we could learn from it, he first took a concrete logical approach and eventually just stopped shaking my hand. I interpreted that this was one way to stop my curiosity and one way to avoid depending on me. He simply told me it "was something that created undue fuss so it is easier to just eliminate it".

I interpreted that he seemed to want to be in control by eliminating it, so perhaps he was feeling uncomfortable about my speaking of our relationship. He said, "I simply shake your hand because I am glad to see you. Nothing more, nothing less".

I asked how he dealt with shaking my hand the same way every time when sometimes he would no doubt be feeling upset in general, upset with me for some reason, or just not in the mood to be so social. He told me he did not see how those things would "prevent him from showing me common respect and a sign of acknowledgement". When I asked him why he wanted to know more personal things about me such as what my hobbies are, if I have a family, and how I deal with troublesome relationships, he said he asks "all his friends and coworkers about themselves to be nice and find out areas of common interest. Also, it is a great way to get pointers on better ways to approach things".

I interpreted, "It is hard to tell if you mean you are glad to see me and feel warmth for me in some kind of unique way to us or if you are trying to find ways to be nice and keep the conversation going. You want us to have common interests and be like friends, but you also act very official and procedural. Maybe it is difficult to figure out how to be comfortable with people in close relationships without being more formal and nice?" Abbott said, "I can't imagine how that would work. I want to respect what the other person needs and not push my moods or agenda on them". I said, "But, sometimes, your mood or agenda might be what makes us close and brings us to a better understanding of things". Abbott replied, "I often feel people are way too much that way, always pushing their wants and trying to have it be their way. My father comes to mind. He has to have everything his way and he is the ultimate selfish person. He is so selfish that he is incapable of realizing he is that way. He just thinks it is natural for me or my mother to be there to serve him. But, what can you do? He is old and he will never change".

I said, "You feel like you have to just accept that you are there to make his life pleasant and never will be able to turn to him or depend on him for your needs". Abbott said, "Yes. That is pretty much it". In the counter-transference, I found myself feeling angry at the father but also feeling handcuffed at how Abbott presented himself as so powerless and unwilling to make an effort to have things go more his way. This masochistic stance of pleasing others and not being selfish was too nice and pretty. I wanted to egg him on to dirty things up a bit and realize he too could have needs and have them met. I noticed these phantasies and feelings in myself and tried to store them for information and keep an eye on myself so as to not act them out.

Abbott was a smart dresser and worked out every day. He maintained a remarkable regime of martial arts, weight lifting, and running. The more I met with him, the more I wondered if these lifelong methods of remaining strong and able to take on any would be attacker were part of an underlying sense of persecution and dread. When I explored this, Abbott assured me that while he felt "completely confident about his safety and presence around others", he "never really felt at ease or calm in life". He told me about always "feeling awkward around others when it came to socializing" and was not comfortable when he was invited out to parties and gatherings. Abbott said he felt like the odd man out and never had much to contribute.

In fact, the more we discussed this, Abbott began to describe how he was shocked at how people seemed very happy "just going on and on about mindless topics for hours and he didn't really see the point". He thought that if a topic came up, it was best to share "whatever data he had about the topic and then let the other person talk". When I asked about how he felt with me, he said it was similar in that he wished I would take the lead and tell him what to do or what to talk about. He said, "It is uncomfortable and different to be asked to just share whatever I am thinking and feeling". This anxiety continued throughout the treatment. We were able to explore how he thought I might be bored, how I might think he was not focusing enough on "the topic", or how I might think he was not working hard enough to get better.

Abbott had a strict diet that allowed very little room for any variety or splurges. In fact, this was one of the areas in which I noticed myself acting out for some time and eventually was able to use this interaction to learn more about Abbott and the ways his phantasy life shaped his internal experiences.

During one session, Abbott told me a coworker had mentioned how "incredibly sparse his lunch was". When I heard about the Spartan items he had like a baked potato with nothing on it and some plain steamed vegetables with plain rice, I thought of how bland and unappealing it was. I pictured a hospital diet that provided no pleasure, only meager sustenance with a bad taste or no taste at all. I felt appalled, like, "Why should he be subjecting himself to this personal poverty?" I asked Abbott why he would need to deprive himself so much. He replied, "It is not so bad. I am used to it. I don't think of it one way or another. In fact, I see food as simply fuel. And, I need to keep it just like that to make sure I am able to increase my muscle mass versus body fat ratio". This last logical controlling departure from any sense of pleasure or humanness and his robot-like adherence to this anatomical goal pushed me to slip into acting out my counter-transference feelings of wanting to fight his rigid restrictions and demand that he allow Abbott more pleasure, need, and flexibility.

I said, "I am no expert, but I am sure you could eat almost anything in moderation, work out regularly, and still be in great shape". He disagreed and told me some of the facts and figures of how to properly increase muscle mass through reduced carbohydrate intake and increased protein intake. Or, maybe it was the other way around but I could not stand it. I said, "You seem to be so rigid about it, but I am sure other people end up just as muscular without putting themselves on a prison diet". Here, I was starting to convince him that no one else does this, he should stop immediately, and he need not be so mean to himself. I wanted him to loosen up and realize he could get something good without so much suffering. I felt compelled to rally for him and debate with him to get him to convert to a nicer, gentler way of treating himself.

Again, Abbott laid out the logic of proper diets for particular body building programs that are utilized to gain certain amounts of muscle mass and maintain specific physical endurance goals. At some point in the escalating debate between us, I realized how frustrated and fed up I was feeling. I really wanted to insist that Abbott stop being so controlling and meager and instead live a little and still reach his goal. As I gathered myself, I was able to find a better analytic foothold from which to interpret.

I said, "I guess what I am getting at is how much you side with the mechanics of it and seem like a robot in training. Food is only fuel, taste doesn't matter, and denying yourself any pleasure is fine since it is for the good of the goal. It all seems so colorless, without feelings. You check off another proper meal on your training calendar. But, I don't see much pleasure or excitement about any of it".

Abbott said, "Well, I see what you mean. It is simply my regime. I am happy to maintain or increase my muscle mass but I don't have much else going on. I think that is what you mean. Actually, I do feel more and I do have moments of excitement about it but I don't think anyone else would really care. To be more precise, I generally don't feel very interested in anything in my life. I don't have any hobbies, interests, or passions. I see other people have that but I feel very empty and lost inside. When I exercise, I feel focused and good. So, with my training, I do feel some passion but I don't think anyone else would care about it. For the most part, I just get out of the way and ask people what they are excited about. As an example, since I don't care about food, it amazes me that people can go on forever talking about the great restaurants they went to, what they have been cooking, or how great the farmer's market was. I try and listen and ask questions but I don't have anything to give back because I am not interested in that. The problem is that I don't feel I have anything to give from any area so I end up feeling very isolated and like I am standing around a group of people who are all linked in to a mutual topic and I have no connection to it or to them".

I asked Abbott about how that was in the transference, how he felt talking to me. He said it was very similar because he "wasn't sure what I wanted him to talk about and he didn't know what to say if it was all up to him. He wasn't sure what was valuable enough to bring up or what would be best to help reach the goal". I replied, "Without the idea of a goal, you feel lost and unsure that I will be happy with what I see or hear. You don't know if you will please me or disappoint me".

He said, "Well, I see how you see it that way. I feel like I don't know if I am giving you the data you need to help me change or not". I said, "So, we are both machines and you don't know if you are putting in the correct data to produce the optimum result. That is a very tight, thought out plan but like your diet plans, it doesn't leave much room for anything else and it leaves you very separate from others, all on your own. You feel self-contained but then very isolated and anxious about how to find a way to connect". He said, "It is true". Then, he said, "But what do we do about it?" I said, "Doing is a way to retreat back to the safety of being a doing robot. It is harder to gradually think about this and come to learn what you feel. Your feelings will guide you to what could eventually be done". He nodded.

Making interpretations to Abbott about what I learned in the counter-transference was a difficult matter, as he took things very concretely and would debate what I proposed from a place of logic and controlled thought, all of which did not allow for feelings, needs, or differences in his tightly bound way of perceiving the world. This sequence of my gradual self-containment of projective identification induced counter-transference states followed by interpretations of his core transference and anxiety laden phantasies helped him to feel understood in a modest, concrete manner. But, to allow himself to explore, question, understand, learn, and change himself meant he would have to be a separate entity willing to confront his disappointment in his object, not cater to them at all times, and express his desire for them to both stop being a certain way and to start being another way to meet his needs better. This triggered unbearable guilt and anxiety so he would fight me off with logic and rationalizations regarding politeness, telling me how everyone had the right to be as they pleased and not have to change just because he wanted something.

Abbott said, "Why should I demand someone be different just for me?" Here, in the counter-transference, I felt myself to be the vanguard of what he deserved and why he had the right to fight for it. I tried to notice that and in the process take something from it that I could learn from and pass on to Abbott. I said, "So, everyone else gets to be themselves and you make sure to respect that and cater to it. But, you don't deserve a turn?" He paused and said, "I don't feel I need anything". I interpreted, "You want to be totally self-contained and not need anything. But, that leaves you feeling like you don't get much in return from your girlfriends, your coworkers, your father, and even myself sometimes". Here, I was referring to when he said he tells me all about himself but I never answer his questions about me.

Abbott's pattern of relating with women was striking and also triggered various counter-transference states that at first served only to intensify the existing phantasies of self and object that Abbott suffered with. But, later, they also helped to direct me in learning more about his internal conflicts and to make some interpretations that focused on those particular areas of conflict. When I heard about the various women he had dated over the years, I was taken aback by the consistent profile of selfish, self-absorbed, "high maintenance" women who wanted Abbott to, in his words, "be their sugar daddy". He said he would go along with this for the most part but if it became too much over time he would end the relationship. So, in that sense, he was not in never ending masochistic bonds that he felt powerless in. But, there was that sort of thread to it. He took care of them and they did not give much back. I thought of his description of his mother and of his father, taking but never giving.

I made what felt like balanced and relatively bias free interpretations about this past situation but mostly about more current relationships including the transference. As a result, we came to learn about his fear of "asking for too much, being pushy or controlling, and not allowing others to be who they are". Indeed, the more we examined this, the more it turned out that Abbott "didn't really understand women, but tried to follow the guidelines and suggestions he read about, saw on television, or had heard about from some of his buddies". These "guidelines" were extremely stereotyped images of how men need to cater to and always provide for women and that women are expected to be very focused on clothes, fashion, makeup, dancing, and expect to be treated well by men with money.

I thought this vision of women was perhaps part of Abbott's internal mother. Was his internal mother so withered, depressed, and unavailable to provide any image at all of what to expect from a relationship with a woman that he had to look for social caricatures to guide him? At the same time, perhaps this was his internal experience of the combined demanding selfish father and a very needy, depressed mother who could never take care of herself let alone give Abbott any attention. I made these interpretations over time and he told me he did feel like he had to "be his mother's nurse most of the time, making sure she was not too depressed and not too beat down by father". This was part of him seeming to feel understood by me but stopping short of using the insights as a way to understand himself and create change in his relationship to either self or others (Steiner 2000). In fact, Abbott told me he did not really see much of a problem in how he viewed women and if they wanted too much and did not seem to be able to give back, he would simply stop dating them.

While on the surface, I believed he was telling me the truth about certain concrete situations with certain women he had dated, I was taken by how he stepped aside from any feelings about these obviously selfish or narcissistic women and any feelings about feeling obligated to do whatever he could to give them the benefit of the doubt even in the face of very distasteful interactions. My counter-transference really surfaced when Abbott told me more of the actual details of his dating patterns over the last few years. Since Abbott was not very social, tended to work long hours, and stayed at home at night or on the weekends, he looked for dates on the Internet.

Not very familiar with the online dating scene, I nevertheless knew from other patients' reports that some of the websites were more cutthroat and vendor machine like than others. To me, it seemed to always be a cold and impersonal way of trying to meet someone but some of the websites were more mercenary than others. So, I found myself feeling it was not too surprising but a little sad or even pathetic that Abbott had put his "profile" on various dating sites and had requested a woman of a certain age, height, and weight, along with a general request for someone who liked exercise and had an active lifestyle. This was all part of the questions on the template offered by the site. I noticed that he emphasized the external and physical and did not request much in the way of more personal or internal interests.

Abbott told me he did not "feel he had much going in those areas so he would have to wait and see what she brought to the table". I interpreted that this was similar to the nature of his transference. He often waited to see what agenda I would set and what aspects of him I would be interested in. When I pointed this out, he replied that he had tried to find out more about me but "I had always turned it around and back on him". I said, "And you are uncomfortable having the spotlight, letting it be about you. You seem to want to turn the attention to me and sit in the background." He said, "Yes. I am good at doing that and feel more at ease that way. I never feel I have much going on or much to contribute. So, I just let the other person lead".

I interpreted that he felt more in control that way but ultimately he was giving control over to the other person and would end up feeling alone and isolated if the other person did choose to make it all about themselves. He no longer really had a choice. He felt more secure and less anxious if he was in the passenger seat but then he never got to drive and never knew where the trip might go or end.

Abbott agreed but said that "once you or someone starts the drive, I might have some feedback and tell you what I think. If I really don't like the drive, I would ask you to pull over and I would get out". I said, "So, you can draw the limits if it gets too bad, but you don't feel you have much to contribute to make it good". He said he "agreed for the most part" and then continued, "I just don't have much to say in social settings. It is not my best asset. I do better when I am by myself. But, then again, I don't really know what to do with myself when I am alone. So, it is a catch 22".

Regarding the online dating, the first thing I noted to myself was that he did not seem to think twice about the custom order style of those websites. It was so impersonal and mechanical, as if one was simply ordering a special ham for the holidays, "medium well done, five pounds, with a sugar glaze but no cloves please". In the counter-transference, I noticed myself becoming judgmental of the whole process and wondering why Abbott would want to subject himself to such a lack of sensitivity in which people were treated like merchandise. I asked him what he thought about using a service that was so much like the bar scene that he had told me he dreaded, "a real meat market" as he put it. Abbott replied, "Well, it is the same but I don't have time to go to the bars with my long hours at work and I can avoid the required dancing and drinking. With the online site, I can just get to the bottom line. I want to find a woman that has common interests, that I could fall in love with, and maybe have a family with".

Here, his comment woke me up out of my counter-transference enactment. In this moment, the enactment was a silent one in which I was going along for the ride, feeling passive and helpless against this website approach. I had stepped away from my role as active interpreter and become like Abbott, a victim of sorts. Specifically, I had started to feel that Abbott was a poor soul who needed a date but was going to be taken advantage of by these selfish women at the online meat market. But, now I was reminded by his comment about just getting to the bottom line that he too was busy picking out his pre-ordered ham. He was filtering out certain types of women and only replying to other types, all in a very sterile manner. So, he was just as much a hunter as a hunted commodity.

Now, I was back on track analytically and out of my projective identification based counter-transference. I interpreted, "So, you have your list of demands as well. You want someone who is this way and that way and not this other way. You usually present yourself as very passive and not able to grab what you want. Maybe this side of things is something you don't normally show me and maybe feel guilty or uncomfortable about. It looks like you are powerful and able to think for yourself some of the time".

Abbott responded, "I can but you make it sound aggressive. I don't think I do it in a way that hurts anyone's feelings". I replied, "You are concerned I think that. I don't. But, you are quick to set the record straight. That might be because you worry about being either passive and nice or too strong and demanding". He said, "Well, I have been on occasion told I get too controlling. But, that was only in a few situations. With the online dating, the women seem to know exactly what they want and are not afraid to ask for it. I have to hope they like what they see. But, I have noticed that sometimes when I meet them in person, they look very different than their online pictures. But, I still give them a chance".

I said, "I think you want them, me, and everyone to give you a chance but you feel scared to come out in the open since it is hard to know what will happen". He said, "Do you mean like I will be rejected?" I said, "Yes". Abbott responded, "I think I try and go slow so I don't go too fast and step on any toes. Also, I am anxious that if I go ahead and just talk about whatever is on my mind, like everyone else seems to be able to do, that I will be boring or fill the space too much". I interpreted, "You are worried about how you will impact me and others so you stay back and be careful for your safety and ours as well".

When Abbott told me about the types of women he met online and dated, I was fairly shocked. He described a series of women who were outright rude and told him that they were "disappointed that he didn't have more rugged features, that he was shorter than they like, that they wanted a man who had more money, or that he wasn't young enough". It was very strange to hear these stories where women were being almost caustic in their feedback to him regarding their initial reaction to meeting him or even after a couple of months of dating.

Now, what was interesting was that these disappointments and rude sounding assessments came in reply to Abbott asking them if they were satisfied with him now that they met him in the flesh and if he was just as good in person as his online profile. So, he was inviting them to assess and critique him, but I was still shocked that he managed to tap into a crowd of such consumer driven women who had a preconceived notion of what they expected from this human convenience store and would quickly and rudely discard anything that did not meet their demands. But, all this was my counter-transference reaction to Abbott not really caring that he was being treated so coldly and not thinking much about how he was essentially doing the same.

Again, I was outraged, he was not. This reminded me of how he spoke of his very narcissistic sister and her demanding behavior and rude remarks. It had to be her way and Abbott had to be ready to serve her or he would hear about it later. It also reminded me of how he described his demanding father who never showed any emotion or caring but was quick to put Abbott down for not being enough for him in a million different ways. But, like I said, I was the one sitting with all these thoughts and feelings while Abbott merely answered my questions in a fairly neutral manner.

As Steiner (2000) points out, the confusion or intensity the analyst feels in the counter-transference can serve to alert him to an important process taking place just out of sight. But, if that total transference situation (Joseph 1985), which includes the counter-transference and all patient references to external issues as well as seemly unimportant interactions during the session, is examined and valued, that purposeful study can help both parties to reduce their mutual acting out and increase their exploration of the patient's phantasies, anxieties, and defenses that are preventing insight, change, and growth.

As Steiner (1996) has established, the goal of psychoanalytic treatment is the re-acquisition and re-integration of projected aspects of the patient's self. To fully accomplish this, a period of decreased control, an acknowledgement of separateness and dependency, and a time of loss and mourning are necessary. This is usually a very difficult and slow process that most patients resist. Conflict is not something we can solve for the patient but something we can help the patient do by re-discovering his or her own resources and mental assets.

Abbott wanted help in this way but he remained in the shadows of his familiar and controlled psychic retreat (Steiner 1993), constructed with logic, denial, and masochistic loyalty. He used splitting and projective identification as his primary methods of relating, characteristic of the paranoid-schizoid position but defending him against a primitive depressive phantasy world of broken and depressed objects, unhappy with him for not providing enough at all times. Abbott tried his best to not have a mind of his own, preferring to deposit any and all desire or opinion in the other. Due to his excess reliance on projective identification, his mental and emotional capacity was inhibited and often lost altogether.

So, as Steiner (2001) discovered, the analyst must integrate information from a variety of sources including the counter-transference to understand the total transference situation (Joseph 1985). Steiner suggested that it is this integration that leads to what we have come to think of as containment (Bion 1962a). Containment provides an experience of being understood, in which the patient's projective identifications are given meaning that then creates separateness and identity in an otherwise diffuse, empty, and fragmented internal experience.

When Abbott told me about how one woman told him he was not rich enough for her to consider dating him for any length of time or making any major commitment to him, I was again outraged and Abbott seemed neutral. I made this interpretation and he again said he thought it was normal for women to look to men to meet their needs. He said, "What she had said was simply her being honest, and that helped both of us know where we stood".

I was able to step out of my minor yet ongoing counter-transference haze to say that he was relating to me in a way that pulled for me to tell him the right way to relate, to give him permission to demand more from women, and to urge him to be ok with pushing back when he felt hurt. I said he wanted me to be a sort of mediating parent who could teach him or permit him to tell his internal father to stop being so selfish and demanding and to tell his internal mother to start paying attention to him and be mothering and caring to him. Also, I interpreted that he wanted me to teach him how to have a relationship that was not a repeat of his parents with him being the helpless, powerless mother and his dates being the selfish, pushy father. However, this would simply make me another person telling him what to do. These interpretations seemed to open up Abbott's thoughts and feelings much more and he was engaged with me about these ideas. We made headway and discussed our relationship as well as how he related to others.

Here, I was shifting from some previous periods in which I had interpreted his actions or inactions with others outside the analytic office to now working through the more immediate here-and-now transference. I was focusing more on the nature of how he was using projective identification with me and the various motives he had behind that method of relating to me. So, as Eizirik (2010) reports, there can be many plausible interpretations referring to a third person or an outside circumstance. But, the most important and transformative interpretations are always the ones that focus on the transference anxiety, the urgency that the patient has in using us in a particular manner.

In the counter-transference with Abbott, more than once I fell into the pattern of trying to make him be someone he was not. I realized I was being pulled by his projective identification based transference to first judge him on how passive and empty he seemed and then to in reaction push him into being more like I thought he should be, active, assertive, and expressive. Thus, I became another bully, another demanding and controlling object in his life exactly like he described his father, his sister, and most of the women he dated. I wanted a better object, much like Abbott wanted a better mother, father, sister, and girlfriend. But, he was too guilty and anxious to own that anger, demand, and hunger. So, he denied ownership and jettisoned those undesirable phantasies into me.

When I did not fall prey to this acting out of his wish to reshape his objects into something better and more fulfilling that he could then respect, admire, and depend on for love and security, I was left with a listless, blank object. In other words, if I did not make him come alive in my mold, he seemed dead and empty. Abbott presented himself to be a victim of sorts, was indeed chronically depressed, and showed no real motivation or confidence to change. So, here I was caught with a lifeless depressed mother object and felt very frustrated and helpless. This was the other side of Abbott's projective identification process.

Rather than become hopeless and drift alone with him feeling angry and helpless, I had to find a way to properly interpret this transference state. I said, "You seem to want me to tell you the answers, give you the guidebook, and show you the way like a helpful, functioning parent who isn't so selfish or depressed to love you. But, without that, without me taking over and controlling you and demanding that you do it my way, we seem to just fall into a fog. You seem lost and without a compass".

Abbott associated to his "entire life but especially the last ten years". He said, "I have felt that way, lost and in the fog, for a very long time. When I am not staying busy with work and taking on special assignments that take up my weekends or when I am not doing something for my sister or my father, I do feel lost. So, I see what you mean about it happening here too, at least some of the time. But, isn't that your job to tell me what to do?" I said, "You want me to be the controlling parent who has you do it my way. I think you are stuck between feeling you are going to have to be selfish and demand that others give you want you want or you will have to be nice and quiet and do things our way". Abbott said, "If I have time to myself and no one else is involved, I have no idea what to do. And, if I can think of something that sounds like it would be fun or important, I never can find the motivation to carry it out. I make some great plans for myself sometimes. But, then I just end up staying at home and really doing nothing. I said, "I think you are anxious to go out there and be yourself among us all. If we aren't calling the shots, you don't know how to fit in. I think you are worried you will bore us, offend us, or not know how to fit in without creating some kind of tension". He nodded and said, "So, my best solution is to do nothing". He went on and told me a few stories about how he has spent a great deal of money on fishing equipment, thinking it would be a lot of fun to take up the sport. He has tried it before and enjoyed it. But, after he purchased a whole array of poles, lines, lures, and other equipment, he never felt moved to go fishing. He said, "If you told me we are going fishing this weekend, I would be ready to go and excited. But on my own, I sit in the living room watching television in a dark room by myself and all the fishing equipment rots in the garage".

Discussion

As the reader can see, Abbott felt understood and seemed interested in much of what I interpreted, but he frequently took up a very passive and helpless position to whatever we discovered or reviewed. Much of the time, just like his description of fishing with others versus by himself, Abbott would sit and listen to me, sometimes engage with a mutual back and forth, but often finish by sitting back in a placid manner and ask me what should he do with what we found or studied together.

Rather (2001) notes how the patients' pleas of "what to do" with the information that emerges in analytic treatment, especially the spontaneous feelings and opinions that emerge, are a defensive reaction away from symbolic thought and symbol formation. Abbott would often say, "Ok. I see. But, what do I do with that? What do I do about it now that I know I feel that way?" He tried to keep us at a robot-like process of data collection and data organization, but stopped short of allowing feelings to flow through him spontaneously via the transference or towards and about himself or other objects.

As Rather (2001) points out, this prevention or elimination of thought and feeling can be because of the dread of depressive experiences engulfing the internal other. In other words, one's own mind and its creation of thought are avoided and attacked for the sake of the other. The mind is felt to be the source of loss and pain so the patient feels they can shut that down and simply rely on the analyst to find out "what to do", thus protecting the other and the risk to the self if the other is damaged. So, this was a paranoid-schizoid (Klein 1946) maneuver of splitting and neutralizing to avoid devastating, depressive (Klein 1935, 1940) experiences.

Ogden (1991) discusses how, in the paranoid-schizoid world, the patient works at separating the endangering and endangered aspects of self and object through splitting and relies on projective identification to experience through others what is too endangering to self or others. Abbott used me to become the keeper of his forbidden thoughts and feelings but reacted in a paranoid manner when I tried to convert those projections into interpretations. He did want to re-own them. Abbott tried to not depend on the object and emphasized how he did not really need the attention or care of the object. He did this as a way to deny how selfish and depressed his mother/father object was and projected most of his need and desire into others. Therefore, he was surrounded by women who were selfish and unavailable.

So, because of this projective identification process and his defenses against the return of his unwanted feelings and thoughts, I had to be careful to not become the source, the messenger of these dreaded experiences of sorrow, anger, and loss. I was always close to becoming a persecutory object; forcing him to face a world of broken objects and selfish unavailable others who had to be cared for instead of providing love. By trying to contain, understand, and gradually interpret these counter-transference experiences, I could avoid acting them out.

As Roth (2001) notes, it can be the counter-transference enactments that are often a bridge to useful transference interpretation that links unconscious conflicts and internal phantasies to how the patient invites or uses the analyst to play out various archaic object relational scenarios.

7

COMBATIVE AND
REACTIVE PATIENTS

The contemporary psychoanalyst in private practice is not seeing many 4–5-times-a-week, on the couch patients who pay full fee out of pocket. Indeed, it is unusual for patients to attend that often and unusual for patients to want to pay themselves instead of using insurance coverage that only provides 20–40 visits per year at a reduced rate of reimbursement to the analyst. Nor do our current patients typically attend for years and gradually work through their neurotic conflicts to a mutually agreed upon successful termination. The reality of current private practice is that we may have one or two such patients (Waska 2005, 2006) but even this is rare and mostly a stereotype of what only may have been a reality decades ago. External factors such as economic problems, time constraints, and either the lack of adequate insurance coverage or the constraints of managed care, make the establishment of a consistent and robust treatment requiem difficult or impossible.

Research (Sabrina Cherry et al 2004) shows that unless the analyst is a training or supervising analyst at a major analytic institute with a caseload of candidates needing supervision and/or a training analysis, most post-graduation analysts are seeing one or two analytic patients and the rest are once-a-week psychotherapy patients or couples and families. Also, the diagnostic profile of our caseload has shifted. Nowadays, we take on the task of assisting individuals with a much more turbulent, fragmented, and slippery psychological profile. These are either the very anxious or severely depressed neurotic suffering from severe depressive position (Klein 1935, 1940) conflicts, patients who are borderline or narcissistic, or those individuals operating in a more psychotic realm.

When meeting with couples and families, the Modern Kleinian therapist offers the psychoanalytic method for a better understanding and opportunity for change from disturbances in intimate relationships. This includes working through the couple's resistance to change and how each may see evolution in the relationship as a parallel to their phantasy of change as danger to the self (Waska 2006). To see couples treatment as somehow not analytic is to be entering the camp of elitism and narcissistic inflation. As De Forster (2006) states, "when an analyst treats couples or families, it is because they reject, without any hesitation, those conceptions of psychoanalysis which are confined to an ivory tower. Our discipline must take a flexible approach, catering to the needs of men and women of our time. If the only therapeutic approach that psychoanalysis can offer is individual therapy consisting of three or four weekly sessions on the couch, our approach to treatment will continue to lose ground in today's society and will ultimately be condemned to death" (page 257).

Kleinian couples therapy and
the search for analytic contact

Overall, there is not a great deal of literature from the psychoanalytic field that articulates a robust, comprehensive, or integrated approach to treating couples. The little there is is a hodgepodge of opinions that range on a spectrum from defining couples treatment as a more psychodynamic treatment to defining it as more of a behavioral intervention or transference manipulation combined with some basic analytic principles. In searching PEP, the electronic collection of the past hundred years of psychoanalytic journals and various textbooks, there is not much on the subject. What does show up are a few book reviews and a few papers that build on the landmark work of Dicks (1967) and Bion (1962a), as well as the clinical and theoretical concepts of Melanie Klein. Certainly, the Tavistock Clinic in England has worked for years with couples, families, and children with a psychoanalytic approach and has published papers and a few books on the subject. But these are not widely available and tend to focus on child treatment.

In this chapter, I will be using clinical material to illustrate my own unique psychoanalytic method of working with couples from a Modern Kleinian Therapy perspective. In addition, because couples work often involves one or both parties entering the treatment process operating within a more primitive and volatile paranoid-schizoid mode (Klein 1946) that contributes to chronic impasses or sudden aborted connections and unexpected terminations, I will present one very difficult, short, and ultimately unsuccessful case for study. These are the sorts of patients who struggle with primitive phantasies of hate and harm (Waska 2010d) that massively interfere with the ability to navigate the ongoing cycles of dependency and individuation that make up healthy relationships.

When using the Kleinian approach with couples, I am advocating the clinical concept of "analytic contact" (Waska 2007, 2010a, 2010b, 2010c, 2011a, 2011b) with couples. By analytic contact, I mean that the analyst should always attempt to engage the patient in an exploration of their unconscious phantasies, transference patterns, defenses, and internal experience of the world. Regardless of frequency, use of couch, length of treatment, or style of termination, the goal of psychoanalytic treatment is always the same: the understanding of unconscious phantasy, the resolution of intrapsychic conflict, and the integration of self↔object relations, both internally and externally.

The Kleinian couple's psychoanalyst uses interpretation as their principal tool with transference, counter-transference, and projective identification being the three clinical guideposts of those interpretive efforts. Viewed from the Kleinian perspective, most couples over-utilize projective identification as a psychic cornerstone for defense, communication, attachment, learning, loving, and aggression. As such, projective identification constantly shapes and colors both the transference and counter-transference and must be constantly tracked, translated, and worked through. Counter-transference, if properly utilized, can be an invaluable aid in the quest for analytic contact with couples. The case material will illustrate this point.

When conducting couples treatment from a Kleinian psychoanalytic approach, there are several moving parts. The technique involves a combination of individual focus on each party as well as treatment of the couple as a unified system. This is where all the fundamentals of Kleinian technique come to bear, including the emphasis on such concepts as love, hate, knowledge, transference, counter-transference, containment, but especially the understanding of projective identification. Zavattini (1988) notes that couples utilize each other for the healthy evacuation and integration cycles that replicate normal mother and child relationships of container and contained. Couples offer each other the opportunity to recognize formally rejected aspects of self and to gradually re-own and value formally rejected and feared areas of internal life.

When the couple enters treatment, we usually meet two individuals in a state of crisis and two people who are presenting with a great deal of anxiety and pathology of their own. It is as if we see two wounded, growling animals placed together in a cage. The result is predictable. They use our office and our presence to act out emotionally violent and chaotic patterns of destructive phantasies regarding multiple issues including persecution, guilt, loss, envy, and separation.

So, in the initial phase of Kleinian couples treatment, I advocate a much closer focus on each individual and their needs. For a while, it is as if there are two individual patients in the room, both requiring individual treatment. So, this is what I do. On occasion, I let them turn to each other and see what happens. If they act like wild adversarial animals confined together in a cage, I stop the interaction and begin exploring why they feel so adversarial and wild, why they have constructed the cage, and how that confinement has served them as well as hurt them.

As we move through this early phase of treatment, there will be numerous opportunities for me to refer to the transference. This might be an interpretation of their transference to each other, their mutual transference to me, or their individual transference to me. It might be an interpretation of a primitive oedipal feeling of envy, hatred, or dread involving me as the father or the lover to the other. It might be a more infantile phantasy of my being the parent to both of them as children. The varieties are endless of course.

So, in the beginning of most couples work, there is some time spent on the mutual couple's projective identification dynamics. But, a much greater deal of time is spent on each party's use of projective identification and other defenses in their own struggle with anxiety, guilt, and persecution. It is a constant analytic observation of the couple together and interpreting their encounter in the moment and then having to separate them as the tension escalates. The Kleinian analyst begins to contain and translate that trouble by focusing on them as individuals until they can develop their own individual secure containment and a new level of individual cohesion in the moment. At that point, we can safely return to exploring their actual relationship or lack of.

In being the psychic referee, the analyst stops the mutual acting out, but also makes interpretations in doing so. So, the analyst may point out how the couple tends to always want him or her to step in as an authority or parent and create some boundaries, definitions, rules, or sense. The analyst may notice one party starting most of the mutual acting out and interpret that they seem to want the analyst to blame them, take sides, or pay more attention to them. Thus, from a Kleinian perspective, interpretation of transference, phantasy, and conflict remain central to the couple's treatment situation.

With turbulent, volatile couples, the analyst is often called upon to create definitions and limits as well as act as container, translator, and guide to working through of the ongoing moments, segments, or phases of each party's pathology. Then, the analyst can direct both parties to move back into a more mutual exploration and see if they use the analytic space as a boxing ring, a bedroom, a fortress, or any other type of mutual creation to negotiate various phantasies of love, hate, and knowledge. Of course, what unfolds would be the next topic for interpretation.

Successful psychoanalytic couples treatment from a Kleinian perspective must always weave back and forth from an individual focus to a couple's format and then to a three person triangle with the analyst serving as the third element in their internal world. One advantage of this approach is that each party can be witness to their partner being vulnerable and having to face or not face certain uncomfortable aspects of themselves and hopefully slowly express their previously warded off feelings they never before allowed into the relationship. A greater compassion, understanding, and acceptance of each other can emerge.

Witnessing

A unique benefit of psychoanalytic couples therapy involves the interpersonal, interactional, and intrapsychic witnessing of each party to the therapeutic relationship between the analyst and the other partner. Each party is witness to the exploration and working through of the other party's transference and phantasy state. Here, the container-contained (Bion 1962a) situation, the analysis of problems with thinking, and the understanding of projective identification dynamics converge for the couple as they are individual observers as well as participants in a parallel process.

A significant curative function of psychoanalytic couples therapy involves the witnessing of the self⟷object struggle in which each party must slowly take ownership of their conflicts rather than blame, deny, or split them off into their partner. It is typical for a couple to begin psychoanalytic treatment in a state where they are constantly blaming each other, only finding fault in each other due to projections of hostility, guilt, and conflict. In this more primitive, paranoid state, each party typically does not view the object as willing to consider their own flaws and thus each patient feels, "Why should I take ownership of my faults if he/she never does?" This is often experienced in an immature parent/child manner in which there is a phantasy of a parental object refusing to be a container and always wanting to be superior to the child, never offering the model of reflection, regret, amends, and resolve. So, each patient is often locked into a projective identification cycle with objects that never admit fault and never want to make it better. These objects only seek narcissistic superiority and sadistic revenge. Other times, in an equally dysfunctional projective cycle, the object is a resentful victim, overburdened and wanting masochistic attention, unable to admit to any contribution to current problems.

If the analyst can engage each party in a therapeutic exploration of their inner world and establish analytic contact with them, the other party is witness to their externalized object's slow transformation. This can provide hope, trust, and increased willingness to do the same themselves. Over time and as a result of the working through of each party's individual issues in front of the other party, more understanding and compassion can emerge, engendering self-reflection, and a desire to help the other and change the self for the good of the relationship. This is the emergence of more healthy depressive (Klein 1935, 1940) functioning.

Certainly, with patients who are gravely disturbed and caught within strong internal conflicts and phantasies, there will be great resistance to internalizing this new view of the object. Envy, guilt, paranoid hostility, and narcissistic independence all preclude these positive witnessing experiences. However, as the analyst notes the negative reactions to being an observer to their object's honest struggle towards change and learning, the analyst can interpret these pathological reactions. In doing so, it can provide a window of understanding for the other party about their resistant partner. In couples therapy, we cannot avoid each party having reactions to the other party's resistance or growth, but we can attempt to interpret it and place it within the context of the individual's internal dynamics as well as the matrix of the couple.

Each partner is distorted in the other party's mind by massive projections of archaic phantasies. One of the central aims of psychoanalytic couples therapy, similar to the goals of individual psychoanalysis, is to help separate the reality of the external world from the patient's personal unconscious vision of the world. By observing their external love object working with the analyst, this psychic separation is easier to allow and to accept. In watching their partner differentiate between what they really feel about the relationship and what feelings and thoughts belong elsewhere, the other party can begin to do the same.

Often, one partner is more integrated than the other. Or, over the course of the treatment, one party is able to begin functioning in more of a depressive state than the other. The partner who has made more progress can often serve as a protective presence or container to the other when they feel persecuted by the analyst or by being in treatment. So, when the first party clings to their projected phantasy states, having the second party present often makes it easier to investigate the resistance to giving up their inner world of wishes and fears because the second partner can act as an encouraging, compassionate, curious, and trusted bystander.

Again, this can also go the other way when some patients are so paranoid or narcissistic that they feel overcome with shame or anxiety at the idea of having their partner view them in distress. Or, the distressed partner may feel the analyst and their partner are ganging up on them. This creates difficult moments but, overall, the presence of another encouraging, containing object can elevate the escalating anxieties and bring about more windows of opportunity in the moment to moment work.

Certainly, it is possible to begin a couple's treatment wherein neither party has any compassion or empathy for the other due to excessive paranoid (Klein 1946) states of mind. In fact, many cases begin in this stormy manner. However, as each party is witness to the one-to-one exploration of their partner's issues with the help of the analyst and is given a window into understanding what sort of internal experiences fuel their partner's view of self and object, each partner can move towards a less defensive posture as they understand "where their partner is coming from" instead of seeing the partner as a faceless foe. This less conflicted view of the external and internal object can lead to a new openness and desire to change.

Etchegoyen (1991) points out the clinical benefits of differentiating sympathy and empathy. This differentiation can be important in couples work and in the dynamic of witnessing. Barugel (1984) defines sympathy as suffering with the other as the result of having feelings that are similar to that of the object. Empathy, on the other hand, is suffering within the object as a result of identification. With couples and witnessing, there can eventually be a healthy degree of projective identification developed in which each party can suffer within the other, reaching a new understanding of the other. Before this progress is made, defensive sympathy in which everything is filtered from one's own perspective is common or a claustrophobic over-identification in which the party reacts defensively to feeling overwhelmed or persecuted by the empathic emersion in the object.

This process of bearing witness and the resulting internalization of new object relations brings about a new ability of negotiation, and tolerance. In addition, it provides a new oedipal experience in which one is able and willing to learn from others, internalize others, and feel supported by the image of a relationship (analyst and the other party) in which tension may arise but things can be worked out. Conflict is ok and resolution of conflict is possible. To be part of such a triangle provides the patient with a level of parental, oedipal containment that might be very different from the oedipal experiences they had with their family of origin.

At the same time, prior oedipal experiences of trauma, loss, and aggression may be triggered by the couple's therapy and acted out in the treatment. In these cases, one patient may try to side with the analyst against the other party, creating unworkable depressive or paranoid conflict between the analyst and the other party or they may feel fearful, envious, or rejected by the oedipal situation in a manner that causes them to retreat or react aggressively. These competitive, withdrawing, or aggressive responses need to be carefully interpreted and followed through to avoid collapse of the treatment setting.

By bonding with the exploratory, curious stance of the analyst, the patient can observe and understand their partner in a new way, from a safe distance. In this way, they begins to establish a sense of seeing and knowing the other, rather than feeling consumed, burdened, or attacked. Part of the new oedipal experience is feeling the analyst/parent offers some buffer or safe envelope from the other party/parent if there is any danger or dispute. The child must trust that each parent will act as a container/buffer if the other parent temporarily fails at being a container/protector. In this sense, the analyst acts as an emotional referee in both an external reality-based manner but also in a very important unconscious, internal manner for the patient who may have lived life devoid of that security, safety, and trust.

Melanie Klein (1928, 1931) wrote about the child's instinctual need to learn as part of normal growth and object relational development. When such development is hindered, this need to learn and to know can become more defensive and become a need to know everything so as to control and master the object. Bion (1962a) elaborated on these ideas and explored the mutual dependency necessary for healthy learning and knowledge to unfold. Bion emphasized that learning comes from the container object being willing and able to be flexible and open to new experiences. The contained self internalizes this flexible, open, yet psychologically defined and separate container object and thus literally learns how to learn. If the object is defensive and rigid to these new experiences, instead of being receptive, knowledge is blunted or blocked.

In psychoanalytic couples therapy, this process takes place within the interpersonal, interactional, and intrapsychic sphere of each party, as well as the combined couple, as they relate with the analyst. Hopefully, over time, one party can become part of the flexible, growth-directed relating. And, as this occurs, the second party is witness to this healthy expansion of container-contained and therefore can be more forgiving to their previously rigid, cruel, or threatening image of their object. As they reduce their hostile or frightening phantasies of their object by reducing their attacking projections, there is opportunity to take in their partner as a more welcoming, helpful container. In a positive cycle, they can then develop the desire to be a warm, healing container towards their object as well.

However, Bion and others (Waska 2005; Joseph 1982; Segal 1981) have noted how envy can play a destructive role in the development of knowledge, the acceptance of growth and change in the container, and the acknowledgement of mutual dependence.

Bion (1962b) points out that envy can create a hatred of any new development in the self or object and phantasies emerge of a hatred rival that must be punished, eliminated, or destroyed. The healing process of psychoanalytic couples treatment that involves "getting to know each other and getting to know oneself better" can only occur when each party can tolerate the pain, fear, guilt, and confusion of not knowing, not immediately changing, or not immediately seeing change in the other. Giving and receiving are part of this, as change in each other involves a natural give and take process. If these dynamics trigger too much guilt or feel too persecutory, the patient may employ massive projective identification attacks on the other party, the analyst, or both. Through these attacks, the patient may try to both deny separateness and create the phantasy of fusion or they may try to create great emotional distance, producing a sense of isolation and alienation in the other. Of course, these pathological processes inevitably boomerang back to haunt the patient with feelings of claustrophobia or loss and abandonment.

As Waddell (2002) notes, healthy learning and knowledge require the ego ability to tolerate never knowing everything, not being able to immediately know, and the uncertain imperfection of sometimes doubting what one knows and being willing to upgrade, disregard, or question what one has relied on up to now.

In this chapter, couples treatment will be discussed as a psychoanalytic procedure equal to that of individual psychoanalytic therapy in value but having some unique points of emphasis. In particular, the analyst works with two patients at the same time individually and later as a unified psychological matrix. In actual practice, this can be a regular back and forth process. Another element that stands out as unique in couples work is the concept of one party bearing witness to the other party's working through process and what that can mean for each party's view of self and object. As mentioned, there are also issues regarding thinking, phantasy, containment, and projective identification (Klein 1946). The turbulent case presented shows how witnessing is often impossible with some more chaotic couples. Often, when working with the more hard to reach couple, therapeutic witnessing can only be partly established. Or, in some cases is not possible at all unless the couple remains in treatment for a longer period and gradually builds more internal and relational stability.

Early phase Kleinian couples treatment with turbulent partners

A and B came to me with a "very happy twelve year marriage that has some very serious issues". While both of them agreed they had "serious issues", they were only able to fight about the possible roots of these problems. Very quickly in the first session, A said to me, "I don't want to sound like I am putting you under a time crunch, but if I don't see results here very quickly, I am going to be ending this marriage". So, right away A was engaged in a transference state with me in which I had better produce, please him, and hurry up or he would leave me.

I said, "It looks like you are putting me on the same chopping block that you put your wife. What is going on that you have such pressure inside of you?" Here, I was interpreting A's projection of desperation, threat, and control onto both myself and onto B. B responded to this by saying, "What do you mean? I never heard you talk about our problems like that". I asked A, "You are essentially threatening divorce if things don't get better really quickly. Is that right?" A nodded and B said, "I can't believe you feel things are so horrible that you would divorce me! What is the matter that you feel that way?"

A shook his head and yelled, "How the hell can't you know how intense and serious this is!? I have told you that if we can't have a regular sex life then I can't stay in this marriage. I can't believe you would not know that. I have done everything in my power to get that message across to you". B said, "I don't really recall that". A said, in a frustrated and furious tone, "Two years ago when we thought about moving here, I told you that you had to decide if our sex life was going to be normal. If so, we would move and continue to be happy with each other. I also told you that if that wouldn't happen I was not willing to move or stay married". B agreed she "sort of" remembered that. Then, A yelled, "And, your memory problems are another thing". Looking at me, he said, "She forgets everything. I end up having the same conversation over and over again". B nodded and said, "He is right. I don't have a very good memory. There are periods I just lose. I don't know where they go. I lose pieces of time over and over".

Here, I could tell I was dealing with two people with significant psychological problems. My initial impression of A and B, based on how they acted, related, and how they pulled me in the counter-transference, was that B was a fragmented, masochistic, and diffused character who seemed unaware of herself and what was going on around her and A seemed to be a very angry, controlling, and demanding borderline or narcissistic character.

Over the next few sessions, I asked more about what was going on in their relationship and what each might be bringing from their past into the relationship. In particular, it seemed obvious that A was suffering from some sort of past trauma. I inquired more about her past. B told me that she had been raped as a teenager and was raised by an alcoholic mother after a bitter divorce. The way she talked about her "aversion to sex" when A was yelling about how frustrated he was about not ever having sex and the strange way she described herself as always reading articles in the newspaper or watching television shows about tragedy and "bad news" around the world, I quickly had the feeling she was suffering from some sort of traumatic breakdown. I asked her about prior treatment and she said she had been in therapy for ten years to "deal with her anxiety and her depression". I asked what she was so depressed or anxious about and B said she "didn't really know but it was constant".

I interpreted, "You seem to be telling me, by the way you are sidestepping our discussions about sex and the way you are reacting to A's anger, that you have some ongoing traumatic feelings about sex. I wonder if you are still reliving the rape and other trauma you may have suffered earlier in your life. If so, it looks like it is now coming alive in the sex area of your marriage". B was silent and then started crying. She said, "I think you are right! I never thought about that and never pictured it still affecting me. But, now that you say it I feel it!"

I asked if that idea had ever been discussed in her therapy. B said it had but not as far as how it might affect her marriage and her sex life. In the counter-transference, I noticed myself feeling irritated with B and her therapist as if they had been negligent in addressing this obvious problem. I thought that this might be an indication of how B might be doing all she could to project, erase, and destroy those feelings from her mind and not own them in any way but she was now a prisoner of them from the outside realm, her external world of the marriage and her sex life. This idea about her transference to both me and to A gradually gave me some insight into B's anxiety. Whenever B asked A to be more supportive or whenever I asked A how he felt about her anxieties and trauma, he would rapidly become agitated, angry, and attacking. He would start to yell at B and me.

He shouted, "What the fuck are you talking about?? I try to be helpful and supportive but I am no doctor! I don't know what to do! What if I do the wrong thing or say the wrong thing? Why am I in this position? This is very uncomfortable and I don't like it. I feel like both of you are not listening to me and are just shoving this at me with no acknowledgement of what I am facing. This is not what I want. I could do something wrong and really screw this up worse. Why the fuck am I stuck with this job? Why are you expecting me to be responsible for this?!"

So, I gradually was able to understand, by listening to A's transference to me and to B that he was overwhelmed by primitive phantasies of having an unbearable task forced on him. A seemed to panic when needing to help, contain, or heal the object. A would yell and scream, saying he was "unfamiliar with what to do" and "did not want to make it worse or do something that would potentially create a disaster". The degree of his anxiety was persecutory, indicating that he was truly unfamiliar with the depressive task of supporting, restoring, or helping the hurt object. All he could picture was a more paranoid vision of creating even worse injury, with things going out of control. So, he felt pressured and forced to administer to the object and then rebelled. B tried to step in and provide assistance. She told A, "All I need is a hug. Just hold my hand and give me a hug!" A replied, "You make it sound so easy but in reality when I have tried that you recoil and pull away. You tell me NOT NOW and turn away. So, I try and then get rejected. I can never tell if you are going to be nice and receive my hug or push me away and reject me, telling me you don't want me! So, I try and try but you don't make it easy!"

These dramatic episodes between A and B were typical of their provocative, combative, and fragmented relating that occurred in this early phase of Kleinian couples treatment. Listening to their projective identification communications, it seemed that A was struggling with more pathological conflicts in the narcissistic and borderline realm. At the same time, B was showing her own needy/rejecting fluctuation that was part of her own scattered, traumatized borderline condition in which she appeared to want to provide A with sex, pleasure, and love but also was prone to withdrawal, withholding, and retreating into emotional coma like states. With A, he seemed to become emotionally crippled when attempting to travel the psychological road from the paranoid-schizoid position to the depressive position. The meaning to him of that emotional transition involved primitive and devastating phantasies of pain that could never be repaired and visions of loss that could never be undone (Brown 1987).

For A, dealing with a malfunctioning or broken object seemed foreign, frightening, and persecutory. In trying to negotiate the depressive position from his primitive projective identification system of control and defense, he encountered his wife as a scattered, fragmented person whom he identified with and therefore internally became a scattered, broken, and fragmented object (Klein 1952a). Subsequently, he panicked and fought back against this phantasy. Part of the reason A felt it to be a persecutory experience, I believe, was that B was using her very scattered and unavailable mind as a weapon. I heard many stories of how she was always late to their important appointments, how she neglected all her house chores, how she had not worked in years, how even though he had requested she clean off the piles of old magazines from the floor of their joint office, she never had, how she would sit with her computer at night for hours instead of spending time with him, and how she would always fall asleep in the living room instead of going to bed with A at bedtime.

I interpreted that while a good deal of these actions might be the result of her terrible trauma, I wondered if it might also be part of an angry and withholding attack on A when she felt resentful or neglectful. B was quite interested in this and gave it a great deal of thought and told me, "I am really going to think about this because even though I don't like the idea, it could be true so I am open to considering it".

For A, the idea of helping the object out of genuine love and concern for a separate whole object was not yet possible. When he yelled in an intimidating way, "What the hell am I supposed to DO?!", he was showing his lack of symbolic function (Steiner 1992) and could only offer a very concrete "doing" to repair the object without much of a genuine empathy, concern, curiosity, or interest.

So, at this point in the initial phase of couple's analytic treatment, I saw a mutual pattern of demand, mixed with a crude and severe feeling of betrayal and abandonment. This was then followed by a mutual sense of anger and aggression. This is a pathological projective identification cycle in which each party ends up feeling bullied, used, misunderstood, and without the very thing they feel they need most. But, this gets played out in concrete action over concrete problems rather than working through the more symbolic, emotional, and complex issues they both have individually and as a couple.

For B, this is the desire for help, soothing, and security when she feels so lost and internally disjointed, unable to find respite from what seems to be an ongoing inner chaos and attack. But, when she receives the hug, the support, or the concern from A, she often pushes it away, ignores it, or devalues it. Also, she seems to attack him with her passive inaction and withdrawal in all the ways I mentioned earlier. Over and over, she sees the object a certain way but wishes it be different and when the object approaches she retreats or retaliates.

With A, he wants the concrete rewards of sex and feels as if he is being deliberately denied that reward and becomes resentful and retaliatory. And, as mentioned, if he does find a way to feel comfortable in offering B support, he feels pushed away or he feels completely overwhelmed by the task of providing it, just as B feels overwhelmed at the task of providing him sex.

So, at this early stage in their analytic couples treatment, much was uncertain and things were very muddled and messy. However, they were able and willing to see me as a potentially useful object and were not overly feeling controlled or defeated by me as their new object. And, as the analyst, I have been successful in containing most of their outrage and outcry, doing my best to study my counter-transference and make interpretations accordingly. Most of my interpretations have been to them as individuals but some have been towards them as a couple in the projective identification cycle I just described. Overall, they are accepting of my words, but do not fully take them in every time as something they can actually think about and reflect on. But, even so, my words serve as limits, containers, and verbal invitations to begin pondering thoughts and feelings that were never considered before or never even realized before. Drama, concrete thought, action, and anxiety can then potentially be slowly translated into something more symbolic, malleable, and transformable.

During the short period of time I met with A and B, there was a shift in their dynamic together. As a result of my questions, observations, and interpretations, B began to be more assertive in the relationship instead of either being a passive victim, immediately blaming herself for most of the couple's problems or simply disappearing emotionally into a profound state of non-being and non-thinking, a zombie like figure who needed A to lead her around almost literally. Instead, she started to have some of her own opinions and questions in the sessions. Specifically, she started to confront A about his anger and asked him, "Why are you always so angry at me? What is really going on with you that makes you always so close to yelling and screaming?" She stood up for herself in a way that was new. B said, "I know I must be contributing most of what causes our problems but you never take ownership of any of it. Don't you think you might be a part of it sometimes? I don't think it's fair that you yell at me all the time". A was both able to hear this and consider it but also quick to dismiss it and justify his anger, yelling in the session about all the things that "obviously make him angry and why the hell can't the two of you see what is so painfully obvious?"

I think that this was a major reason A reacted in such a violent manner two weeks later. He called me and said, "I am informing you we will not be returning". I asked why. He said, "I don't need to tell you, just consider yourself fired!" I said, "You are being rude and angry with me. Why are you so angry?" A said, "I am NOT angry! I am just sick of your pathetic ways. It is obvious you are not very smart and have little to no skill as a therapist. I could tell that from the first visit. I won't be needing you anymore". I said, "The way you are treating me is exactly what seems to be happening in your marriage. So, maybe if we continue to meet, we can find out what makes you so unhappy with me and with your wife". A said, "Like I said, I have no use for you. You are fired!" He hung up the phone and that was the end of the treatment. I felt completely abused, outraged, and amazed by his behavior. I was feeling all the things B was only starting to realize about her childhood trauma as well as the condition of her marriage. And, A remained desperately out of control, demanding the world deliver what he wanted but in the end he only felt cheated and empty.

8

EMBEDDED ENACTMENTS AND EMOTIONAL TRUTH

Modern Kleinian Therapy is a contemporary hybrid of classical Kleinian psychoanalytic techniques. It is a clinical approach to working with the more disturbed or complicated patient in a private practice setting under less than optimal conditions. These external obstacles include various restrictions from insurance companies and third party agencies involved in the treatment, limited numbers of sessions available and/or a enforced termination date, a more severe or complex diagnosis, and, most often, a reduced frequency.

In the outpatient setting, most psychoanalysts and psychotherapists in 2012 are rarely seeing patients 4–5 times a week on the couch. It is much more common to be seeing individuals 1–2 times a week or couples 1–2 times a week (Cherry et al 2004; Waska 2005). Typically, our patients have been in a marked state of distress for quite some time before entering treatment and often have some current external crisis going on. The treatment profile is often quite messy from the start and optimal frequency unavailable. There is immediate acting out in various degrees and forms creating a lack of stability in the overall therapeutic frame, psychological states of mind that are fragmented and fragile, and the severe or exclusive use of splitting and projective identification in the transference. The external crisis or chronic external troubles these patients bring with them create realistic obstacles to much needed deeper exploration but also serve as challenging defensive retreats for the patients to find refuge and control in when they are reluctant to join the analyst in looking at their lives in a deeper or broader manner.

Clinically, we see many patients who tend to quickly subsume us and whatever we do or say into their pathological organization (Spillius 1988) with its familiar cast of internal characters. Modern Kleinian Therapy focuses on the interpretation of this particular transference process by investigating the unconscious phantasy conflicts at play and highlighting the more direct moment-to-moment transference usually mobilized by projective identification dynamics. Bion's (1962b) ideas regarding the interpersonal aspects of projective identification, the idea of projective identification as the foundation of most transference states (Waska 2010a, 2010b, 2010c), and the concept of projective identification as the first line of defense against psychic loss (Waska

2002, 2010d) difference, or separation all form the theoretical base of my clinical approach. Taking theory into the clinical realm, I find interpreting the how and the why of the patient's phantasy conflicts in the here and now combined with linkage to original infantile experiences to be the best approach with such patients under these more limiting clinical situations.

In doing so, the main thrust of the analyst's observations and interpretations remains focused on the patient's efforts to disrupt the establishment of analytic contact (Waska 2007). We strive to move the patient into a new experience of clarity, vulnerability, reflection, independence, change, and choice. Analytic contact is defined as sustained periods of mutual existence between self and object not excessively colored by destructive aggression or destructive defense. These are moments between patient and analyst when the elements of love, hate, and knowledge as well as the life and death instincts are in balance enough as to not fuel, enhance, or validate the patient's internal conflicts and phantasies in those very realms. These are new moments of contact between self and other, either in the mind of the patient or in the actual interpersonal realm between patient and analyst. Internal dynamics surrounding giving, taking, and learning as well as the parallel phantasies of being given to, having to relinquish, and being known are all elements that are usually severely out of psychic balance with these more challenging patients. Analytic contact is the moment in which analyst and patient achieve some degree of peace, stability, or integration in these areas.

So, analytic contact is the term for our constant quest or invitation to each patient for the found, allowed, and cultivated experiences that are new or less contaminated by the fossils of past internal drama, danger, and desire. These moments, in turn, provide for a chance of more lasting change, life, and difference or at least a consideration that these elements are possible and not poison. Paranoid (Klein 1946) and depressive (Klein 1935, 1940) anxieties tend to be stirred up as the patient's safe and controlled psychic equilibrium (Feldman and Spillius 1989) comes into question. Acting out, abrupt termination, intense resistance, and excessive reliance on projective identification are common and create easy blind spots and patterns of enactment for the analyst.

While there have been many compelling texts that demonstrate the theoretical and clinical aspects of Kleinian psychoanalysis with patients attending 5–6 times a week, there is almost no literature on the application of the regular Kleinian technique to difficult and disturbed patients only able or willing to attend once or twice a week (Waska 2006, 2011b). I will demonstrate with clinical material how there is no real need to modify the technique. However, in low frequency cases, certain aspects become highlighted.

The Modern Kleinian Therapy approach is a clinical model of here-and-now, moment-to-moment focus on transference, counter-transference, and unconscious phantasy to assist difficult patients in low frequency therapy to notice, accept, understand, and resolve their unconscious self and object conflict states. Projective identification is often the cornerstone of the more complex transference state (Waska 2004) and therefore is the central target of therapeutic intervention and interpretation.

A good deal of patients being seen in today's private practice settings are mired in the primitive zone of paranoid and narcissistic functioning without access to the internal vision of a pleasurable object to merge with without catastrophe. These are patients who often are using vigorous levels of defense against the more erotic, pleasurable, and connective elements of relationship just as they are massively defending against the fears of conflict, aggression, and growth. And, this is a state of psychic conflict so intense it may in some cases create psychic deficit.

While Modern Kleinian Therapy is fundamentally no different from the practice of Kleinian psychoanalysis, due to the limitations of reduced frequency, more severe pathology, and external blocks such as health insurance limitations and personal financial limitations, a greater flexibility is required in the overall treatment setting. Also, there is a greater need to notice the ongoing and immediate impact of unconscious phantasy, internal conflict, and transference that occurs in the analytic relationship. Careful monitoring of the counter-transference for clues to the presence of projective identification based communication and the importance of combining interpretations of current here-and-now transference and phantasy with more genetic links as a therapeutic hybrid approach is also a modification of sorts. However, this is more a question of emphasis than a new or radical theoretical shift or unique technique.

Due to the specific pathology and conflict state the hard to reach patients usually exist within, many cases fail, others prematurely end, and others terminate with only partial resolution. And, they often do not have the resources or motivation to attend 5-times-a-week psychoanalysis. However, I think these patients are helped in ways far superior to simple suggestion provided by behavioral therapy or counseling. So, the way of judging success is also something to consider.

Because of the lower frequency of treatment, many might call my model psychoanalytic psychotherapy. In that sense, my approach is not radically new when you consider the vast offerings of psychoanalytic psychotherapy that exist today. Indeed, many psychoanalytic institutes do far more training in this area and have far more candidates for that than their training of classic, on the couch, 5–6-times-a-week psychoanalysis. Many articles, workshops, books, and classes have been available for many years now by well-known psychoanalysts who all advocate this low frequency approach.

Unfortunately, for many decades and still continuing, there has been a great deal of political and theoretical debate in the field of psychoanalysis over the differences between psychoanalysis, psychoanalytic psychotherapy, and supportive therapy. To this day, the debate is usually but wrongly simplified to defining everything as either "proper" psychoanalysis, watered down psychoanalysis combined with supportive techniques, or suggestive/supportive therapy.

There is the smaller group who see a place for psychoanalysis being practiced at a reduced frequency with or without the couch and it still being considered psychoanalysis. This was the stance of Merton Gill (1994) in his last book on the subject. I agree with this view. However, I am unique in practicing a Kleinian model from this theoretical vantage point and hence it is called Modern Kleinian Therapy. I use the word therapy to avoid the ongoing debate over analysis versus psychotherapy.

Modern Kleinian Therapy involves the establishment and maintenance of "analytic contact" (Waska 2007). This includes constantly looking for how both the analyst and the patient may try to deny, delay, decay, or destroy the intimacy, truthfulness, and vulnerability that analytic work creates, demands, and discovers.

Overall, I believe good, sound Kleinian psychoanalytic technique, as practiced both by classical Kleinians such as Hanna Segal and refined by newer Kleinians such as Betty Joseph and Michael Feldman, is transferable to low frequency cases, to couples therapy, and to work with more disturbed borderline, narcissistic, and psychotic patients.

Modern Kleinian Therapy is about working in this deep analytic fashion with the less than ideal patient population we all encounter these days. While the therapeutic result is often more messy, more complex, and prone to more enactments by the analyst, the work is still possible and often successful and transformative.

The countertransference is more complicated and the patients often end treatment abruptly or prematurely with some remaining symptoms and conflicts. However, a great deal of change can be created for the external symptom profile the patient suffers with as well as a modest or sometimes profound change of their more fundamental internal psychic structure and the profound conflicts that exist within.

Embedded enactments

In the past few decades, there has been much needed exploration into the interpersonal and intrapsychic struggles the analyst faces in the counter-transference, especially with the more disturbed and disturbing patient (Cartwright 2010; Gold 1983; Steiner 2006). These are more fragmented, reactive, and primitive patients who are prone to use action and acting out, both internally and externally, to avoid the unwanted and uncertain contact with reality, with themselves, and with others. Through projective identification, these patients exert a great deal of pressure on the analyst to join them in certain archaic patterns of defense, desire, and repetition (Bateman 1998; Feldman 2009; O'Shaughnessy 1992; Segal and Britton 1981; Sweet 2010; Williams 2010).

There are many motives and aims behind the pressure a patient puts on the analyst, and the ways he or she tries to trigger various enactments. The hatred of reality (Anderson 1999) and the envy (Spillius 1993) some patients feel towards their perception of others leads to the use of pre-thinking, non-symbolic states of mind attacking any attempts of the analyst to introduce learning and knowledge. Growth and change are avoided and attacked (Waska 2006). In this sense, one aspect of enactment is the creation of a death instinct zone of repetition and stagnation (Rosenfeld 1987; Segal 1993). This anti-life mentality can draw the analyst into psychic detours, away from the investigation and working through of central anxiety and core phantasy conflicts. These are the dreaded enclaves and excursions (O'Shaughnessy 1989) that unfold within enactments.

While difficult to notice as they occur because we are an active partner in them, enactments are cycles of projective identification (Feldman 1994) that must be directly faced and understood with the patient in order for the foundations of transference based anxieties to be solved. In this sense, I think of enactments as part of the total transference (Joseph 1985) and the complete counter-transference (Waska 2011a). Normally, enactments are thought of as moments of diversion in the clinical situation and periods of imbalance in the therapeutic setting that can be useful when understood. In addition, I believe there are more extended forms of enactment, embedded enactments that are sustained and essentially make up the entire transference for long periods of treatment. These are times when the projective identification dynamics are at their most intense and create an interpersonal and interactional process between patient and analyst that can be difficult to acknowledge, difficult to step out of, and difficult to resolve (Joseph 1988, 1989). These are matters that strain the normal limits of communication and containment in the analyst process (Steiner 2000).

In more low intensity, brief, or transitory types of enactment, there can be a division between when the analyst is participating in the enactment process and when he can step back, reflect, and regroup enough to begin making helpful interpretations. However, during the embedded enactment cycle, there is not much room to come up for air. The analyst is almost always in the midst of or on the verge of feeling engulfed in some sort of rigid and restrictive pattern that makes up a very predictable but almost unavoidable dynamic between patient and analyst.

Similar to Friedman's (2008) idea of the artificial separation between the proper non-acting out work of analyst and the "other" temporary acting out phase of analysis, an artificial and unrealistic expectation or ideal, I believe the embedded enactment situation is one in which there is little time or space for the analyst to freely consider a neutral or proper mode of interaction. The embedded enactment is a type of transference pressure that calls the analyst into the trenches and interpretations must be made while the bullets are flying, not later during a peace treaty. Analytic observations (Waska 2012) are necessary in combination with more traditional interpretations. These are comments about how a patient is positioning the analyst or using the analyst in their object relational phantasy. This complements the use of interpretation to help a patient see why they are using or positioning the analyst or themselves in certain ways within the therapeutic matrix.

So, in the case material, I will illustrate the countless times that my patient invited me, pulled me, or emotionally kidnapped me into participating in an ongoing, sustained enactment regarding a variety of internal phantasies about self and other. It was only when I could begin making consistent observations and interpretations within those embedded enactments that we were able to work through the meaning of such projective identification patterns and start to see what made it so threatening to change.

Sandler (1976) has noted how patients are always unconsciously attempting to turn the analyst into an archaic object, generating a role responsiveness in the analyst's mind and behavior. Spillius (1988) notes how projective identification is the vehicle this takes place in. I believe the difficulty of the embedded enactment lies in how the patient is so persistent and loyal to the mission to convert both analyst and self over to a limited number of very static, controlled, and rigid ways of relating or non-relating.

Regarding the case material, I could have presented a case of either individual or couples treatment that went much better. But, I deliberately choose the details of a much more unstable and chaotic case. I do this so as to enlarge the truth of what actually takes place in contemporary psycho-analytic practice and demonstrate the effectiveness of Modern Kleinian Therapy. We all have many cases that go very well and follow the expected phases of anxiety, resistance, defense, interpretation, insight, working through, and change, unfolding with the traditional psychoanalytic clinical ideal we all are trained to strive for. However, there are many other much more unpredictable, rocky, and often only partly successful cases we have to encounter. In fact, there are numerous cases that terminate abruptly and prematurely, with only small change and a general feeling of dissatisfaction for both parties.

However, I believe even these very vexing and turbulent cases deserve to be studied for two reasons. First, we hopefully can learn from them and do a better job next time. Second of all, I think that when we work with difficult and troubled individuals or couples who have years of distress, ongoing emotional collapse, and severe and chronic internal conflict under their belt before walking into our offices looking for immediate relief, sometimes we are able to provide some degree of resolution over time, some degree of insight, growth, or change while still ending on a sour note or a job only partly finished. This is painful to admit and hard to accept but it is the reality of the work we do. This type of loss and fall from any reachable ideal is inherent in the psychoanalytic process. Once we accept and integrate this reality, we can begin to feel grateful for the success we do have and the genuine help and healing we provide, even if in small and scattered pieces throughout our caseload.

Case material: The slippery search for emotional truth

Warren and Jill came in with what they termed "a crisis point" in their marriage. During the first session, Jill seemed very anxious but also emotionally liable. She went from being very angry to crying and yelling to being quiet and withdrawn. Also, she acted stubborn and withholding. In his physical posture, Warren was very rigid and he remained very quiet. He looked to Jill for cues, glancing over to her for when he should say something. Overall, there was a good deal of tension in the room as we began.

When I asked what brought them in, Jill explained that Warren had cheated on her twice over the period of several months with two different women. She had found out about the first one and after a great deal of painful fighting and discussion, Jill "believed Warren when he promised it was all over but then he lied to my face and went out and did it again!" Jill told me this was devastating and created a great deal of trauma in the marriage. She had brought up the possibility of divorce. At that point in the session, Jill began sobbing.

Warren started talking. He told me the affairs were somehow "all an awful accident". He said it was somehow a result of the medication he had been on for depression. He said it "made him not know what he was doing".

Here, I responded to my feelings in the counter-transference and said, "So, you are saying the pills just made you go out and have sex with another woman after you had promised your wife to never do that again? It seems you are not owning your own behavior". Warren was quick to say, "Oh, I am completely to blame. But, I was taking a new antidepressant medication and I was drinking quite a bit at the time. I just was not myself". I said, "Again, you seem to not want to consider your own self in this. You may have been impaired in some way, but you choose to find a girl, have sex with her, and keep it a secret from your wife". Jill added, "He kept it a secret from me just like the first time. But, then I caught him texting her right next to me in the car just as he was acting nice and loving to me. I can't believe he would lie like that and destroy the trust we had, not once but twice!"

Over the course of the first two sessions, I learned more about the affairs. In the first one, Warren had been away on a trip. He met a girl in a bar and went home with her. They continued to meet for sex during the following week. Initially, he told me it "was just a one night stand and very casual". I had to point out that he was filtering the facts. In fact, it was a "one week stand" that looked much more calculated so I wondered what made it so hard for him to tell me the truth. I noticed myself thinking about how he was lying to me but not doing a very good job of it. It felt like he was very anxious but also not caring enough about Jill or I to even construct much of a lie.

At first, Warren said, "I am just forgetting the details. You are right. But, it wasn't like I planned each day. It just sort of happened". I pointed out that just like the medication story he was making himself sound like a victim to circumstances and trying to escape the obvious, leaving me to catch him and call him a liar. Warren said, "I just feel so bad. I don't except her to believe me at this point. But, I am very sorry and I know I will never do something like that ever again. I just am so sorry I have put her through this".

In response to this, Jill seemed both angry and hurt and said, "I want to believe you and want to not have this in our lives, but I can't stop thinking about it. Why would you do this to me? Am I not exciting enough, not sexy enough? Why would you do this?" Warren said, "I don't know. I don't have a good idea. I had no reason to do such a terrible thing". I said, "I think you did have a reason to do what you did both times. Maybe it is hard for you to find the reason and face the reason. We can do that here. But, you did choose to go out and sleep with two other women". He nodded.

I slowly learned more about the details of these two affairs. As mentioned, he had met the first girl while away on a one week business trip. His wife found out after finding various items in his suitcase when he returned and by checking his cell phone records. After a great deal of tears and fighting, Warren convinced Jill he was truly sorry. He told her he had done this almost "by accident" and that it would never happen again. Yet, a month or two later he ended up doing exactly the same thing. This time, it was with a girl his wife had actually met before and Warren ended up having the affair over the period of about one month this time.

In the session, we discussed how Warren lied about being done after the first time and never doing it again. I said this was obviously a lie and it sounded like he just wanted to get Jill off his back the first time and he was obviously still in the mindset of wanting to do what he wanted. He did it again so in my mind it sounded quite sadistic and thoughtless. I left that as a question mark.

So, as we began to investigate all of this, I was struck by how on one hand Warren kept talking about how "this was all in the past", how he "has moved on and really understands the gravity of the situation", and how he was "really ready and willing to try and be different". I felt he was claiming too much too fast and I interpreted that. I said that he seemed anxious to make it all ok and that he seemed to not be genuine in the process. I said he seemed to be trying to convince Jill and me of how sincere he was.

Warren said, "No. I am just saying that I understand how awful I was and I am really ready to make it better and be different". He went on to say that his actions were part of "his old self". He added that he drank a great deal in the past and at the time of these two incidences he was taking an anti-depressant medication that he said made him "feel very fuzzy and not himself". It seemed like Warren was putting a lot of the blame on this medication "fuzziness" and the drinking so I remarked that he seem to be placing blame on those things and not really taking accountability.

At the same time, I confronted Warren with how he was so quick to say all this was in the past and he was a different person now. He wanted me to see him as "fully recovered and better" and that he had "learned his lesson". I said he was so busy "learning his lesson" that he seem to not be aware of the wife's predicament and how awful she still felt. Also, I said he did not seem interested in understanding what led him to these actions. Finally, I said that all these ways of relating to me left me to be the one who points out his faults and he to be the one who comes up with excuses or quickly apologizes. Here, I was noticing the counter-transference echoes of enactments that were taking place and using that information to inform my interpretation of his transference and of the object relational climate he was creating in the room.

This transference theme emerged fairly often with Warren taking a controlling, forceful, and anxious retreat into "how much better he was" and how it was "all in the past". As a result, I felt he was manipulating Jill and me into seeing him as reformed and considerate. I would make the interpretation that, in effect, I was catching him in another lie because now Warren was minimizing things and claiming to be "moving forward". I said he was trying to look nicer and reformed to me as a way to avoid feeling blamed or judged.

Warren agreed but quickly added that he was different now. I said that in his haste to be different, he seemed to be making sure to not stop and really take a good look at what he did and what led up to it. That just led me to chase after him and him to feel judged. Thus, we were acting out this sadomasochistic cycle. I would interpret it and then we would act it out a bit and then I would interpret it again. This is the essence of the psychoanalytic work necessary when faced with embedded enactments, clinical situations that demand thoughtful interpretations in the midst of unthinking acting out.

I talked with Warren about how he seemed to be lying to me and distorting the facts, thus putting me in the position of being the authority who labels him. I noted that he seemed to be maintaining the role of a small child who says, "It is not my fault, please don't punish me anymore", hoping I would have mercy on him. Warren would take my comment and allow himself to consider it for just a moment. But, then, he would turn away from it and reply as the little boy who was either apologizing, lying, or saying he was all better now.

In describing the marriage before his affairs, Warren said it was common for him to hang out in the back room drinking while Jill cooked dinner and did chores. He said she "nagged him to do chores and help her out". Jill seemed to be very anxious during most of the sessions as well as angry and controlling by the way she talked to me and to Warren. On one hand, Jill seemed to really impress upon me how upset she still was, how she "cannot get this terrible thing out of her mind", and how she cannot believe he would have lied to her. To Warren, she yelled and cried, "You betrayed me not once but twice!" While Jill was sobbing about this, she was also very quick to demand immediate solutions from me and expected a quick resolution to all of their problems so she could "move on and get back to feeling okay".

So, I interpreted how Jill was reluctant to really stop or slow down and examined what led up to these events in the marriage and to begin to learn. I said she seemed to want to forget about it all and magically "move on" to pretending everything was ok again. And, she was angry I was not helping her do so. I added that it made sense she is very upset and does not want to have to face this pain but we must bear it together in order to learn what really happened. Jill was ok with this idea for about five minutes and then began shifting back to telling me it "was useless and pointless to have to focus over and over on what Warren did". Instead, she wanted to know "what to do to enable them to move on and go back to the way it used to be".

Here, I said, "You can never go back to the way it used to be. That is over. You are having a hard time tolerating that. It is different and we have to find out how the two of you will be in this new stage of the relationship and how to learn from the troubles that led up to the affairs". Jill shook her head and said, "I don't know if I want to do that. I don't want to look at the same thing over and over again". She was angry and agitated and Warren alternated between looking anxious and fading into the background to agreeing with her and joining in her stance against me as the one "making them stay stuck in the past". This was a difficult moment of mutual transference in which Jill and then both of them wanted to avoid the painful mourning and loss characteristic of the depressive position (Segal 1962) and to instead have the magical power imagined in the paranoid-schizoid position (Segal 1962) of simply turning back time and returning to something without having to notice that it was ever changed, altered, or damaged. While I made many interpretations in that direction, Jill and sometimes Jill and Warren collectively were too anxious to tolerate that internal realization. Instead, they attacked me as bearer of bad news and painful reality.

As I attempted to find out more about Warren and Jill's marriage, more about each of their own psychological states, and more about how these internal worlds interacted, I noticed certain transference states emerging. Warren would often look like a scared rat just scurrying for cover to avoid getting caught by me or by Jill. This anxious persecutory way of relating to me alternated with the more controlling, manic state in which he assured me that he "totally understands what he did and how wrong it is. Now, he's a new man who is really trying hard". Warren told me in a forced and pushy manner that he had turned a new leaf and feels good about how he has changed.

I would try and engage him in exploring these ways of relating and reacting to me. I asked him to join me in being curious about what his motivation was behind these seemingly panicky and artificial ways of interacting with me. He would sometimes be able or willing to ponder this and reflect for a moment, but quickly shifted back to one of these default ways of shaping our relationship.

Meanwhile, Jill continued her angry stance of, "Why do we have to keep going over the same old thing and why do I have to come here and feel this pain every week?" I interpreted that it was more comfortable seeing me as the source of all the pain and blame than to have to wonder what went wrong in the marriage and to slowly consider how they both contributed to things not going well. When Jill was not putting me down for causing her all her pain and suffering, she became overwhelmed with sorrow and confusion. She looked lost in trying to "figure out why he would do this to me" and trying to understand "what went on for you that caused you to do this to me?!" Part of this seemed genuine and heartfelt, her feeling betrayed and devastated and then wanting to understand it. But, part of it felt more accusatory and bent on finding a concrete reason that she could control, understand, and eradicate. This more mechanical, action orientated style of finding the problem, fixing it, and "moving on" seemed to be a way she avoided her internal feelings and conflicts that she had no control over.

In exploring Warren's transference states, I interpreted that he immediately felt he was like a child who was going to be lectured, branded, and looked down on. One way this occurred included his physical manner and the overall interpersonal aspect of his projective identification. Warren sat there looking very timid and very nervous, with his eyes open wide. He looked at me and Jill with apprehension about what we would say or do next. He was clearly feeling like he was the target or soon would be the target. I interpreted this fairly often, especially when this transference seemed to escalate. During the first three of four sessions, Warren put himself in that position more and more and it looked like he was very having a very hard time being in the room without feeling severely judged.

So, I said, "It looks like you probably don't want to be here given how you're about to wear the Hangman's noose. But, I wonder why you're seeing Jill and me as suddenly against you instead of us all learning more about what happened". I continued, "When you claim it was the drinking and the medication that made you do it, it seems like you do not want to look into these things more deeply, maybe exposing what was really going on for you in the marriage and with your own life. Instead, you are saying you were powerless and helpless and then you can simply say I'm sorry and promise to never do it again. I am hoping we can talk more about what really went on and create something better going forward". This interpretive containment (Sandler 1984; Schafer 1997) seemed to reduce Warren's anxiety and his immediate attempts at talking his way out of the problem with general, global remarks and grand statements about his insight and change.

However, this brittle opportunity to reflect and learn was quickly shattered when Jill would stiffen up, be strangely silent, and then start asking in a demanding way, "So, what are we supposed to do? What am I supposed to do? What do you recommend how we get over this? How do we move ahead, how do we move on?"

This was done in a very tense, controlling, and aggressive manner that put me on the spot and left me feeling defensive. I acted out some of this by saying, "Well, I don't even know you yet but you want me to tell you what to do with your life. I have no idea. So, it's interesting how you want it all fixed and done and over so quickly. I wonder why?"

Jill responded by breaking down, sobbing, and saying how devastated and hurt she was. She could not believe he had done this to her and she just wanted to know why. She yelled, "Why? Why? Why?" I talked with Jill about her complete shock and surprise over these two events but very quickly she would turn back to this controlling demand of "So, what do we do about it?" She told me she does not see the point of "Just talking about it over and over and over. It only brings me more pain. I just want to move on, find out a way to fix it, and be done with it. I don't see the point of talking about it".

In the counter-transference, I tried to be very patient and stabilize myself to avoid lashing out in some form as a reaction to the way Jill was treating me. So, I talked with her about how she seemed to just want to erase this event, check it off her list of "to do" items, and move on in a very controlled way. I said I understood that she was hurting and did not want to hurt anymore but when she said talking about it only makes it worse and only makes her sad, I said that perhaps this was one of the issues in the marriage. I suggested that there was not a lot of talking with me or maybe in the marriage as she felt it was hurtful and never led to anything healing or to any helpful discovery. I said that talking seemed to be uncomfortable for both of them but perhaps we could learn why being vulnerable in this way was so unwanted.

This seemed to reduce their mutual anxiety and open things up for a while. They described how in the marriage there "was a lot of talking". They said they "got along wonderfully, they really love each other, and they both really like their marriage". But at the same time, there was Jill's description of Warren as this child who sat in the back room, on the computer, drinking beer all the time, ignoring Jill, and never helping with chores. After she said that, Warren quickly agreed.

Jill is the breadwinner of the family. She told me she comes home and ends up doing all the cooking and the chores. She nags Warren to help out and he eventually does but there is resentment on both sides. I interpreted that they have a hard time looking at what might be in the middle. Everything seems to be very black or white, similar to the mutual transference in which they both sat there and waited to have me fix them. They wanted me to tell them what to do, to explain what was going on, and to have some kind words of wisdom. They waited for me to instruct them on what is going on and what they should expect next. While they had been able to take in what I was saying up to this point, now they sat there and looked at me in a very passive yet demanding and expectant way. So, I interpreted that what I had just said was now being demonstrated and played out in the room. This analytic observation (Waska 2012) helped to slow them down and get them to back off a bit before reloading for another mutual attack and joint demand for something other than having to look at themselves.

After about the eighth or ninth session, Warren came in by himself. There had been no discussion about this although it was not a total surprise as Jill had become unhappier with showing up. She had continued to tell me that she did not see any point to therapy. She just wanted to be told what to do and how to proceed. So, it did not quite surprise me when Warren said Jill "was sick of it and didn't see the point". Then he said, "I'm the broken one. I'm the problem, so I am here to deal with me and my problems. After all, I caused all the problems".

I said, "That is the way that you're quickly relating to me and to Jill, that you're the problem. You are fast to take it all on when it's really two people contributing to everything. Yes, you are guilty of the actual infidelity and the lies around both events. But, both of you are in the marriage. So, it's interesting that you're quick to take over the entire blame and see yourself as the bad person and her as the innocent one in the relationship".

Warren was able to take this in to some degree. As a result, he was able to settle in for the next two sessions by himself and explore things in a much more reflective manner. Warren brought up his childhood and made some important links to his present state of mind. As a child, his parents moved around the country every two or three years for business. Warren said he felt he never fit in with friends or at school and always felt he was the outsider. So, as a way to better fit in, he began lying about all sorts of things and to everyone he met in these new locations. He told me he ended up building this pattern of lying to get by and to feel better about his place in life. While this all felt genuine and honest, it perhaps became too much of a vulnerability because then Warren shifted his manner with me. Almost out of the blue, he said that "perhaps it's now just a habit", referring to the trouble in the marriage. This was said in a much different, aloof, and devaluing tone.

I confronted Warren on this habit idea. I said it was not a "habit" that made him cheat on his wife. Rather, it was a deliberate act. The more we talked about his active role in these events, Warren relaxed and gradually shared that he liked the attention he received from the other women.

Warren said he felt he had not been getting enough attention in the marriage and that he liked the "power and attention" with these two other women. At the same time, he said he "still doesn't understand what came over him and that he would never do it again". I said, "You said that after the first affair and then after the second affair. It makes sense why Jill is having a hard time trusting you". He said, "Yes, of course. But, it'll never happen again". I told Warren that it appears he is trying to convince me just like he is trying to convince his wife but that we do not know how long it will take for her to forgive him or for this rupture in the marriage to be repaired. I suggested he wanted to leap over that difficult fact and just "move on". He said, "I know it will take a while and that makes sense".

Here, I was interpreting his struggle with the unknown aspects of the depressive position in which he would have to deal with loss, grief, repair, reparation, and possible forgiveness but all with a painful and frightening sense of uncertainty. He wanted to control all that with a magical immediate switch to everything being ok right away.

In general, the way Warren related and responded to me left me feeling uncomfortable. From the beginning of the treatment, there were moments in talking with him that I was left feeling very uncertain about the capacity for honesty in him. I sometimes felt very uncomfortable and even scared about who this was I was sitting with. For example, during the second session, I thought to myself, "He might be an actual sociopath!" I also pondered, "Is this someone who is intrinsically evil? Is he a liar that cannot be treated? Is he essentially just out to get what he wants and will do anything it takes? Is he somehow corrupted internally?"

Other times, I was less uncomfortable and suspicious so I had room to wonder why I was having these eerie counter-transference feelings and where they were coming from. I wanted to give Warren the benefit of the doubt but also kept in mind that these sudden reactions were important information. It was not just to the fact that he cheated twice that I was reacting to. It was the way that he was with me, the way that he was relating to me interpersonally.

Along the way, in each session, I caught Warren in quite a few lies. I would interpret, "The way that you are describing things just does not make sense. You seem to be brushing over the details to paint a rosy or positive picture but when I ask for the details the story looks quite different. I have to pin you down and ask for details and then it turns out that you are making it sound a certain way to your favor. Other times you say things to me and to Jill that make you look guilty and like a liar when it seems you are telling the truth. So, in both ways you are getting me to be the heavy and call you out as a liar and then you have to defend yourself or admit to being a bad boy. This is the same type of relating we talked about in the marriage".

So, here I was interpreting the transference in which Warren was a lying little boy who got caught by me and had to confess or just continue to try to lie his way out of it. I was left with trying to decide if I was with an evil little misfit or if he was just a confused little boy that I needed to tolerate until we could make sense of things. Again, this was helpful counter-transference information that helped me notice, understand, and manage the inevitable enactments that resulted from this transference so strongly based in his projective identification dynamics.

In almost every session, Warren appeared to be setting himself up to look badly. At other times, he was deliberately trying to pull the wool over my eyes and make things look better than they were or leave certain details out of the story. Then, I would catch him in a lie by noticing how he first said one thing but the next time he would say it quite differently. Essentially, I would say,

"Hey, wait a minute. You said this before in a different way". He would say no, so I then I had to call him a liar. I pointed out this very predictable transference structure to Warren over and over, which did two things. First, it underlined my acting out of the punitive authority telling him what his crime was and him feeling caught and punished. This was the embedded enactment that was unavoidable and constant. But, second, my interpretive persistence in the midst of this emotionally combative or wartime climate did gradually allow a working through of this transference and a more reflective and less defensive reaction on his part.

An example of this was when Warren told me he smoked pot on a regular basis, drank almost every day before being found out with the second affair, and that he thought the drinking and the medication were "probably to blame for all of it". I pointed out that one thing he could do is immediately stop drinking, stop smoking pot, and to also get rid of the pot he said he still had around the house. In response, Warren was quick to tell me he did not have a drinking problem and he did not want to get rid of his pot because he "had just paid for the latest batch and didn't want to waste his money by throwing it away". I told him that if he believed these things had so much to do with why he cheated on Jill it was interesting that he did not want to immediately get rid of those problems. But, as soon as I brought that up to Warren, he would become very defensive and try to explain how he was not using the pot too much, it was only recreational, and it would be a waste to just throw it out.

So, I then interpreted that Warren was setting us up once again for me to be the lecturing authority who is catching him at doing bad and telling him to do things my way and he was the accused little boy who felt falsely judged and picked on. He reluctantly agreed and seemed to somewhat allow my comments in but mostly seemed to go along with my authority. As a result of this capitulation, Warren did agree to stop drinking altogether and apparently was successful for several weeks. He also disposed of the pot.

At the start of a session in which only Warren attended, he told me, "I want to be honest with you. This thing happened". I noticed how the "thing happened" was once again a passive "not me" way of speaking, but I chose to just listen. He told me about how he had been alone doing some gardening while Jill was at work. Warren said he "was sick and tired of not drinking" and "just wanted to have a beer and knew he could with her not there" so he did. I interpreted that he "felt free and easy from being under the cloud of her control and wanted to do as he wished. So, he did". Warren agreed this was a major factor in his drinking. I added that this shows us he may have an alcohol problem as well as a rebellion problem. He said, "Maybe".

Apparently, Jill came home and became suspicious of how many beers were left in the refrigerator. After she confronted him, Warren admitted to her that he had indeed broken his promise and drank. While he had "admitted" to me and her about the drinking, I noticed I had to really pull for any details about the whole thing. I commented that while he was openly sharing this story with me, it seemed like I had to be the one who was quizzing him for the details. He reluctantly agreed and told me a little bit more.

Then, about ten minutes later, he added, "Oh yeah. I guess I should finish the whole story. A week earlier, I also drank and never told her". I added, "and never told me either". He said, "Well, I am telling you now and I didn't really think of it as an issue to talk about until she caught me. Then, I decided to go ahead and tell her about the time before. Now, I am doing that with you too. So, I am trying to be honest with you".

I was aware of a slippery back and forth honesty⟷dishonesty going on and me having to be the detective again. I made this interpretation. Also, I told Warren it was difficult to treat the marriage when Jill was not there. I said I understood he felt a wish to focus on his own issues with me and that was an important step. I said, "You may be lying some of the time to me or to Jill, but you are here. You showed up". He said, "Exactly!" Due to my comment about her not being there, Warren urged Jill to attend the sessions and she showed up for the next visit.

One intense and challenging aspect of Jill and Warren's mutual transference was a strong stance of "we don't need to be here, we're fine and always have been fine, we've moved on, and we've always been happy". Jill especially, but sometimes Warren individually and sometimes both of them together, would literally repeat those phrases over and over. This strong stance created significant tension in the room as they felt captured, persecuted, and made to face something in themselves they dreaded.

This would unfold when Jill, in a provocative and angry manner, demanded, "Why are we still here? Why do you want us to be here? We don't need to be here. Why are you making us be here and why are you telling us something is wrong with our marriage?" I would interpret how unbearable their feelings must be and how hard they were trying to move away from the pain but their retreat from facing conflict and difficulty was perhaps exactly what happened in the marriage to begin with. Warren and Jill would temporarily be able to take in or allow for this painful knowledge and slow down a bit to begin reflecting on themselves.

But, for the most part, they would move very quickly back to this paranoid stance of "Why are we still here? There is nothing wrong with us". I would then have to interpret that when they were not able to face or tolerate their pain and vulnerability, they passed on the blame to me and felt forced to be in my office and forced to face this pain. This means they were pulling me into being this accusatory person who was reminding them that it was only two months ago that he cheated on her and it was only two weeks ago that Warren lied to Jill about drinking. My interpretation of the couples transference and the underlying object relational dynamic was helpful but only temporarily as Jill especially was so aggressive in discharging her anxiety and sorrow in this persecutory projective process.

Right away, this paranoid transference escalated when Jill came back with Warren for the next session. She said, "I didn't want to be here, I cannot see the point. I want to know what I am supposed to do to feel better and how to forget all these things". I told her she clearly must be very troubled and in a lot of pain because she is trying so hard to forget what happened. But, she is unable to escape the pain of betrayal and grief. Jill broke down and started crying in a genuine manner, momentarily feeling the full weight of her grief, anger, and hurt.

But, then, unable or unwilling to bear it anymore, she quickly switched to "Of course, I'm in pain! I can't believe he did it! But, now we are doing fine and Warren seems to be better. I'm sick of having to come here and be reminded of all these things and have to look at what happened. These are things that I don't want to have to look at! Why are you making us look at these? What is the point? It just makes it worse!"

I interpreted to Jill that she was using me as the emotional wastebasket for all her terrible feelings and she saw therapy as the place where all the bad memories were. So, if she were not in therapy, she would never have to think about it or feel it. But, I said, "I'm sure you do feel it and it goes with you every day". Again, Jill broke down sobbing in response but then quickly escalated to say she was "set up" by coming to the session and, "It should be all about Warren anyway. He's a problem, he is the bad one!" Looking anxious and wanting to make peace, Warren quickly agreed and said, "Yes. I'm the one who is broken".

So, I had to interpret that once again they were setting up a process of her being the mature one, in control, who never did anything to contribute to an unhealthy marriage and he was the unhealthy one who was broken. I interpreted that this was in fact the old dynamic they were so used to and here they are falling back in it again because it seemed quite comfortable. But, in fact, all of it was a probably a two-way street. While Warren had indeed done the action that was so hurtful, they probably both contributed in many ways to things that they both were unhappy about and could do a better job at if they tried together.

Jill repeated her accusation about Warren being the broken one and Warren immediately agreed. She got very angry with me, saying, "I don't know why you're making me be here? I do not want to be here!" In the counter-transference, I felt bullied and blamed. These feelings were strong as Jill was constantly yelling at me and loudly accusing me of forcing her to be in therapy and deliberately making her feel bad.

I lost my therapeutic balance for a bit and was pulled into saying, "I'm not making you do anything. You don't have to be here if you don't want to. But, you're asking for my advice, my recommendation, and my insight into what's going on in your marriage. It is probably helpful for both of you to be here and learn about the marriage in a way that might help going forward". At that point, Jill got even angrier and walked out leaving me and Warren in the room. We were also out of time so we ended with me saying to Warren, "I will see you next week".

He came in for the next session by himself and let me know that Jill was not going to come anymore because she felt, "All we do is focus on the bad things that happened, which just makes you feel worse". He told me she said "She had never left a session feeling better, only worse". Interestingly, Warren added that since the last session she's felt very depressed and is thinking constantly about the events on her own. He told me she was very upset and angry about what happened and angry with him. Then, he just sat there looking uncomfortable.

In the past, he would remain silent and then start to feel anxious about not knowing what to do and about not doing what he thought I wanted of him. This "pressured to perform" transference to my authority and his phantasy of my demand was now considerably less as the result of our work on it. Warren said, "As you know, I have a hard time starting".

I interpreted this statement was progress because in the past he saw me as the one demanding and commanding him to have a certain topic and to fill the space in some special way. Now, he was not immediately consumed with that idea and more able to realize this anxiety state was his own. It was self-generated. This was a move away from more paranoid functioning to more whole self and whole object experience.

Warren told me he was able to "catch himself" feeling "on the spot" and then he was able to find a way to "rebalance". Then, having finished saying what was on his mind, we sat in another moment of silence. I asked him what he was feeling or thinking and he said, "Do you mean about something specific or in general?" Suddenly, he seemed to again feel compelled to answer my questions implicitly and specifically. I said "just anything". So, with "my direction", he began talking about how he feels he is doing much better and that he is moving in a better direction. He said his life is improving.

What I noticed and thought to myself was that this was the same line of thought about getting better that he and/or Jill would often bombard me with but it was not said in the usual manic or pushy way. I did not feel he was yelling, "I'm cured, I'm all better, there's nothing wrong with me!" This was more thoughtful, slower, and somehow more truthful. I could believe him. I did not feel he was as much of a liar. So, this was an interesting transference/counter-transference moment.

Warren went on to tell me about how he has realized that throughout his entire marriage he would "say anything, whatever it took, to placate Jill and just have her go along with the program so I could get my way, avoid conflict, or feel somehow powerful". Again, this was a new way of relating to me and to himself. Part of this was that without Jill present, he did not feel as threatened or pressured. But, it also seemed like it was simply working through some of his defensive posture and rigid pathological organization (Steiner 1987, 1990, 1993). Obviously, this was only the very beginning of any significant working through and lasting growth, but it was an important start.

Warren told me there were multiple reasons he lied or "bent the truth", but he said he "just had a habit of saying whatever it took to get his way and to make her happy". I said it sounded like he had lied his way through the marriage for a variety of reasons. He agreed and went on to associate to "that's how I made my way through my childhood". Warren went on to explain that he moved around every few years so it was very hard to fit into school and have friends. He said, "So, I made a point of saying whatever it took to make my way through and make myself look better and more important. Also, I did it to avoid conflict. Since I didn't live in any one place too long, they could never check the facts or examine the evidence. I could do whatever I wanted or say whatever I wanted and I got away with it".

I told Warren that he did his best to cope as a child and deal with a very difficult situation and he found a lot of advantage in that style of relating that he continued today. Warren said, "Well, yes, up until about six months ago because that's when I realized what honesty was. It was the first time I ever stopped and realized what it is to be honest". I said this was an example of him saying something that is a red flag and I have to become the suspicious authority and interrogate him. I said, "You said what you said just in passing, very casual. But, let's get this straight. For 15 years of marriage you didn't know what honesty was and you just lied and cheated and didn't know you were doing anything wrong because you didn't know what honesty was. But, suddenly six months ago you learned what honesty was".

Then, Warren backtracked and said, "What I meant is that I finally started to see the consequences of my actions so I tried to do better. Before that, I never saw the consequences of my actions. After the two affairs, I did see the consequences so I tried to change". I asked him if this seemingly blind state of not knowing could be somehow connected to how both of them seem to always be quick to convince me that the marriage was always great and then suddenly he cheated on her twice but now they get along fine. I said that probably there were years before this cheating of things not working well between them and things that we need to understand that led up to these events.

In response, Warren began to describe how he had been unhappy with himself for years, feeling a "complete lack of confidence, a lot of drinking, a general retreat in life, and not really participating in the marriage, with chores but also emotionally. I just generally withdrew from life". After Warren told me this, I repeated it back to him, saying, "It does sound very lonely and painful. It sounds like you really were withdrawing and ended up unavailable emotionally, unhappy, and drinking all the time. Being so unavailable to her, I wonder what her part was in all of that. She must've surely noticed or maybe she tried not to notice that you were not emotionally there for her".

Warren quickly said, "Well, I wasn't really withdrawn like that. I wasn't drinking that much and I wasn't really unhappy all the time. So, I don't think she would have noticed". I interpreted, "You are basically taking back everything that you just said and now I have to run after you and show you the evidence. I have to be the detective again and tell you it seems like you are not fessing up to something or that you are lying your way out of something. Now, I have to pin you down and call you a liar. This has happened several times in almost every single session. You seemed pretty defensive so maybe you are demonstrating what you described about your childhood as well".

Warren said, "Well, I think I am defensive because I feel criticized". I asked how and he said, "Well, you seem to be calling me out on everything. You're always calling me out on everything". On one hand, Warren was correct. This is the ongoing acting out that is part of the embedded enactment process. Within this enactment dynamic, the analyst must find a way to make therapeutic interpretations, monitoring them so as to not just be making comments that are part of the enactment process but also useful, thoughtful comments that the patient can use and learn from. With the embedded enactment, we are constantly swimming about in the pool of projective pathology but trying to find a way to come up for air and make a helpful assessment of what is going on and provide the patient with a moment of integrative insight before we go underwater again.

I said, "It seems to be a bit of a vicious cycle because you will say something and when I either repeat it or ask for details you become evasive or retract what you said. So, then I have to pin you down about it and find out which version is really true. Then, you feel criticized by me. So when I ask questions about what you seem to not be upfront about, you take it all back and I have to call you out on it. Then, it looks and feels like I am the heavy who is calling you a liar. I have seen this very thing happen between you and Jill and now between the two of us. I think you're still working the room like you did as a kid but I am catching you at it and calling you out and then you feel like I am being mean. I wonder if initially you want me to learn about you and find out what's going on inside of you but then you feel like you revealed too much, get anxious, want to rewrite history, and take it all back. But, that means that I feel like you are lying to me. So, maybe you are honest at first but then get anxious about the results of being honest".

Warren said, "I want to let you know me but I don't know if what I show you is what you want". This was quite revealing as he was describing a phantasy of me as someone demanding him to be a certain way to please me and him desperately trying to please me but failing. Also, he was describing a phantasy in which he wants me to really know the true Warren, the real him, but he is anxious that I will not accept or want that and I might want some other portrait of him, possibly a false, untrue version of him that catered to my needs more than his needs. I made these interpretations and he seemed somewhat interested. They seemed to help him and provide an expansion of possibilities in his mind. He seemed less anxious and less psychologically restricted.

In the next session, Warren started off in his usual manner, telling me how he was "doing so much better, really lending a hand around the house, and communicating with Jill". I noticed my urge to speak up about this rush to assure me or convince me but I stayed silent and listened. I wondered if this was him truly revealing himself or just trying to figure out what I wanted and deliver it.

Warren told me he had noticed the urge to have a beer a few times but resisted it and was "still staying with the no drinking thing". Here, it did seem like Warren was describing something he was reluctantly going along with. I said that and Warren predictably said, "Oh no. I really don't want to drink anymore. I can see how it was creating a problem". I asked when these times of wanting a beer occurred and he said mostly when Jill was still at work and he was alone at home. I said, "I wonder if those are times you feel you can get away with it, times when you feel like a rebel". Warren replied, "Oh no. I just happened to want a beer. Her not being there has nothing to do with it. I don't feel like a little kid with her anymore. That whole parent/ child dynamic we discussed has changed and I feel we are operating as equals now". Again, I had the sensation that he was trying very hard to instantly change things into a harmonious and conflict free zone, with cures and changes happening overnight.

Next, Warren told me he was "starting to get with the program of working in the kitchen as Jill suggested". I asked him what he meant. He said, "She is prodding me to cook more so she can come home and not have to immediately do more work. She wants me to pull my weight and I am finally learning to now. I get it and I am doing my duty as I should! So, it is working out well". I said, "The way you say that it sounds like part of you wants to help out and another part is reluctant, like you are just going along with what she says. That is what we discovered about the pattern in the marriage before the affairs. Do you think that is going on?"

Warren replied, "Oh no. I am over that. I see us as equals now. She is asking for help and I am stepping up as I should. She told me to do it and I am doing it. I am fine with it". Here, I felt like, once again, I was becoming the detective and searching out the pieces of a crime and he was busy hiding those pieces and denying any guilt. I said, "It seems like you sometimes say something that sounds like you are not happy with the relationship. Then, when I comment on it, you feel like I have found you out and you quickly retreat and say the opposite. Do you notice that?" Warren thought for a moment and said, "Well, I can sort of see how you would see it that way. But, I feel I am doing what I should as a grown up and a husband. I know I have it in me to be lazy. If it were up to me, I would come home and relax and read for a while. But, now that she has told me what I need to do, I can see how that is the right way and I am willing to come home and start working in the kitchen immediately. I am slowly learning and coming on board with the program".

132

Here, I once again felt like Warren was a kid who had been lectured to do his chores and he is trying to act like he is grown up and believes in the goodness of chores while really feeling other things as well. So, I said, "It seems you are having a hard time finding any middle ground between being a lazy rebel who only wants to relax and read or becoming a responsible grown up who is trying to please your responsible wife by getting down to business. I wonder what makes it difficult to own some middle ground in all that? I am guessing if it were up to you, you would read a bit first and relax before going into the kitchen. That would be your way, not my way or her way but your way".

Here, I was interpreting his splitting dynamic and his avoidance of revealing his true self for fear of punishment or judgment. Warren was trying to convince us of his new found harmony and responsibility and in the process possibly avoiding conflict if he owned his differences and individual way of doing things.

Warren responded, "Sure, I would like to just do nothing. But, I am trying to not be that lazy person. Jill wants me to join her in taking care of things so I am hearing the call. I am starting to feel more comfortable in the kitchen. At first, I felt very anxious and stiff. She is a very good cook and has high expectations. I didn't know if I could pull it off. I try and take a lot of deep breaths when I am in the kitchen to calm myself down. I am slowly learning more and it can be fun sometimes. I am starting to see the value in it".

I tried to engage him about his anxiety, his fragile self-confidence, and his fear of not meeting her expectations. As predicted, Warren denied much of what he had just told me and said he did not feel that anxious and Jill was not that demanding of him. I said, "Maybe she isn't, but you seem to feel small and uncertain and then see her as big and intimidating or demanding sometimes". He was quick to say, "No. That might have been true in the past but not anymore. I feel good now!"

Here, I wanted to remind Warren it has only been about three months that he has been trying on this new way of being but I refrained. I said, "You seem to be engaged in two different paths. On one hand, I think you try hard to please me and Jill and sometimes feel anxious that you are not meeting our expectations. That is when you start saying something and then take it back. But, at the same time, you are trying to learn about yourself and find a better way of living that you personally enjoy more. Evidence of that is that you continue to come to see me on your own". Warren said, "Exactly. I plan on continuing to come because I want to be a better person and a better husband. I want to make changes".

Discussion

This is a case in which the Modern Kleinian Therapy method was used to treat a volatile couple comprising of two difficult to reach individuals. In many contemporary psychoanalytic treatments, the analyst encounters quite unstable patients prone to acting out with turbulent transference states. In addition, there is often sudden, reactive termination. Frequency is usually low and the road towards analytic contact slow and tedious, marked by many roadblocks, detours, and retreats. However, if the analyst can remain open and flexible in their technical approach, yet adhering to the ongoing exploration of unconscious phantasy and transference as well as the defenses of both the paranoid and depressive positions, progress and change are possible.

Jill and Warren exhibited severe problems regarding containment (Bion 1962b; Steiner 2011), the pathological use of projective identification, and conflicts of knowledge and learning. They did not seem able to offer or provide an ample emotional container for each other and instead projected a variety of bad objects and anti-container phantasies into each other and into me as the analyst. As a couple, they had certain limitations in their capacity to love each other and themselves (Kernberg 2011). These included troubles with trust, mature interest in the interests of each other, inability to truly forgive, and the sense of gratitude and appreciation over the need for control and the resulting issues of resentment.

Jill could not picture Warren as man enough or mature enough to provide a shelter for her more vulnerable side, the more tender dependent side of her that she seemed to despise. Warren did not want to share his lack of confidence and uncertainty with me or Jill for fear she or I would judge him and take advantage of him. He also seemed to want to protect and reserve that rebel and manipulative side of himself in case he wanted to retreat to it as some later date.

Specifically, the two of them projected the phantasy of an object who would take away what they favored (Britton 1989), a rebellious, angry, and devious child in the case of Warren and a controlling, bossy parent who got her way in the case of Jill. They both feared learning about themselves and gaining knowledge of the object. They would rather construct false profiles of joy and harmony than face the unfinished, unhappy, or controlling aspects of self and other.

As demonstrated in the case material, the transference with more troubled patients such as Warren and Jill tends to be quite chaotic, alternating between different split off sets of self and other in phantasy conflicts of contrary formation (Clarkin, Yeomans, and Kernberg 2006). Interpretation is an uphill battle with countless cycles of conflict repetition and vigorous revisiting of the core conflicts being clinically necessary but very taxing and easily subsumed into the enactment process. It is easy in the counter-transference to either want to give up altogether or to force the therapeutic message into the patient once and for all. I had to struggle with the latter with both Warren and Jill. Both these states are key areas in which embedded enactments are played out with difficult patients. For Jill and Warren, their interpersonal use of projective identification was quite strong and relentless, creating a transference state that was formidable and challenging.

With Warren, his method of not being honest, of saying one thing and then switching to another or taking back what he had just said, created a system of lying and manipulating as well as a cycle of either getting away with something or being chased and caught. I found myself being a detective, constantly on the watch for his shift in speech and ready to catch him in his crime. This made me another authority riding over him, much like he saw his wife and much like he related to her. He was a child caught shoplifting, and then trying to talk his way out of it.

In the short time spent so far with Warren, it seems his lying and his appearing to lie are a combination of phantasies about and compromise solutions for various unconscious conflicts. His distortions of the truth and his manipulation of communication seem to be a vehicle for power and grandiosity but also a way to retreat, camouflage himself, avoid or reduce conflict, and defend against a powerful and dreaded object that he is trying to impress and appease. With this excessive and pathological projective identification system, Warren becomes involved in a vicious cycle in which he has to lie more as he feels more inferior and more attacked or more ignored. These lies might be about what he wants, about what he feels the object demands, or how he feels about pleasing the object.

In the sixteen sessions I have been seeing Warren, first with Jill and now by himself, I understand him to be struggling within an intensely divided internal world with quite opposed views of self and other. I believe he is showing me, through the transference, a specific set of unconscious conflicts.

Warren seems to be alternating between the experience of being a sneaky and sinister little boy wanting his way and not wanting to participate with the object. To be open and honest with his object, he imagines he would have to reveal himself, give to the object in ways he would resent, or that he would have to grow up and lose his identity. On the other hand, he seems to feel like a scared child who is constantly trying to please a demanding object that could easily judge him or punish him. This dread and anxiety leaves him on the run and without any core self-identity.

So, at times Warren is like a lazy boy who likes to do nothing or simply likes to do things his way and not listen to the expectations or rules of others. This side of Warren tries to control and manipulate others by lying or by twisting what he says at any given time. As he told me, for years he said anything he needed to manipulate his wife and get her off his back. I interpreted that he did the same in the transference. In this mode, Warren felt a great deal of aggression and strove to do things his way and avoided doing things the object wanted.

But, when I confronted him on this or interpreted his fears and desires in this realm, he was quick to deny all of it. Indeed, there was a frantic flight into convincing me or Jill that he was cured and that he was now a good boy just like he should be. This more crude manic defense shifted recently to the more shady and questionable pronouncement of him "finally growing up and starting to like the things he was told to do and should do" in the context of working in the kitchen.

At the same time, Warren seemed scared of his vision of Jill and me as authorities who expected him to act and speak in proper ways that we determined. He would be nagged, lectured, or punished if he did not meet our standards. This transference was played out to some degree in how he projected these object relational conflicts onto me and then spoke in contrary and suspicious ways that pulled me into chasing him and calling him a liar. He was in fact lying to me and Jill but the way he went about it served other projective identification functions such as feeling powerful, hidden, defended, noticed, and able to avoid conflict as well as to retaliate against perceived demands.

It was also a desperate yet twisted cry for help and a hope I might see him as more than just an evil liar. When I recently interpreted this fear and anxiety over being expected to perform in the session with me or with Jill, he was quick to deny any sense of persecution or inferiority. So, this again triggered the cycle of me chasing him and pointing out the details of how he was scared and how he was feeling inferior with us. But, then he would deny it or tell me how he used to feel scared or bullied to please me and to please Jill but that he had "gotten over that and past that".

When in this scared child transference, Warren also tried to convince me and himself that he was happy and grateful that Jill was teaching him how to be a better person and that I was showing him the ways he was avoiding being a responsible adult. But, he said this in a way that was partly genuine but also partly false. I would interpret that he is trying to talk himself into believing he likes being trained to be an adult but really has mixed feelings about it. I would also interpret that he is anxious about whether I could tolerate him having mixed feelings about slowing changing but still holding on to some of his past ways and feelings. This is an interpretation of the death instinct and his persecutory anxiety over shifting towards the depressive position.

As he has throughout the treatment, Warren assured me this was not the case and that he did not feel that way. However, I believe this is a core element in his ongoing object relational struggles. So, I continue to interpret his denial of the existence of a little boy who still rebels and tries to dominate with getting his way and manipulating others. But, this same little boy wants to escape the grip of a demanding authority (his superego) who will not respect him or see him as ever capable of ever growing up and having importance in his own right. I interpret that Warren does want to grow up but he wants to find his own unique way of being an adult, sometimes doing more and sometimes doing less, but always fitting in and feeling loved and respected.

So far, this is too much for Warren to acknowledge or allow me to work with. But, I believe we will slowly get there by the interpretation of his shifting, yes/no, true/untrue transference and his way of positioning us in familiar yet restrictive and destructive ways. I could go along with his method of growing up but then I would be colluding with him feeling he has become an adult under the authority and direction of others who see him as needing to be trained and him as seeing himself as being inferior and needing this dogmatic and devaluing treatment. I would have to go along with the falsehood of him having no reservations about giving up his little boy ways and along with the punitive idea that his little boy ways are always evil and wrong.

I must stand up and say no, you are lying. You do have these other sides to yourself that sometimes create problems but they do exist and do not have to be eradicated like a poisonous disease. Instead, they are simply parts of you that have emerged as the result of past conflicts and experiences and can now be integrated and modified in ways you choose, creating potentially positive elements of personality if better understood and mastered. He wants to use action and primitive non-thinking attacks based with defenses of the death instinct to eliminate this potential new knowledge and change. Warren fears and hates to know the reality of what is and what could be. He is not an omnipotent rebel who can escape responsibility and the domination of authority, but a man who will have to give up some of his desires and childish power and he will have to confront the object's power and control, asserting himself as a respectable equal with different but valuable opinions and methods of living, establishing himself as unique and important among others.

While this analytic treatment is only getting under way, there has already been a great deal of psychoanalytic work accomplished. Using the Modern Kleinian Therapy method, a chaotic and ultimately collapsed couples therapy has shifted to the difficult yet promising once a week psychoanalytic treatment of an individual suffering with severe depressive and pre-depressive anxieties. Interpretation of his internal phantasies and his transference state has proven very challenging but helpful. We have established numerous periods of analytic contact and are slowly working towards meaningful object relational change and a healthy, non-reactionary, and new view or knowledge of the self and other.

9

THE LIMITS OF OUR VALUE AND
THE VALUE OF OUR LIMITS

Cooper (2010) examines the analyst's enactments of feelings regarding the analytic process. He examines our personal expectations of how the patient should be able to sort through their problems and how much or how fast they should be able to modify and change their prior pathology.

Also, Cooper looks at the idea that psychoanalysis should be defined by the analyst's intentions, not by external criteria such as frequency, diagnosis, or use of couch. This is very much in line with the central tenets of Modern Kleinian Therapy. By using intention as the issue, the process may take many forms and different arrangements, but to understand and treat the unconscious conflicts that plague the patient remains the goal. So, in my first case presentation, having my patient's mother attend each session with him or have my second patient struggle with his paranoid and psychotic state without "doing something" to control him and only seeing him once a week due to his financial problems might seem to not fit the traditional psychoanalytic model. But, Cooper (2010) reminds us that, regardless of the theoretical approach the analyst uses, what remains is the desire to inspire and elicit the patient's curiosity in their conscious and unconscious experience. Cooper reminds us that the patient will then make specific and unique uses of that intention that, in my way of thinking, may be in the favor of the life or death instincts.

Waska (2007) has written much on the matter of intention and the creation of analytic contract under all circumstances. It seems clear that our field will only survive if we stop idealizing our work, promoting a caricature of it that is impossible to obtain, and to accept the limits of our value and the value of our limits.

When termination is occurring, feelings of loss, the nature of limits, dashed dreams and angry disappointment, and the difficult acceptance of partial change and unreached desires all come to bear intensely for both parties. Primitive guilt and persecutory anxiety, fueling a variety of desperate phantasies, can cause patients to leave treatment abruptly. Even if it seems like they just fizzle out and leave out of boredom, closer examination shows a more jagged and chaotic internal state. Depending on how we are able to work with and contain these turbulent emotional disturbances, the patient's state of mind can create destructive, regressive, and angry exits or a difficult, painful but insightful and reflective goodbye that leaves both parties still thinking and open to learning.

There is always a fragile balance in which both analyst and patient can either terminate within a restricted and hurtful paranoid-schizoid position (Klein 1946) or end within a sad but grateful depressive position (Klein 1935, 1940). With many of our more disturbed and hard to reach patients, it is very difficult to find a footing in this more secure and hopeful place. Even if the patient leaves in this fragmented and stormy manner, we must strive to preserve our own healthy grief and remain contained and able to think clearly enough that when and if the patient returns, or when the next such case comes along, we can be present for them and read to join them in their challenging quest for psychological freedom from inner turmoil.

For some patients, it seems what we can offer them is never enough. They demand more and indeed seem to need so much that they present as an interminable project. These are the borderline, narcissistic, psychotic, or severely depressed patients who barely function emotionally and often have a very difficult time coping in their day-to-day external lives. Due to the turbulent internal climate they exist in, they occupy complex transference states and utilize complicated defensive patterns in how they relate or not relate to their objects.

As a result, some of their treatments are short and chaotic with abrupt endings and others may be long, arduous, and fizzle out without much of a sense of success or closure. All these circumstances can be very trying on the analyst, leaving us feeling frustrated, ashamed, depressed, and powerless. We easily feel like failures and can end up blaming ourselves or our patients. One way of escaping this guilt and persecution is to say the treatment was only psychotherapy and not true psychoanalysis. This is just another way of avoiding the feeling of not having done enough or not having done something in an adequate manner.

This chapter uses the case material of analytic work with two difficult to reach patients to explore this very common predicament. The chapter proposes this sort of less than ideal, often spotty and rocky pattern of some gains and some losses to be fairly common in psychoanalytic practice even if not often reported. When working with patients who live with very distorted visions of self and other, constantly in some sort of destructive or dangerous union or separation, it is common to only be able to access restricted portions of the patient's mind at any given time. Even after many months or years of successful treatment, certain areas of object relational turmoil, conflict, and collapse may still exist and remain unreachable.

Thus, we face the limits of our profession every day with such patients. Issues of giving, receiving, taking, dependence, envy, persecution, severe loss and grief, and angry grievance are but a few of the psychological issues that bring the transference to a state that makes a full psychic recovery out of the question. However, we can do a great deal to help such individuals to mend, change, and transform their inner lives and this is indeed the very rich yet limited value of the psychoanalytic method (Waska 2010a, 2010b, 2010c).

Case material: Tom

Tom was 30 years old and shuffled into my office carrying a check his mother had given him for me. She cooked his meals, washed his clothes, woke him up in the morning, drove him to most of his appointments, and sat with him during every session. Tom would never have come to see me nor would he have sat through any sessions if she had not been there by his side. Most of the direct analytic work was with Tom. However, I spend a good deal of time working with both of them around the over caring mother/demanding infant relationship they seem so embroiled in. Also, there was some discussion of the dysfunctional state of the marriage and the unhealthy family dynamics that seemed to be played out in Tom's pathology.

Tom was an intelligent man but had never completed college classes because of what sounded like a complete mental collapse. He had been in several day hospital programs and was put into the inpatient unit twice before. Over the last ten years, he had attempted suicide by cutting his wrists, drinking bleach, and taking pills. Currently, he felt his life "was useless and a waste" and he "thought of jumping off the bridge or a building". Tom insisted his only problem was "social anxiety" and "only wanted to find out how to be more social". When I noted that he was on anti-psychotic medication as well as antidepressants and anti-anxiety medications, he yelled, "That is for social anxiety!" He had seen numerous therapists over the years but never stayed with any because he "didn't like them and they never helped him". Tom lived with his parents and had no friends. He had worked a few part time jobs over the years but none of them had ever worked out. His two older brothers lived out of state.

Working with Tom was immediately a challenge. When he sits down at the start of a session, he appears agitated, irritated, and impatient. He looks at the floor and then at me and back at the floor. After a few seconds, he yells at me, "What? What the fuck!!?? What do you want?" In trying to engage him in exploring his internal experiences, I find him stubborn, anxious, frightened, and aggressive.

Overall, Tom is extremely demanding and feels anxious for and entitled to "the answers" and he wants them "right now". If I do not deliver the goods, he is furious and in the counter-transference I fear he will discard me. I take this to be an important piece of information about how he regards his objects and the way he views himself. When Tom tells me about his extreme anxiety, I interpret that his constant projection of hatred, anger, and demand makes others seem either totally useless so his world is lonely and empty or it makes others seem intimidating and scary, which makes his world persecutory and vile. So, to facilitate analytic contact, I immediately began confronting his transference of anger, anxiety, and demand.

Tom seems to always be very angry when I ask questions and always yells, "I don't know!", "I don't know the answer!", or "I don't know what to say!" This is followed by grunting and cursing. In the counter-transference, I felt the victim of such a withholding withdrawal and angry dismissal that I wanted to pester Tom with questions and really put him on the spot. Noting this emotionally and also observing myself acting this out to some degree by the amount of questions I asked, I interpreted this transference and counter-transference dynamic by stating, "You seem to have brought us to a place where I am the constantly questioning father and you are the one-word withholding teenager. We are in a total standoff". Tom responded, "Just like my fucking father".

I asked for details and over the next few sessions learned of an abusive and rocky relationship between him and his father when he grew up. But, back to us in the moment, in noticing this standoff, I was then able to see that the pressure I felt might be the pressure he felt and I especially thought of how he sounded when he said, "I don't know what to say!" I pictured a torture victim yelling out that they did not have any information to give, no secrets to provide. So, I interpreted, "I wonder if you feel pressured to perform, to give me the goods and you don't know what the goods are. You look like you are being tested and feel very anxious and worried that you are failing my test". Tom immediately relaxed a bit and said, "Yes. I do feel like that. I have no feelings or thoughts and I don't know what to tell you". I interpreted this hollowed out, empty core result of his projective identification process by saying, "Maybe by always having to focus on me and what you think I am demanding, you lose sight of everything inside of you". Tom nodded and was silent for a moment.

Later on, Tom talked about feeling very isolated, bored, and lonely. He told me that he had no friends and he always felt extremely anxious when around other people. I suggested it might be that he saw others as he saw me, demanding him to perform immediately and he was left feeling empty and not knowing what to say. He said, "That could be". I asked him if there was anyone he likes to hang out with, or wishes he could hang out with like perhaps his father. Here, I was thinking of the probable ambivalence he would have with his father, both wanting a close relationship and avoiding it at the same time.

Tom said, "No. I don't get along with him at all. But, I like to do things with my mother". I asked him about that. He said, "I really like to hang out with her and do things with her. We have fun. But, when I look around and see other 30-year-old men, they are not hanging out with their mothers. They are with their friends, girlfriends, or wives". He was quiet and looked sad. I asked him what made him feel sad. He said he felt like he "had wasted his life and has nothing".

141

Then, Tom fell silent and gradually grew agitated and finally said, "What! Shit! What do you want! I know all this shit! How does that help? I need to know what to do!" I said, "You are upset telling me about these painful things and feeling like you have wasted your life. Maybe it is easier to get angry at me than to have to join me in investigating these painful issues". Tom yelled, "What the fuck? It is the same crap I have told all the other therapists!" I said, "I wasn't there then. This is me and this is you and me. I want to know the details. I need more from you". Tom rolled his eyes and grunted and threw his hands up in the air and said, "Fine!"

Here, I was using my counter-transference experience of him being the one that holds the power and has everyone come to him. I was reduced to always pleading and wondering and waiting for him to come to me. I realized this was an important aspect of the transference and his phantasy state so in my interpretation, I was taking back my rights to be taken care of, to be listened to, and to be given to. I was also demonstrating my boundaries and exerting my belief that it is ok to have a give and take relationship that is formed around help and care instead of a violent back and forth or a deadened one way street. The result of this interpretation was a sudden reduction in his anxiety and a momentary acknowledgement of "fine!" that indicated his allowing us to be together for that moment instead of separate in his normally harsh and adversarial manner.

Another session found us discussing Tom's job. He felt "stuck in it and unhappy with it". He had been fired from his last job for not showing up on time. He told me he was bored and fed up with this current one. I said, "You are telling me you feel unhappy and stuck but you are not telling me if you do anything to change that". Here, I was interpreting the transference dynamic in which Tom was presenting himself as this passive victim and looking to me to "do something" and give him the answers. Tom said he had looked online for "a while" for better jobs but after not finding anything he had given up and now his mother continued the search for him. He said this in a way that seemed dismissive, arrogant, and entitled. I interpreted that he was demanding immediate answers from me and wanted immediate results from his job search. When he became fed up with having to make his own efforts, he looked to me and his mother to be his personal fix-it crew. I interpreted that if he pressured himself so savagely to know what to say to me, he probably was savage in the way he looked for a job as well or even in how he wanted a girlfriend and a social life. He wanted it all NOW. When it was not immediately delivered on a silver platter, he became angry with himself, very anxious and lost, and then lashed out at others for failing to fix him, rescue him, and make his life the one he wanted.

Technically, I also noticed that the way Tom demanded so much right away from me left me as the powerless object needing to feed Tom on demand out of intimidation. I was only the delivery boy and he had all the rights to request, demand, and own. So, I noticed that it was helpful to point this out in my interpretations when he refused to answer questions or acted smug and devaluing of my inquiries. I told him, "I want more. You want something from me and from being here. So do I". This was a step towards positioning myself as a whole object that deserved attention and had the ability and right to gain something in life. This was the opposite of what Tom thought of himself and what he imposed on himself and his objects.

At the same time, this was a tricky process in the total transference situation (Joseph 1985) and the complete counter-transference (Waska 2011a). I had to be watchful about the repeat of a sadomasochistic dynamic Tom seemed so familiar with and comfortable in. So, when he was withholding and angry about my questions and inquiry, I also interpreted that in him being so silent and withholding, I was now pushed to be the demanding one, insisting he provide what I wanted immediately and therefore he was the one who was failing, the one who was bullied. But, he also got to be the withdrawn silent bully who refused to give and be in control through not giving and only demanding a fix.

The analytic treatment with Tom continued over the following months much in the same manner. We still struggled with his sense of entitlement, detachment, distance, and devaluation of anything but a master/servant relationship in the transference. However, it appeared that with my consistent interpretation of his fear of facing the lonely devastation of having no one and being nothing to anyone, he slowly relaxed his grip on having to be special and entitled at all times, constantly projecting all his anger, hate, and demand into others leaving him alone and without. Bit by bit, he seemed more willing to interact and sometimes allow himself to emotionally and mentally consider what could be possible if he mourned what was never possible. He was less anxious and psychologically combative but still extremely cautious and challenging. Overall, Tom continued to be extremely resistant to treatment and probably would never had continued if it were not for his mother's assistance and presence. He was still very turbulent in the transference, being extremely withholding and relying on projective identification to a severe degree.

As Kernberg (1992) notes, it is always important to look at all developments in a patient's life including those outside of the treatment setting and the patient's experiences in the past as well as the present. This was part of my stance with Tom as I sought out his feelings and thoughts about his life in totality, his day-to-day life, and the life or lifelessness of our therapeutic relationship. The Kleinian approach embraces this constant examination of both internal and external reality based on Klein's (1952b) discoveries of how the transference is always derived from a combination of real and phantasized aspects of the past and present as well as defenses against both the real and the imagined. This makes it vital to stay close to the immediate nature of the patient's here-and-now transference state and the nature of the analytic contact (Waska 2007) that is being fostered, cultivated, or fought off. With Tom, he constantly fought off any lingering moment of analytic contact as it seemed to mean he had to give instead of receive.

The current status of Tom's analytic treatment is helpful to consider when examining the limits of our work and the sense of success, failure, or generally turbulent struggle that emerges as we try to assist our patients. It is always an unsatisfactory journey we elect to undertake with our more difficult patients in terms of mourning our hopes and desires for cure and total repair of pain and tragedy. We may do our best in each session and we many hold onto certain hopes and goals for the encounter. However, the nature of the patient's phantasies and their unique defenses against whatever paranoid and depressive anxieties they have will often be the ultimate decision maker. We can offer to help the patient look within to realize the possibility of change and improvement. But, sometimes, the desire to retain their internal psychic equilibrium (Joseph 1989) and their utilization of the death instinct to ward off separation, difference, or need is hard to go up against. For some patients, the life instinct represents an overwhelming shift in their current psychic equilibrium and they resist any change as it is experienced as great danger to their entire being (Waska 2006).

Tom was very much fused to the idea of mother as permanently available breast and his entitlement of being cared for no matter what, based on what I thought to be a very ancient grievance with his father. All of this came head to head with a new external reality.

Over time, Tom's mother put plans into place that would enable Tom to move out of his parents' home into an assisted care setting. Whenever the mother brought this idea up, which was seldom and watered down as she feared hurting his feelings and making him angry, Tom immediately told me "I am not ready for that. I will never be ready for that. I am too anxious around other people!" I interpreted that he was very scared and was trying to retain a sense of power in the face of enormous anxiety over separation and loss of his power over his objects. He told me, "I feel nothing!"

During a recent session, Tom's mother told him she was in fact putting things into place and he might end up moving out in a matter of weeks. While Tom looked very concerned upon hearing this, he told me he "felt nothing" and "didn't see it happening". In the counter-transference, I noticed myself wanting to be forceful or even cruel in getting him to see the reality of his situation. In an interpretive enactment (Steiner 2006), I said, "Well, whether you see it happening or not, it is happening!" In my immediate reflection on what I said, how I said it, and how I felt saying it, I realized I was participating in a push/pull debate. Tom would say, "No, I am not leaving home" and I would say, "Yes, you are whether you like it or not".

So, I used this internal information to formulate my next interpretation and made a comment about how he was digging in his heels and making things a standoff between us. I said, "It is like you are saying I won't do it and you can't make me and then we have to make you". He was silent. In addition, I attempted to talk with him about how much he was trying to escape the terror of being alone and without the breast he felt he deserved but that had otherwise been taken away long ago, now replaced by his use of parents as loyal servants that he could never be close to or feel loved by.

Tom did say he "felt the whole thing was rather disturbing" but then said "I don't care" and "I don't know what you are talking about". At this point he seemed to eradicate our link and our discussion so completely in his mind that he truly forgot what was going on. He said, "What are you talking about? Why are we here?" So, Tom stopped engaging with me at that point emotionally and cognitively.

After the session, Tom drove himself to a nearby bridge and started to peer over the railing. He was taken to the hospital by a policeman who asked him what he was doing and Tom said he was going to jump. Tom has been in the hospital for a week now and it is unclear if he will return to treatment. He may be placed in an assisted care program as his parents have said they do not want him back home.

In the counter-transference, I have gone through a sense of hopelessness, helplessness, and frustration. I have blamed myself for not being a better analyst and somehow helping him to "grow up" faster. But, I recognize this is a guilt-based, critical, and aggressive parental stance that is similar to his mother's. In other words, I am feeling he "should" grow up immediately and stop acting like such a stubborn child. Therefore, when I am not being demanding and critical with myself about that, I feel like blaming Tom for being so resistant and so stubborn. This is my projective identification based counter-transference window into understanding some of the complex layers of object relational pathology that made up Tom's methods of relating and non-relating.

In addition, I have blamed his parents for not being involved enough at any time in his life. While this is probably true to some degree, again I found myself wanting to find someone accountable, be it myself, Tom, or Tom's parents. It was as if blaming and battle were more important than understanding and patience. Understanding was the victim of expectation. This in fact was one of the central ways Tom related in the transference. He did not want to understand anything, he only wanted immediate results or he would walk away. So, through his projective process of immediate expulsion, I came to feel his same angry expectations and critical ways.

Tom allowed for no hope, no joy, and no sense of discovery in his life and this was projected into our therapeutic relationship. So, along with the aggression and blame, I also felt this blame shifted into apathy. I found myself feeling like I could never help him and that he was doomed to be lost in the fractured social service system where he would be unable to function in life forevermore. In my worse moments, I felt I was stuck in a career of not reaching those who are unreachable. When I noticed this sense of despair growing, I was able to pull myself up into a more balanced sense of doing the best I can in a very difficult situation. I realized that perhaps if Tom is placed in an assisted living situation, he will have the opportunity to continue to see me and he will have the chance to find out what it is like to be more separate and independent.

Perhaps in this very troubling and sad story, there already has been a bit of growth or at least a bit of assistance given. Maybe at a later time there may be a chance to offer Tom additional opportunities to work on himself. Until then, I must be content or at least accept and tolerate the fact that this is a rough road without a map and that we have made some headway in some direction. We cannot fail at something if we are simply striving to go forward and learn as we proceed. We can make an effort and see if that effort is helpful and of value. In the process, we must accept the loss of desired omnipotence and realize we may not be able to do much for some people and they may not choose to or be able to do much for themselves. But, if we wade into that sometimes painful river, we may be able to save a few along the way. To do so, we must face the frightening currents and know how to not be swept away ourselves.

Case material: Larry

In the time I met with Larry, I often felt he never changed. I think this is my own counter-transference-based struggle that is induced from his projective identification based transference. He is a patient whose disturbed and disturbing ranting has become very familiar to me over our five years together. His chanting of misery is predictable and I can almost literally recite what he will say each session, word for word. Over and over, he tells me, "I have no money, everyone else has money. Why don't I have money? What is wrong with me that I have no money? All this psychological crap is useless. I just want to die. I want to kill myself. I need money! If I can't find a way to support myself with money, I need to kill myself. It would feel so much better than this agony they call life! Can you kill me? I want to die. I should spend the rest of my money on a gun. I hate life. It is all about money. Why am I so miserable all the time? What is wrong with me? I just need money. Money would make it all better".

After seeing me for five years, Larry stopped due to a complete collapse of his finances. Actually, it was the most current collapse of many years of near crisis and several actual bankruptcies. He lived a marginal life running his own small business because he "wasn't about to work for those shitheads out there!" He would rather barely make enough to pay his bills and often go further into debt than feel like he was giving over his life to those who "thought they had the right to live the good life and treat others like shit". At the end of our time together, he was very far in debt and barely able to maintain his apartment. This was the same precarious external state he was in when I met him.

146

After about a year of meeting with Larry, not only did I know what he would say in each session almost verbatim, but my interpretations were fairly predictable as well. I say this with both positive and negative implications. I believe I was able to analyze Larry's transference and phantasy struggles to the degree that I could provide ongoing interpretive understanding, confrontation, and translation of his emotional chaos. This persistent attunement provided him with a new stability and a chance to examine himself in a less persecutory and primitive manner. Tom had a repetitive way of inflicting us with the same intense aggressive grievances regarding demanded love and care that never came about because of his desire for complete and immediate care without any back and forth reciprocation. This had the effect of pulling me into a pattern of relating to him in which we were both keeping our distance from each other and from his core anxieties. But, overall, I think my diligence to what I saw as his core fear and desire to extract love and justice from his objects was helpful in grounding him in a more integrated experience than his normally agitated, persecuted, primitively guilty, and ready for annihilation way of living in the world.

So, as Larry is yelling his complaints over and over on the analytic couch, I find myself being pulled to subtly blame him with interpretations about how if he wants more money he should charge his customers more regardless of how guilty he feels about it. Guilt is a crippling matter for Larry but in a persecutory manner. Over time, I was gradually able to see how my patient's projective identification process was affecting my counter-transference and pushing me to be a bully to him rather than an understanding object. Then, I was more able to make helpful interpretations based on what I learned from these feelings in my counter-transference instead of attacking him in these guilt-ridden interpretive enactments.

Over time, in thinking more deeply about the nature of my reverie and the enactments I slipped into, I have found new ideas and images I can use in my interpretations. Only when I am more aware of how I am being pulled into being a critical, distant, bad mother object am I able to regain my therapeutic balance and utilize my reverie state or counter-transference play as I call it. So, as Larry practically chants "I have no money, where is my money!" I sometimes drift off into a state where the words change to "Where is my mommy, I have no mommy! Everyone else has a mommy! I should kill myself. I want to die. All I think about is death. If I can't find mommy then I must die, there is no other choice!"

Using my reverie, sometimes I will then make the interpretations that he is really suffering from the loss of his mother and is angry and demanding that I and others become his mother. I interpret that, on one hand, he angrily tells me over and over that he will not accept any help, will remain a helpless orphan, and wants to simply protest and resent all those who seem to be so lucky as to have a loving mother who takes care of them. I comment on his suicidal threat and wanting to call attention to himself, demanding my immediate rescue and love.

On the other hand, I interpret that Larry desires and demands that I and others take over his life and become the all mothering agent who will make everything ok. But, for this reward he has to enter into a passive sadomasochistic relationship and hope I dole out enough nourishment. He had better be a good deserving child and act according to my wishes. Larry responds very well to these sorts of interpretations for a while and is able to begin thinking about himself more before slipping back into this concrete grievance about money.

Of course, my reverie state is influenced by the transference and my knowledge of his childhood with a violent alcoholic father and a psychotic mother who was in and out of institutions from Larry's birth to her recent death. His two brothers are also psychotic and one has recently killed himself.

My example of reverie is a Kleinian use of counter-transference play in which I allow myself to float within a free association state with my seemingly random dream like thoughts and feelings. The patient's excessive projective identification based transference creates particular states of mind in the analyst (Joseph 1987; Waska 2011a) that can then lead to interpretive enactments such as my blaming Larry for not charging his customers more and for not asking for more in life. This is a thinly veiled blame for not wanting more from his weak and broken mother, even though he has always felt too scared and guilty to ever do so.

And, I was able to use my counter-transference play state to make more useful interpretations that led to a reduction in Larry's anxiety and an increase in his ability to ponder, think, and shift his view of self and object temporarily (Waska 2011b).

When Larry chose to stop treatment after five years, he did not see this as a choice but something he was forced to do by wicked outside forces. This was in line with how he viewed the rest of his life.

I find myself sometimes feeling like I failed him as a mother and other times feeling tired of dealing with someone who does every possible thing to never own any sense of self, personal strength, or desire for autonomy without shifting to his rigid defiance. Then, I regroup and realize that for Larry, we have managed a great deal. Before I met him, and hopefully now without me, he has managed to survive many times over. Sadly though, Larry keeps things at a "just surviving" level and fights off his persecutory and guilt-ridden aspirations for more than mere survival. But, we managed to keep the therapeutic boat drifting forward ever so slowly. We never sunk. Accepting that a ghost ship is what we have instead of a submerged wreck is not a great feeling but an important one for this analyst to realize and own so that I can continue to be ready for Larry's return and to be ready to help him in the same way, inch by inch and sometimes a motionless ghost ship still afloat, rather than a sunken wreck.

Discussion

Winnicott (1974) has written about patients who fear some terrible calamity or breakdown in the future so they avoid relationships, live very narrow lives, and suffer from intense anxiety or panic attacks. However, these patients are really projecting the past internal breakdown and psychological collapse they have already suffered into the future as a way to avoid experiencing the pain currently. This is in line with Klein's (1952a) belief that the death instinct and the life and death conflicts with primary objects create a fundamental persecutory anxiety. This poisons the early ego unless and until these phantasies of collapse and danger are mitigated by more depressive phantasies of safety, resolution, and hope. The patients I am outlining, illustrated by the cases of Tom and Larry, have not successfully reached this inner lighthouse, the safe haven of the depressive position. They are still lost in the choppy waters of their object relational uncertainties and the unsafe and unpredictable nature of the paranoid-schizoid experience especially when colored by excessive reliance on projective identification dynamics.

For Larry, he projected his childhood collapse, the collapse of his psychotic mother, and the collapse of a safe and reliable father object into his present and future life. Thus, he saved himself from the agony of his broken and terrifying bond with his family by creating an ongoing chamber of emotional horrors in his adult life. This is a historical emotional camouflage based on intense projective identification. It has dire consequences for mental functioning and is a flimsy and fragile psychic retreat (Steiner 1993) that is either always on the verge of failing or is in a constant state of fragmentation.

The work of Kleinians such as Hanna Segal (1993) affirms Freud's concept of the life and death instincts as a purely psychological conflict and clinically useful when viewed as such. Birth confronts us all with the experience of needs and Segal thinks that in relation to that experience there can be two reactions. One is to seek satisfaction for the needs that is life-promoting and leads to object seeking, love, and eventually object concern. The other is the drive to annihilate the need and to annihilate the perceiving experiencing self, as well as anything that is perceived. This is the death instinct. We all are in constant struggle with the two and our lifelong conflicts regarding love, hate, and knowledge are shaped by this. However, the patients I am describing are much more pathologically entrenched in this psychological turmoil. The death instinct is much more clearly an issue that colors their transference as well as the various ways they view and relate to self and other.

Both patients in this chapter wanted something in the direction of life but were pulled away from it by their opposing and destructive feelings. In parallel, there were many times when I would make life affirming observations or inquires about how and why they might be holding themselves back or sabotaging themselves. They would turn it around as a persecutory control, attack, or judgment, creating something more in the direction of the death instinct.

The phantasies my patients were struggling with were often life avoiding retreats into defensive control and withdrawal that then shaped the transference situation. Perlow (1995) states that phantasies are wish-fulfilling expressions of instinctual drives, specifically the life and death instincts. He says they are the medium by which the life and death instincts are experienced and are very little influenced by external reality or relationships. They are experienced directly either consciously or unconsciously.

I think that Perlow is correct about phantasies not being influenced by external reality and that is why the transference can be so jarringly out of synch with the reality of the therapeutic situation and the external world. And, of course, this is why reassurance and trying to be a better object than the patient's bad objects is doomed to fail. However, I also think that the patient's core phantasy world and conflicts influence external reality by the means of projective identification and therefore our interpretive methods can gradually have a positive effect in reversing or modifying the nature of those crippling phantasies.

Yet, for some patients, such as Tom and Larry, the nature of their phantasies and the value of maintaining psychic equilibrium regardless of how ultimately destructive this strategy is creates a formable if not impossible wall of opposition that we sometimes cannot do much with. This we must accept without giving up. Instead, we must proceed with a sense of realistic optimism and realistic pessimism.

The type of patient I am examining is typically thought as residing within the spectrum of the borderline, the narcissistic patient, the psychotic, and the severe neurotic all caught in a web of persecutory guilt and chronic psychic loss (Waska 2002). Many are unwilling to budge from their flimsy but familiar psychic retreats (Steiner 1993) and their excessive reliance on projective identification (Waska 2004). Some are able and willing to stay in treatment for extended periods while others exit fairly quickly. In both cases, it is rare to include a smooth termination process, one that is discussed and worked through. It is usually an announcement in a session that "this will be my last". This sudden abort of trust, connection, and legacy cannot usually be worked with sufficiently as these types of patients quickly feel that request to be another way we are capturing them, obligating them, not understanding them, and using them for our own benefit. Clearly, a paranoid vision of the analyst as warden, judge, and needy parasite emerges and these phantasies are part of previously worked on conflicts between self and object.

While most patients revisit their original inner drama during termination, this is more of an intensified continuation of an ongoing struggle and battle. The analytic work with such patients feels like a constant peace negotiation in a tent positioned in the middle of the battle field. There is rarely a moment of clarity and hope that prevents or modifies the internal world for very long.

However, the importance of psychoanalytic treatment with such difficult cases is that if the analyst persists, there is a gradual reduction of the enormity of distortion, a diluting of the internal poison, and a shift in the fundamental gravity of both paranoid and depressive anxieties. It is a difficult job that is never completely satisfying but a job worth doing.

10

KEEPING THE FAITH WHEN WORKING WITH TURBULENT PATIENTS

Our more difficult patients have typically spent their lives cultivating, maintaining, and then enduring intense internal and interpersonal turbulence through excessive reliance on destructive projective identification processes. As a result, the analyst must be constantly aware of these shifting and complex dynamics. Turbulent patients, by definition, create a vicious internal cycle of projecting toxic mental conflict, reacting to it as if it is an outside force threatening them, and then creating more defensive projections to protect themselves.

In the Kleinian approach (Segal and Britton 1981), the understanding of projective identification has led to a greater attention to the interaction between analyst and patient. Historically, this has added to those sources of information already available for interpretative use such as the patient's verbal and nonverbal behavior. Now, interpretation can include the analyst's perception of himself via his patient, his own emotional experience of the session in the counter-transference, and both his and his patient's tendencies to action. Often, the core of the transference with such patients will be projective based phantasies that pull the analyst into very narrow roles the patient expects, desires, and fears. The case presented in this chapter illustrates many moments of this type of uncertainty and misstep on the analyst's part and the struggle to regain balance.

Slow to thaw patients such as the one followed in the clinical material struggle with enormous levels of anxiety concerning conflicts over love and hate as well as the psychological meaning of knowing more about themselves or their objects. For example, the patient in this chapter unconsciously felt knowing more about his mother and knowing more about his own feelings towards his mother was very dangerous and therefore to be denied, avoided, or eliminated.

In response to these internal threats regarding knowledge, love, and hate, these difficult patients tend to have excessive and destructive methods of projective identification, manic denial, and splitting that provides temporary psychic shelter or pathological retreats (Steiner 1993). These methods of relating and reacting create intense transference and counter-transference climates. Joseph (1978) has pointed out how the more the patient is using primitive defenses against anxiety the more the analyst is used by the patient unconsciously, which in turn means the more the analysis is a scene for action rather than understanding. I like to think that Joseph means this is a threat for both parties so the analyst must constantly be on watch for ways he and the patient may be trying to act out rather than understand, think, feel, and know. By working within the complete counter-transference (Waska 2011b) and the total transference situation (Joseph 1985), the analyst has a chance to not be overcome by the same demons the patient has succumbed to and gradually interpret the nature of the patient's unconscious conflicts. As a result, the patient has a new opportunity to possibly work with their paranoid and depressive visions of self and other and find some degree of emotional freedom and peace of mind.

Case material

F had seen me for nine years when he suddenly stopped attending. Now, this sudden termination was not entirely a shock. Throughout the length of the analytic treatment, F had often questioned "why I am still coming in here when I feel just fine". His "feeling fine" states were often fairly short lived followed by a return to a marked depression. By our working together, F would realize he was in a manic state of denial and begin to face a variety of feelings and conflicts that he felt less than fine about. But, at that point, he would feel anxious and claustrophobic about owning these less than perfect feelings and would project his critical judgments and controlling desires onto me. Then, he would struggle with "whether he really cared enough about all those issues to work on them", "was he just facing normal problems everyone has and therefore has no need for help", "was he just being bullied into staying when he really wanted to quit but felt guilty that he wasn't working hard enough", or "was he possibly hurting my feelings by stopping and leaving me hating him as a bad patient?". Along with these transference states, F had ongoing phantasies and conflicts about whether he needed me or not that came out in how he would "draw the line" by cutting down how often we met. So, we met three times a week, twice a week, or once a week depending on how F was able to tolerate feeling exposed and not in control. It was not my choice how the frequency changed, I had to go along with his anxiety and his controlling way of making sure he was in charge.

F was a 40-year-old homosexual accountant working for a law firm. When I first met with F, he engaged in rampant sexual activity, including live computer camera masturbation with strangers, random sexual "hookups" at bathhouses, and the use of online gay sex sites to meet random men several times a week. He would stay up until three in the morning so he would arrive to work exhausted and like an alcoholic, vow to not do that again until he rested, and then he went back to the same behavior.

Along with having this anonymous random sex several times a week, F was also prone to manic schedules of activity with friends and various social clubs. So, in any given week, he might be meeting friends for dinner and a show one night, going to a fundraiser the next night, and going out dancing another night. In-between, he would meet men at his place or their apartment for sex. This was all done in a very mechanical, greedy, or controlling manner where he simply pressed a button to get all his needs met regardless of who it was with. This was a symptom of how desperate and lonely F had been for most of his life.

Over the nine years we met, F often started to fall in love with one of these many men and became entangled a very complicated jungle of feelings in which he would be conflicted if they were "the right one" or "a big mistake due to their flaws". He would become caught up in all the pros and cons of why he should or why he should not plan on spending the rest of his life with them, picking them apart for fatal flaws or signs of perfection.

Just as F demanded so much from the world in these perverse ways, in the transference he often felt I could either magically cure him overnight or else I was bitterly disappointing him over and over. Likewise, he wanted me to see him as my favorite hardworking patient but worried I was sick of him and frustrated with his lack of progress. As a consequence, there were many periods of his on the couch analytic treatment in which F "didn't want to feel judged anymore, didn't want to feel pressured to change, and didn't like feeling as though I was thinking he should be working harder at his job and in therapy".

These persecutory (Klein 1946) transference feelings were part of a projective identification process in which F put his lifelong adherence to what he called "the rulebook" into me and then felt obligated to come up to my expectations. He thought I would be as demanding as he was.

It was not unusual for F to spend many sessions telling me about how other drivers on the road were rude and not paying proper attention, people at the grocery store were not respecting the lines at the cashier correctly, people's mode of dress was too informal, and manners were not being adhered to pretty much everywhere. These unrelenting sets of standards were something F collared others with but he himself felt most collared by. So, in the transference, he would put them on me by becoming impatient and irritated that we "hadn't cured him yet" and that "I hadn't told him the easy one-two-three way step to happiness yet". But, he also felt I was impatient and unhappy with his slow process and his constant complaining.

Also, F felt stuck and helpless in life without all those things others seemed to have such as relationships, money, importance, or attention. F wanted them but felt unable, unwilling, and unsure how to go about achieving them. He would bring up these feelings of frustration, dissatisfaction, and envy with predictable phrases such as, "Why doesn't a rich prince come along and take me away from all this? Other people seem to get lucky and have it so easy!" When I would bring up his obvious displeasure, sadness, or anger about this "lack of luck", F would not acknowledge it or own it. Instead, he felt I was "forcing my agenda" on him.

This persecutory guilt phantasy came up frequently in several situations. F had worked as an accountant for years and often was bored. He spent hours playing online bingo games. As a result, he felt guilty that he was being lazy and irresponsible. His company essentially wanted him to do two jobs because of their budget problems so he was overworked and also hated his assignments. When he tried to "do his job like I should and take care of business like they pay me to", F felt overwhelmed by the number of hours it took. When I would point out his displeasure, frustration, and his resulting sense of helpless acceptance about it, F would feel I was "wanting him to quit his job and do something better". He would become upset with me for not being ok with him as is. In other words, when I voiced the projection of his wish for more and his displeasure with what he had, he felt guilty and anxious and immediately denied that projection belonged to him. Instead, he tried to see himself as "normal" and me as wanting too much.

F said, "I don't like my job and I am fed up with it. I have been for years. But, the only other jobs out there are exactly the same so I should just accept what I have and realize I will be in this situation until I retire in twenty years". I replied, "You definitely don't sound happy about it when you say that. In fact, you sound a bit resentful". F would become even more anxious and angry with me and say, "You don't seem to ever be ok with someone not liking aspects of their job and having regular ups and downs. You want me to walk away and find something perfect. Well, that isn't out there!" I replied, "If I bring up my observations that you sometimes feel trapped, unhappy, or frustrated and try and explore those feelings with you, you immediately think I am demanding immediate change, some immediate action, or I will be disappointed with you".

F would agree in a concrete manner, agreeing that "I was being mean". But, then sometimes he was able to reflect on what I said. He said, "I think I see what you mean. If I look at my feelings I don't necessarily have to do something with them right then and there but I might feel better just talking about it". I replied, "Yes. And, you might figure out something you would like to do or not do as a result of talking about it. But, you get worried I see you as bad if you don't do something with your feelings".

F agreed in the concrete way again and said he does in fact think I am always pushing him to change and improve his life. I interpreted that this sense of demand and rush might be his own sense of expectation and his own desire for change that he struggles with. Here, I was interpreting the projective identification process he seemed so stuck in. I said he might be dealing with a feeling of either having to put up with things he does not like, or to having to take a scary, rushed, and dangerous plunge into the unknown. He may have a hard time finding some middle area. F calmed down when he heard this and said he "thought we might be on the same page after all".

The other way these transference feelings and phantasy conflicts would emerge was in his other relationships. On one hand, F craved a deep, committed relationship with someone who "could be his soul mate". He felt lonely and empty and wished for "that special someone". However, whenever I drew attention to this, whether externally or in the transference, and tried to explore his deep despair followed by his sense of hopelessness about it, F would feel I "was pressuring him to date, pushing him to find a boyfriend, and expecting him to find a partner right away".

Then, F would tell me he "didn't see what was wrong with just accepting that he would never find that special someone but that he could have a fine time anyway". So, there was this quick retreat from need and unhappiness when he had to own and feel those conflicts. There was a rapid dive into justification, denial, and pseudo-acceptance of his plight. Then, if I questioned this "normal level of frustration in life", he felt I was being hyper-critical and expecting too much. F tried to be in control and to not ever have to see himself as failing or lacking. Indeed, this was one interpretation I made that seemed to help. He defined himself as either reaching the ultimate level of love, money, and achievement or he was trapped in shameful failure and loneliness. So, then to recapture his sense of control and not wanting to have to experience the envy he had about all the other people he pictured who had reached these pots of gold, F had to manically build his fortress of normality and defend it with everything he had.

These cycles of emotional hunger and resentment followed by denial, justification, and defensive self-assurance were part of F's struggle with the death instinct and chronic feelings of envy (Klein 1957) for what others seemed to possess that he was never allowed to have. So, he had to deny ever needing it and then he clung to his phantasy of feeling fine with what he does have. Breaking "the rules" or wanting more in life was a constant conflict involving feeling angry and deprived versus feeling guilty, hopeless, and having to accept what is.

When I first met F, he was always trying to adhere to "the right way" of doing things but felt he was often failing. He felt guilty for having a promiscuous sex life but was quick to justify it and tell me how "he was simply honoring his sexual nature". While F was prone to crippling bouts of depression as well as intense anxiety, he had never really seen these feelings as part of any unconscious conflict. He had been in the hospital and had numerous emergency room visits for depression, panic attacks, and thoughts of suicide. The few times over the last decade he had tried to stop taking his psychiatric medication, he experienced immediate and extreme relapses into depression. So, he considered his depressive problems merely a "chemical imbalance" that was corrected with medication.

As we went along in the analytic treatment, F revealed elements of his early childhood that seemed to have shaped his current psychological views of self and other as well as contributed to his depressive problems. Growing up, F reported his father as a "nice man who worked all the time to support the family. He had to travel a lot for his job so he was never home. When he was home, he was always quiet and went along with what mother said". This memory was often played out in the transference. I interpreted that F was both himself as a child combined with his passive dominated father and I was the more pushy, dominating, and unsatisfied mother that left everyone feeling pressured and controlled. This line of interpretation was only possible during the last few years of treatment when F did not hold his mother up on such an idealized standard where she did no wrong.

During the first few years of analytic work, F described his mother as "perfect in every way. She was the most dedicated mother one could have and really matched the classic picture of a 1950s mom baking cookies for all the kids and taking care of everything in the house". Over the course of several years, I had the impression from F's recollections that he remembered a mother who left him feeling a mixture of love and upset, gratitude and resentment. But, any time I brought up my observation that he might have mixed feelings towards his mother, F was steadfastly against it and "felt I was trying to make him think negatively about his childhood when everything was just fine".

So, here was another way that my curiosity and inquiry was experienced as persecutory and damaging. I think a projective identification process was at work in which F deposited his dangerous feelings of unrest, unhappiness, and desire concerning his mother's care into me and maintained a conflict free zone of idealization. Over time, I also interpreted that F strived to keep himself to that standard of perfection, always going by the rules, watching his manners, and trying to please others. However, at the end of the day, this left him feeling alone, empty, and often resentful and envious of all those who did not have to abide by these strict standards.

On one hand, F would quickly debate me on this, saying, "There is nothing wrong with being on time, holding the door for others, and saying yes to any request for help from others". On the other hand, F was able to acknowledge his envy and sad helplessness when he watched others enjoy relationships while he faced the weekends without a date and lived alone. But, soon after becoming vulnerable with me and sharing this unhappiness with me, F quickly went back to using his intellectual defenses and denial to tell me that he was very busy most of the time going to functions with friends and "practically didn't have time to be dating".

F's view of his mother was so hardened and one dimensional that it seemed to rule his internal life and constrict his ability to consider anything about his mother outside the realm of his idealized, always good intentioned view of her. So, any observation, speculation, or interpretation on my part of any type of irritation, anger, or general unhappiness inside of F directed at mother was met with an immediate denial and a doubling of efforts to emphasize how he "understood" and "accepted whatever had happened with his mother without any sense of ill will".

However, in the fourth year of analytic treatment, we were talking about a memory he had of his childhood and F suddenly jerked his body on the couch and froze in silence. After a bit, he said, "I have always thought of my mother as the most perfect, nice, and caring person possible. She was always a hard worker and never made father feel bad or never was mean to any of her kids. If she ever was mean, I am sure it was because we did something to provoke her and test her. But, otherwise, she was the sweetest person possible. But, now as we are talking about this time when I came home covered in mud and she yelled at me, slapped me, and made my nose bleed, I had the idea that maybe she wasn't the perfect mother. Maybe, she might have had some flaws. This thought has created the strangest sensation throughout my entire body. I feel like some sort of electrical jolt just ran through me the minute I questioned my mother's true nature. This is really weird!"

Over the next few years, F began to think of his mother as someone more human, with both flaws and positive attributes. He began to remember numerous incidents in which his mother was obviously overworked, tired, and angry and then took it out on her kids. These memories revealed F's hurt and angry feelings over being subjected to his mother's temper and mood swings. Now, in his mind, she was not just wonderful and loving, but also strict, controlling, and demanding of everyone around him. She had a "rulebook" that she felt very righteous about and expected others to follow. I pointed out that F had followed mother's footsteps in many of these traits with his own "rulebook" that he and others had to obey.

Over time, these rulebook ways of experiencing life emerged in the transference. F was very diligent, loyal, and punctual in his appointments with me, his payments to me, and his overall way of relating to me. When I tried to explore this, he told me it was "simply polite to be on time and pay for services rendered". However, he was also overwhelmed on occasion with phantasies and feelings of being chained to the treatment, obligated to have "something to talk about", and pressured to "be changing his life and working on things even if he didn't see anything wrong with his life". F would lapse into intense modes of feeling bullied by me or by his own guilt of "not wanting to be a bad patient and not wanting to look like he wasn't motivated".

F thought I wanted him to be a certain way or to change certain things and then felt pushed to take action on those matters or to be talking about them even if he felt they were not a problem. Over time, I interpreted that there was a link between the way he tried so hard to be loyal, diligent, and punctual with me, always playing by the rulebook, and this sense of feeling chained down and obligated to please me at all times. I also noted that he grew up following mother's rulebook but now he had written his own rulebook and seemed to be a prisoner of it. F would relax a bit when I made these observations. My interpretations seemed to reduce his anxiety and guilt long enough for him to begin to reflect and think about these ideas instead of feel a victim to them.

Over the course of our nine years of analytic work together, F made many changes in his life, both internal and external. As a result of our explorations, F felt much less depressed and anxious. When I met him, he felt suicidal much of the time. He was on high doses of several antidepressant medications and an anti-anxiety medication. There were many days when he would barely be able to get out of bed, frequently failed to go to work, and spent the day in bed. As part of this depressive cycle, F would overeat and became quite overweight. In addition, he was out of shape and rarely worked out. Life was meaningless and hopeless for him.

Because of his gradual analytic progress, when F stopped treatment he was no longer on any medication and rarely felt depressed or anxious. After the first few years of treatment, he would feel fine for the most part but quickly crumbled back into a black depression if certain disappointments occurred such as a relationship not working out or a frustration at work. Now, after nine years of treatment he was able to weather these choppy waters without falling apart. His remaining problem is a fundamental stance of denial and manic self-sufficiency that surfaces when he realizes he feels stuck, unwanted, or unhappy in some way. In other words, wanting more still brings about a sense of hurting mother and being punished for violating the rulebook by being greedy or envious. Of course, when he denies those desires, he only ends up with more envy, guilt, and persecutory anxiety.

Rather than face the initial feelings of helplessness, difference, or anger, he is quick to tell himself and to tell me, "I am fine with it. Life is full of ups and downs and I am just accepting that I can't have everything". While this sounds fine, it is a thin veneer that hides his anxious discomfort underneath, the unhappiness that would be against the rulebook of being a good citizen, a good Christian, and a good son. Now, this global bubble of manic denial is certainly an improvement over the debilitating depression that used to result. But, it still is an impairment to F's full enjoyment of life and his ability to rely on himself and others for security rather than feel despair and envy, followed by a defense of false optimism and manic undoing. For F, the grief, mourning, and the ownership of healthy desire that are part of the depressive position (Klein 1935, 1940) remain an uncomfortable and unreached area of development.

Over the course of treatment, F changed much about his approach to coping with his internal emptiness. When I first met him, he was having random sex with several men each week and staying up until the wee hours searching the Internet for new sex partners. He would be exhausted the next day but would manage to wake up enough to go at it again the next day. When I tried to investigate this destructive behavior he would try to pass it off as "just an ordinary gay lifestyle". But, over time, we were able to see how it was a desperate effort at finding control over his internal hopelessness, loneliness, and lack of contentment. He was constantly searching for "the one" and hoped to find the "perfect soul mate to spend his life with".

For the most part, F engaged in safe sex, but on occasion when he felt he had met "Mr. Right", he desired to be in an instant merger or bond with them and "forgot" to engage in safe sex. Our exploration of his demand and despair to find "the one" had resulted in less anxiety, less desperate searching, and a greater sense of self that he could rely on instead. Therefore, he was less prone to this type of acting out.

In the process of exploring this acting out, we examined his life long search for an ideal maternal object to merge with and give himself over to completely. However due to very complicated core sadomasochistic feelings this often resulted in him feeling victimized, ignored, or unloved by that object or him devaluing and rejecting that object. In his acting out, this meant that he frequently exposed himself to a deadly and punishing internal object and externally it meant that he put himself at risk in his sexual relationships. Unfortunately, in the last year of treatment, one of these times of acting out resulted in F being diagnosed with HIV.

Parallel to this compulsive, desperate sexual acting out, for the first four years of treatment there was a similar acting out in which F compulsively shopped and went into great debt. He bought all kinds of things including furniture, art, trips, and beauty supplies. But, mostly, F spent a great deal of time and money buying clothes. He often would buy ten shirts at a time and then feel guilty and stupid later. He would return most of them but kept a few. As we began to understand this pattern as a way to hide his loneliness and anxiety and as a way to fill an internal void, he stopped the manic, compulsive shopping and started to consider each of his purchases more. For a while, he would tell me "it was excruciating to see something on sale and tell myself no to buying it". As mentioned before, part of this had to do with his intense envy for "all that everyone else has. They have more money to spend as they please and will be able to retire while I will still have to work and save". But, after a while, F was able to remind himself that he "already had a similar pair of pants and even if it was on sale he would be going into debt to buy it".

So, I interpreted that to not freely feed at the breast of excess was at first painful and felt like a cruel punishment. He could not have the wonderful fusion with perfection and the bliss of having what he wanted. But gradually F came to realize he was still secure and full from his last feed and did not need anything more. Bit by bit, F was more accepting of his current station in life without feeling frozen in failure. He saw he could work towards a promotion at work or avoid increasing his debt by not overspending but still buy things when he really needed them. In these ways, he was in fact more in line with those others that he envied so much. This was more of a genuine acceptance and contentment than the other state of false contentment or bravado he usually showed about his job or being single.

In the last few years of treatment, when I inquired about the details of his feelings, it was much easier for F simply to share them with me. This was because he felt much more stable and genuine internally and trusted that I would not see him as a sinner, a lazy patient not doing my bidding, or a greedy bad boy breaking the rules. However, there were still many moments when he became defensive, guilty, and anxious and resorted to his more fragile, thin, manic conviction that "everything is fine". During those moments, F would say, "Everything is just fine and I am ok with accepting what I have. Sure, I would like to live on my own desert island with lots of money instead, but who wouldn't? I don't see why you keep asking me about it. I am fine. Yes, my job isn't perfect and I would like to finally find someone to be in love with but that just isn't going to change and I am fine with that. It is normal to not like certain things and I don't know why you can't see that!"

F would be very worked up and irritated by the end of this proclamation. He would be quite agitated as he felt I was interrogating him about why he was not going to do something to change his problems. This debate could go on for weeks until we worked through these phantasies and he was able to see that I wasn't forcing him "to reach for perfection" but that he was projecting his unhappiness or frustrations into me and then claiming everything was just fine.

F also shifted his formerly rigid and strict way of wanting others to do things his way. When driving, he used to feel that everyone on the road was "inconsiderate, rude, and impatient". He would become very frustrated and "think bad things about all the other drivers who obviously didn't pay attention to the street signs and the stop signs". Now, F was more tolerant of others and gradually realized with our exploration that it was he who was often the impatient driver, demanding everyone else move out of his way and drive at his speed. However, this more accepting stance would still break down as he felt the anxiety of owning these more outright aggressive and demanding aspects of himself. F would end up telling me that people "should pay more attention to the road and spend less time on their phone. There are rules to follow and those rules are there for a reason". But, overall, he was able to maintain a less rigorous and less strict view of others and this made his world a bit more enjoyable and less constricting.

Another area that improved over time with F was his intense quest for "a soul mate". For the first five or six years, he was able to fend this desire off when I inquired about it by telling me he was only after sex and a good time. However, every once in a while, one of his random sex partners showed F some tenderness or kind words. F would start to imagine how wonderful it would be to date this person, move in with them, and live with them for the rest of his life. F would become excited and enchanted with every last detail of what that person said and did and how his wonderful life with them would be in the future. The more this intense fusion and relational emersion took place in his mind, the more claustrophobic he became. In other words, the more he mentally drew the person inside of himself, initially he felt whole, safe, and satisfied. But, very soon, F was so consuming and controlling of that person that he was a casualty of his own excessive projective identification mechanism. He felt taken over and intruded upon.

In the counter-transference, I noticed myself having a variety of reactions and feelings to F's transference states. There were predicable and familiar transference cycles in which F would alternate in seeing me as ideal and then as failing him. He would see me as a magical chance at radical positive change and later feel I was an obligation he was burdened by. And, F felt pressured to please me by seeing me even when he thought our work was useless or "something that forced him to look at things he would rather not have to deal with". These states of mind created intrapsychic and interpersonal patterns that invited me or pulled me to be a certain way or to feel a certain way (Joseph 1985). So, F would see me as "a real help and a new way of looking at things", "a guiding light", and "a very important friend who helped him grow and change, someone who cares and listens". He told me he really looked forward to seeing me and that he was "very grateful for my help and patience".

I noticed I felt secure and content in how F seemed to be attached to me but I also felt there was a sort of static, false, concrete, and deadened quality to those same moments, as if no life was present in the room. He talked a great deal and told me many details of work and activities, but something felt dead or missing. I believe this was a counter-transference experience engendered by his projective identification process of putting his own lifeless state into me, a state of mind in which he controlled his objects by staying distant and perhaps repeating what he felt was his mother's controlling and emotionally restricting ways with him in childhood.

F also had a pattern of telling me how he dreaded our meetings and felt trapped by them. He said he felt "obligated without any real sense of interest or reward". I interpreted this as part of his narcissistic demand for instant gratification and immediate answers without having to feel or do anything. With this aspect of his transference, I often felt my own sense of dread, anger, and defiance, a reaction to feeling trapped by his demands and complaints. I felt a dread of how in any given session, he might fill the entire time with his "questions of what he is really getting out of it, never getting any input on what to do, constantly wondering why he should continue, if he isn't really just wasting his time, and how it would be so much nicer to simply go home and relax than have to drive all the way to my office and dwell on all this stuff without any real outcome". F would sometimes add that he resented feeling "he had to come to please me and do his duty". Much of the time, he would pester me with questions about "What should I do?", "How can we fix this right away?", and "I want you to tell me what to do so I don't feel this anymore". When I would say, "You want me to hand over the magic cure without you having to do anything. I am your magic pill", he would say, "Yes. Are you going to fix me today?"

As a result of all this sandpaper like transference, I often felt irritated or fed up and wanted to tell F off by saying, "Fine. If you don't like it then stop complaining and get out. Either participate or leave. If I am so worthless then find someone else but stop bothering me". This counter-transference frustration and desire to retaliate alerted me to the way F acted very passive with me and his other objects but was actually constantly demanding they give him more and more. When he felt they did not deliver, he wanted to throw them away. But, he often also felt scared and guilty about those strong feelings so he adopted a more masochistic profile to tolerate and deny his narcissistic hunger. But in the meantime, he still stewed in his envious juices for the ideal object that would provide more, better, and quicker. F would then try to either intellectualize those feelings, neutralize them, or eliminate them by projecting them into the object. So, then his objects carried out his dirty work and were filled with these unacceptable states of mind that he could deny and feel above.

This ongoing pattern of manic bliss and magical merger with the ideal object followed by claustrophobic entrapment and disappointment occurred in the transference as well as his external life. Not so long after telling me how the latest person he had dated seemed so perfect and how they could "easily spend every waking moment together", F would start to tell me how he was worried they did not like the same music, they lived too far apart, they had different political views, and they made different salaries. The list became so big that he would start to see the relationship as doomed. Meanwhile, it was unclear if the other man was actually even interested in dating F. In fact, what often happened was that the other man never returned F's calls or told him he just wanted a "sex buddy".

At first, F would feel emotionally jarred or terribly rejected. But, very quickly, he tried to regain control by telling me, "It doesn't matter really. I don't think it would have worked out anyway. We didn't have much in common". So, over time, F became less "star struck" in these ways but still had a very difficult time exploring the underlying loneliness and desperation that he felt for a "soul mate". Using his manic and narcissistic defenses, F instead withdrew and stopped looking for someone special. He gradually tried to convince me and himself that he did not really need anyone. When F relied on this defensive retreat, he became less and less interested in sex and essentially gave up on finding love.

When F developed HIV, this intensified. He decided no one would ever want to be with him so he resigned himself to be single forever and "just accept that. Since I know I would never want to be with someone like me, I know no one else would want to be with me either". So, F decided he was once again unlovable according to his standards and his rulebook.

However, by my continuing to explore this psychological barbed wire stance, over time F did decide to go on several dates and did end up having sex with a few of the men he met. I interpreted that he was allowing himself to be lovable to the object even though the rulebook said otherwise. I interpreted that perhaps he wanted to rewrite the rulebook even though he idealized it. F said, "Maybe a couple of pages".

However, overall, F took the position that the love and sex area of his life was now closed and he tried to be content with just doing activities with friends and having occasional sex with random partners he found online. When I brought up this resignation, F would become agitated and feel I was pushing him to change something "he already felt fine about". So, here I came up against the resistance of "I have changed to the point I want to and I don't want to face anything else. I am fine as is!"

F thought of himself as a "plague victim with AIDS that no one would want to touch". So, he was amazed that others would want to have anything to do with him. I interpreted this to be a reflection of his anger and disgust with himself. This included his analyst in the transference. He thought I must think he is "so ignorant and foolish to have done something like that". So, we explored these feelings of having been "so stupid" and "not using common sense". I interpreted that he was sure we all agreed with his punitive view of himself and hence did not want anything to do with someone so "stupid" and "disgusting". I interpreted that he had a hard time allowing me to be a compassionate person who was trying to understand him and instead put his rulebook between us, making it hard to have contact.

F sometimes was lost in his concrete, rigid, black and white thinking and other times he was able to see past this cruel vision and consider a more loving and curious view of himself and of us together. The concrete thinking was F's lack of as-if symbolism, broken by excessive projection, in which he was essentially saying, "Well, yes! I think you are right about my stupidity. I am sure you do see me as a total loser that way". Steiner (1989) has noted that borderline patients slip out of the symbolic ability to think or communicate rather easily and when they make gains in this area it is fragile.

F ended analytic treatment with a much more balanced view of himself, of me, of others, and of his mother. He still was severe in his judgments and confined to his rulebook in many ways, but much has shifted in nine years. Now, when thinking of his mother, he allows himself to see her in a more realistic and human way, with faults and flaws as wells as wonderful qualities. Equally, he ended analytic treatment seeing himself, myself, and others in less of a punitive, demanding, and exacting light. Since his phantasies of self and other were less cut-throat and persecutory, his projections onto his objects rendered them less persecutory.

In the end, after nine years of analytic work, F still was sure I might be unhappy unless he "did it my way". Unless he quit his job and found something better, unless he started dating and working to find his soul mate, unless he worked hard at feeling more confident, and unless he came to see me several times a week "forever", I was disapproving of him. He could allow for some degree of reflection that these were his remaining rules from mother's rulebook and that I might simply be curious about his feelings in these areas of continued conflict and discontent. He could accept that "I simply wanted to know more about his feelings". But, his acceptance was thin and quickly crumbled as he talked about it. He assured me he "was fine and would contact me in the future if he needed it" but that "for now he was done and was living a life he was happy with". In the counter-transference, I had to accept this as is. This was my struggle to stay in the depressive position and grieve what I could not have and what I did not have without having to deny it or force it upon F. I could not make him want more and I could not make him be more curious about his current state of acceptance. How much was genuine and how much was a false, defensive, and envious retreat remains an unfinished question for both of us.

Discussion

It is not unusual for turbulent patients like F to terminate abruptly with many tense standoffs along the way. In this sense, I think of treatment with such individuals as a series of small, ongoing negative therapeutic reactions in which the patient's need to control and feel superior is played out through projective identification cycles (Rosenfeld 1975). These create a sense of persecution in the patient and a sense of frustration and anxiety in the analyst. To the extent that the analyst succeeds in modifying the patient's narcissistic control, contact is made with a dependent part of the patient. Then, there can be a gradual working through of the raw and unprotected feelings and the core phantasies of loss, abandonment, and neglect. However, once the patient is in touch with this current state of psychic breakdown, they quickly return to the negative therapeutic state as protection against emerging feelings of dependent vulnerability and helplessness. So, they are slow to thaw and quickly return to a frozen emotional state if threatened.

Daniel (1992) notes that from her work with young children, Klein had found the rich, imaginative world of unconscious phantasy peopled with internal objects. These internal objects were distinct from the actual parental objects, although in interaction with and influenced by them. Daniel (1992) reminds us that for Klein, this world of inner phantasy objects was alive and actively determined the transference. This meant it can be modified by interpretation.

Klein found that the primitive superego is extremely harsh and cruel, but she also found that its strength could be reduced by interpretations, particularly of the underlying anxiety and guilt. This was the ongoing effort with F that was sometimes successful and sometimes blocked by the harsh and cruel aspects of F's superego. His superego was partly his internalization of some of his mother's attributes that he distorted and shifted in parallel with his own love, hate, and quest for knowledge.

Etchegoyen (1991) notes that the Kleinian approach sees transference as the externalization of current internal phantasies regarding self and object, not just a recycling of past object relational conflicts. While Kleinian theory sees integration in the paranoid-schizoid mode as the gradual blending, tolerance, and accepting of the good, giving object and the contented and satisfied self with the frustrating, withholding, or hurtful object and the frustrated anxious, or injured self, some of our patients such as F have not found their footing in this more stable emotional plane. This makes the transition into the depressive mode much harder and fragmented. Thus, for F, acceptance of himself as living in the full spectrum of being hurtful, giving, sadistic, and guilty towards an injured, grateful, betrayed, and repairable object was the developmental challenge.

F is an example of how some patients attempt to take on this psychological advancement into the depressive position as a defensive stance of pseudo maturity. They claim to themselves and to the analyst through their actions and words to have this broad view of self and other, but it is false and brittle, easily crumbling. This was the case with F, in the beginning of his analytic treatment but also somewhat at the end.

When these types of more hard to reach patients operate within the proximity of the depressive position, their fear of disturbing the object with their own displeasure, hunger, or identity is so great that it must be denied in a more desperate and manic method such as F illustrated, and when their defensive idealization of the object breaks down, the despair of no object/no self is extreme, fueling the overwhelming and crippling depression that F suffered from. In order to avoid that, he had to engage in manic cycles of sex, shopping, and exaggerated optimism.

The classical Kleinian method of interpretation consists of the analyst attending to anxiety whenever it reaches a critical stage in the patient, whenever it becomes overwhelming to the patient with either paranoid or depressive conflict. At that point, it is important to offer interpretations of the phantasy and/or transference state that brought that anxiety into its critical level. Here, Melanie Klein is a true follower of Freud's quest to make the unconscious processes conscious and understandable to the patient.

Contemporary Kleinians, particularly those who side with the technical direction of Hanna Segal, see a complete interpretation as eventually linking the past, the present, and the here-and-now transference state. With F, I attempted to interpret the difficulties he had facing the lack of a nourishing, available mother figure in his early life and his avoidance of anger and deprivation by substituting an ideal and perfect, by the book, mother in his mind. He avoided being an angry, lonely, and desperate little boy by remembering his mother as a classically available "leave it to Beaver" mother. I interpreted how this paralleled his present life struggles and his often rule bound, striving for ideal perfection way of relating to himself and others as well as his way of relating to me and the treatment.

As Bion (1962a) notes, when the infant or adult feels overwhelmed by deprivation and envy for the better, available breast but must cling to something less satisfying for security and nourishment, the fragile ego relies on enforced splitting. Bion explains this as a controlled, defensive process in which the patient allows for the contact, nourishment, or interpretive connection with the analyst, but denies the emotional experiences of it. Symbolism is crippled and a voracious but always unsatisfied experience emerges. As in F's manic patterns, the thing, the sex act, the shopping spree, or the quest for immediate "progress" in treatment all become sterile goals but with no emotional value attached. So, there is never a sense of being filled up and content.

Etchegoyen (1991) notes that we do not try to eliminate our patient's anxiety and guilt. But, over time, through assisting them to understand, own, and learn from their internal experiences, the patient can come to reduce, face, and manage these experiences. F demonstrated how some more difficult to reach patients feel this invitation to better know themselves and their objects as very dangerous. They feel as though the analyst is taking away something important, their control and sense of things, and instead introducing something threatening, unknown, and out of their control.

Regardless of the turbulent and faltering nature of some of our more difficult analytic cases, I am advocating focusing on Freud and Melanie Klein's clinical discoveries: the understanding and working through of unconscious phantasy and the warded off object relational conflict. In this view, consistent exploration of transference and phantasy defines the goal and the modality. Rather than frequency, use of couch, duration of treatment, or the type of termination, the working through of unconscious conflict and defenses, created by core object relational phantasies, becomes the bedrock of what constitutes helpful and successful psychoanalysis.

Many clinicians have extended Klein's (1946) intrapsychic concept of projective identification to include the interpersonal and interactional aspects of the analytic situation. Joseph (1988) and many other contemporary Kleinians have noted the patient's unconscious ability to stimulate and provoke the analyst to pair up with the specific object relational phantasy embedded in their projective identification process. I have provided examples of this with my work with F. My moments of counter-transference enactment verified Spillius's (2007) observations that the technical relationship between counter-transference and projective identification is as important if not more important than the patient's verbal associations. Careful examination of my counter-transference feelings, thoughts, phantasies, desires, reactions, and acting out helped me to understand the motives (Rosenfeld 1971) F had in his use of projective identification, including communication, discharge, attack, plea for help, and invasion of the analyst's body and mind.

The key Kleinian concepts include the total transference, projective identification, the importance of counter-transference, psychic retreats, the container/contained function, enactment, splitting, the paranoid and depressive positions, unconscious phantasy, and the value of interpreting both anxiety and defense. In my work with F, most of these concepts came alive clinically. He retreated into manic optimism because of his sense of having no containment. But, after allowing some more depressive feelings such as anger, desire, and hunger, he felt a persecutory containment. Due to splitting and projection, he felt persecuted by my interest in his conflicts. So, I tried to consistently and gently explore and interpret his anxiety and defensive reaction to a set of intense core phantasies regarding envy, deprivation, and guilt.

Hinshelwood (2004) notes the three key elements of current Kleinian technique to be interpretive interventions aimed at modifying the source and nature of the patient's anxiety, an understanding of the inevitable enactments that emerge as projective identification based transference states infect and shape the analyst's counter-transference, and the effort between patient and analyst to jointly discover and create new knowledge about the patient's internal world and thus promote new ways of thinking and feeling. Of course, the more disturbed patient will react to knowledge and change as something dangerous to either self or other (Waska 2006) and show corresponding transference styles of perverse relating or destructive non-relating. The use of projective identification as a vehicle for the death instinct in evading or eliminating threatening knowledge and new ways of thinking or being can immobilize the treatment and erode effective analytic contact (Waska 2007, 2010a, 2010b). When a patient is addicted to such massive evacuative methods of projection, we see the patient ending up empty and robotic like, internally and interpersonally (Sweet 2010; Willams 2010).

For F, our focus on knowledge was extremely disturbing, whether it was prior knowledge that he denied or the gain of new knowledge about himself and his beloved objects. When he began to allow himself to know more about his mother, he was filled with guilt, anxiety, and fear. By our work together and my specific interpretations, he started to know more about himself and how he came to feel so depressed as a result of his own demanding rulebook. F came to know more about how he made others into critical and unloving bad objects through his projection of the rulebook. However, F would only allow and tolerate a certain amount of new knowledge about himself and the world and when it began to shift his psychic equilibrium (Feldman and Spillius 1989), he pushed back and rebuilt his psychic retreat. Ending analytic treatment was another such retreat into comfortable yet false optimism. We gained a great deal of ground and learned quite a bit. F decided to not allow any more learning or change at this point. Perhaps, at a later point in time, he will tear another page out of the rulebook but for now, we must allow for what is, what isn't, and the unknown of what could be.

We always seek to find a mind of our own (Caper 1998) in which we can still share and experience the patient's provoking and recruiting transference aspects of their internal phantasies. We may at any given time feel extra comfortable, unusually awkward, strangely excluded, lustfully pulled into, curiously greedy, carelessly uninterested, sadly unimportant, or outright angered by the different ways we are used or not used as a transference object.

11

PHANTASIES OF DREAD, DEMAND, AND DESIRE

In private practice, the contemporary analyst faces a great variety of patients in various degrees of primitive or neurotic functioning and acting out in often strong and persistent fashion. This can be taxing in the counter-transference, and enactments are common but hopefully helpful in learning about the patients' unconscious motivations. Projective identification is considered a cornerstone of the transference from the Kleinian perspective (Waska 2004, 2005, 2006) and with the more primitive, paranoid-schizoid (Klein 1946) or disorganized patient, this dynamic is often the primary vehicle for much of their inner life as opposed to more organized depressive (Klein 1935, 1940) conflicts that utilize higher level defenses.

When patients come to us in an intense state of anxiety and agitation and are in some type of external crisis as well as having lived a life of chaos and a childhood of unpredictable pain of one sort or another, it is very difficult to find a place of balance and clarity in the clinical situation. For some patients, such as the couple in the first case report, the intensity of their unconscious phantasy state is so disorganized and savagely in motion that it seems only a matter of time before all breaks down and the treatment comes to a fiery end with archaic conflicts being acted out without any insight being allowed or endured. This is a common but very confusing and frustrating clinical scenario that analysts encounter in their day-to-day practice (Waska 2007).

For other individuals, such as the patient in the second case report, there can be a significant amount of insight and some degree both of internal and of external change or shift. However, that growth or change is not well rooted and can easily fall apart or become stagnant. The intensity with which the patient's psychological sands shift can be reduced, but that is not always a lasting change.

The second case report shows how the splitting process and pathological projective identification processes can constantly undermine the analytic work and ultimately and suddenly derail the entire treatment process. The conflicts with loss and abandonment create severe persecutory and depressive phantasies that are acted out in the transference (Waska 2010c, 2010d, 2011a) and foster pathological organizations (Rosenfeld 1987; Steiner 1993) or psychic foxholes

169

(Waska 2010a, 2010b) from which the patient attempts to master and defend their chaotic inner world.

With some of these difficult cases, there cannot be much else done. Perhaps another analyst could have done a bit more or found a way to engage the patient for a while longer, but I believe these sorts of ticking bombs and unraveling balls of knotted string are unavoidable. We must simply hang in there, learn what we can along the way, and do our best to impart what we see and feel to the patient in a manner that is therapeutic (Waska 2011b).

In the two cases presented, the degree of pathological projective identification being employed to manage unbearable primitive internal conflicts led to very difficult therapeutic standoffs. Initial attempts to offer therapeutic containment were often either thwarted by the patients or abused and overused. But, once the patients began a projective process and once the transference was primarily centered around projective identification based cycles of internal phantasy, they were extremely reluctant to give up the container aspect of the analyst.

More turbulent patients resist the giving up, the working through, and the taking back of their projective worlds, often made up of sadomasochistic role reversals. Rather than experience the grief and loss of letting go of often lifelong manic and omnipotent projections, they would rather continue to act out their phantasies and avoid the pain of a new reality.

CASE MATERIAL 1

This case has been previously described in "Early Phase Kleinian Couples Treatment With Turbulent Partners" in Chapter 7 (pages 107–111).

Discussion

Rosenfeld (1987) has been instrumental in discovering and describing the different manifestations of projective identification. He has outlined how it may be an instrument of communication for some patients. For others, it is a defensive mechanism in which they rid themselves of unwanted feelings and aspects of their personality.

Rosenfeld describes a third method of projective identification used by more disturbed patients in which they force themselves into the analyst in phantasy and feel they have omnipotent control over their object but in doing so feel a loss of self from this fusion, dependence, and surrender into the analyst. They panic and deploy intense defensive reactions involving attack, retreat, and manic independence.

Here, in this cycle of evacuation and annihilation, the purpose of the projection is not to share unbearable unconscious experiences but to deny them and place them permanently into the analyst. This creates a transference in which the patient presents as quite narcissistic, aloof, and unreachable and as a result of projective identification, the patient often feels the analyst is being that way as well. This was the case with A.

In discussing the value of here-and-now interpretations, Arundale (2011) notes how the patient's internal objects, which are what we encounter in the transference, contain the essence of all historical past and ancient conflict. Therefore, interpretations that involve the past need to be made after more in the moment transference work has taken place. In the case of A and B, their acting out was so intense and deliberate that there could be no precise fix made on the source of these conflicts and the past nature of their phantasies and distorted histories. I believe even the here-and-now transference interpretations with them could offer only meager containment and understanding of the present or past internal anxieties due to the enormous degree of evacuative projective mechanisms they employed (Joseph 1987).

However, after the combative transference that they both presented with me and to each other and the modest in-the-moment work we manage, we were led to important historical material about B that seemed to influence the here and now.

In discussing Betty Joseph's (1985, 1989) work, Arundale (2011) points out how essential it is for the patient to eventually find or re-find the good object in order to mitigate the pangs of either persecutory or depressive anxiety. However the patient's hostile, envious, or defensive phantasies can kill off, prevent, or neutralize any evidence of a good object that could be sustaining and healing. In the case of A and B, there were fleeting moments in which they seemed to recall, allow, or accept the other as a good object they could depend on and trust but this in turn seemed to bring on such renewed anxiety, resentment, and aggression that a perpetual battle was all that was possible.

This became true in the transference as well. I could be seen only in fleeting glimpses as a possible helper or potential aid to understanding and change. This was quickly contaminated by their projected hostility, blame, and constant demand for something other than what the object was offering. The husband, and then both of them as a unified blaming team, came to see me, almost from the first session, as a withholding, unhelpful, and unnecessary person in their lives who should be used up and gotten rid of.

They emotionally climbed into me with their particular style of chaotic possessive projective identification. Once inside, they took what they could and then felt cheated and claustrophobic. Retreat and omnipotent rejection was the solution. For a moment, B was able to step out of this mutual mindset, which then caused A to fragment, escalate, and protest.

CASE MATERIAL 2

Mary came to me for help with her "job stress and her confusion with her boyfriend". Mary was a 30-year-old woman from a Latin American country.

Her family moved when she was three years old and she has been living in America ever since. Mary worked as a dentist for a clinic specializing in high end cosmetic dentistry and had been there for a few years after she left a non-profit agency where she was "happy but underpaid".

The first month of treatment, twice a week on the analytic couch, was taken up with her discussing her boyfriend and her confusion about their relationship. All her friends told her he was a "bad guy and was probably cheating on her". She thought it might be possible given how aloof and emotionally unavailable he seemed but she also thought he "was just going through a tough time". At times she literally begged him to talk to her but he was "too shut off to respond". This frustrating and barren type of relating had been going on for more than a year.

I explored her place in that frustration and over time we came to an understanding that she was trying to help him, fix him, and make him into the caring object she could be close to. I explored her desire to turn a cold stone into a loving source of security. In the process, we began to find out about other issues.

In the transference, Mary alternated between two ways of seeing me. She said, "I really looking forward to seeing you. I really need to be here. I need someone to talk to and confide in. My friends are always trying to tell me what to do and I know they mean well but I end up feeling like they are just telling me what they want. I need this kind of sanctuary for my mental health".

On the other hand, Mary told me, "I don't like the idea of being dependent on you and needing you. This doesn't feel comfortable. I am thinking of stopping and just trying to trust myself. After all, that is really what I need. I never have been able to figure things out for myself. So, maybe I need to just take the time to listen to myself and not rely on everyone else for everything. The more I come here the more dependent I feel and that can't be right. I should not have to go to someone every week to figure out how to live my life".

We began to investigate this quick switch view of myself as either trustworthy, warm, and someone to depend on or some cold stranger running a business, an outsider, and someone she was getting too dependent on. I pointed out how she seemed to feel safe and then unsafe with me, wanting my advice and support but then feeling like I might be "manipulating her" or "simply stringing her along for more cash". At some point in this exploration of her transference conflicts, she mentioned the parallel to "some feelings with my mother".

When I asked Mary for details, she began to share with me stories of her upbringing that we discussed over the next few months, along with other topics that emerged. Mary's parents divorced when she was four years old and Mary has never seen her father since then. She remembers her early years as "very strict and we did everything according to exactly what mother wanted".

Mary had one other sister and they both felt very "nervous around mother and tried to avoiding setting her off or starting up one of her moods".

When I asked about what this meant, Mary explained that when her mother became angry, which often was for no predictable reason, "there could be hell to pay". Mary's mother would slap them in the face, throw pots from the kitchen at them, hit them with wooden spoons from the kitchen, and "sometimes throw chairs at them". She would scream and tell them they were bad children who were never grateful enough.

When Mary was in her teens and early twenties, as well as just in the last few years, her mother could be just as explosive and abusive but the "moods" seemed to jell around specific topics. From what Mary told me, it was mostly around how Mary should live her life in terms of marriage and career. Her mother suggested, underlined, and often demanded Mary become a lawyer or doctor and marry a lawyer or doctor of her own ethnic background.

As Mary grew up, if her mother found out that she was dating a man who was not of the right ethnic background and/or not in the right college pursuing the right degree, her mother became violent and abusive. There were many stories of being slapped in the face, of her mother waving a knife around and yelling, and of various items being thrown and smashed against the wall.

When Mary went away to college and graduated as a dentist, her mother started telling her she needed to move back home and take care of her. This involved a great deal of guilt as well as more verbal intimidation. As a result, Mary felt extremely fragmented and confused. She felt guilty for wanting her own life and for leaving her mother behind in the process. Mary felt like she was making a big mistake not moving back home and caring for her mother, who was in fine health. She told me that she feared that if she did not do that then when she was "old and infirmed, no one would be there for her and she might die on the streets".

From the ways Mary talked about these issues, I interpreted another aspect of her thinking that was not being brought up. I interpreted that she might feel powerful and important to her mother if her mother seemed to need her so much and wanted to depend on her so much. I added that while this power might be inviting, it also seemed to be scary in that her mother depends on her so intensely.

Mary agreed with my comments and expanded on them by telling me about how her mother and her mother's sisters have always seen Mary as the authority when it comes to anything medical even though she was a dentist and not a physician. Her mother and Mary's aunt would often call her to consult about various medical issues. When a cousin was in the hospital for a serious condition, Mary flew out to be with her aunt and offered professional advice and medical opinion. In telling me about these matters, I noticed that Mary was only slightly able to reflect on them as being unrealistic or strange and for the most part was just conveying facts that she saw as normal. So, over time, this combination of sadomasochism, narcissism, omnipotent independence, and dread of deadly dependency emerged.

In the transference, I felt Mary alternated between intense dependency and passivity and a narcissistic distance in which she did not want my advice and almost resented the idea that she would need me or the support of her friends. When I made interpretations about these conflicts and phantasies, Mary tended to respond very concretely and then alternate between telling me she did need me or she did not need me. Here, I was working in the here-and-now clinical moment, staying with how she was using me as her object or locating me in her internal world.

Over the course of six months, there were several major external situations we followed and explored as they unfolded. As mentioned, she felt her boyfriend was someone who "eventually might learn to open up" so she kept hoping and trying to have a relationship with him. Interestingly, Mary told me that "every single one of my friends have told me he is bad news, that I could do way better, and that he is probably cheating on me". When her boyfriend announced he "didn't think things were working out" and moved out, Mary was stunned, depressed, and sad for several weeks. She was even more upset when she found out that he had moved in with another woman.

We talked for weeks about how she may have not wanted to see certain clues along the way and instead tried to make him into what she hoped for. But, ultimately, Mary was very disappointed to find out he was someone very different from what she had wanted. I interpreted that this might be part of a very complicated and confusing internal struggle that was a jumbled composite of her troubled relationship with mother. Mary seemed interested and we explored the possibilities. Here, I was linking the patient's phantasy conflicts with her internal experience in the past with her primary objects.

Rather quickly after this breakup, Mary started to date again. I had the feeling that this was somehow a mechanical move in which she was not really in touch with her feelings but more so just wanting to find someone to be with. I made such comments and she told me she was aware of that possibility and was "trying to stay aware of not just getting into a rebound relationship". After about a month of reporting good feelings and a "real attraction" to this man, he announced he was going to go on a two month backpack trip with another woman whom he said was "simply a good friend".

Mary went back and forth for weeks about feeling "uncertain, unsure, and uncomfortable about it" and also trying to trust him and take him at face value. In the counter-transference, I found myself thinking that she was being very naïve and was letting herself be taken advantage of. On one hand, I felt like telling her off as from her description it seemed obvious that this man was going off with another woman, especially since he never even asked Mary to go with him. When I brought that up, she told me, "Well, he knows I have a job so he knew I couldn't go for that long".

Based on these and others interactions, I began interpreting how she seemed to want me to be like the intervening caring and knowledgeable father she never had but she also did not want to believe that someone might be manipulating her and using her. She would have to separate or break up with that person if she let herself realize what she really felt and thought. There would be conflict, friction, separation, and she would be alone again.

I interpreted that she avoided that by letting me or friends be the messengers of bad news and then she could ignore us or sometimes heed our warning. She also controlled me by making me be the one who spoke up on these sensitive matters. Here, I was again establishing analytic contact by attending to the total transference situation occurring in the moment (Joseph 1985).

A similar situation emerged around Mary's job and her relationship with her boss, the manager for the large dental clinic she worked at. Mary had been there for more than a year and saw it as a place where she was doing good, helping people to "look better and feel more confident about themselves". The clinic specialized in implants, braces, and cosmetic dentistry. When Mary was in dental school, her friends warned her about the "cut throat corporate money making scams" that were prevalent in such clinics but when Mary interviewed there and the manager assured her that the clinic's mission was to "help people overcome their ailments and provide them with methods of reaching their optimal health", Mary felt encouraged and positive. But, after almost a year of working there, she began to receive critical feedback from her manager.

Evidently, Mary was spending as much time with each client as they needed and performing whatever procedure she thought was best for their dental health after extensive discussions with the client. There were many times in which she told the person they "may have heard great things about implants and how they were the superior product, but in fact they were often a much more expensive and unnecessary choice when other procedures were just as good in their particular case". Mary told me she prided herself on being completely honest and strictly adhering to what was best for each person's physical, emotional, and financial wellbeing. This struck me as being delivered, in the transference, in both a naïve and superior manner.

Her manager began sending her emails and having lengthy discussions with Mary about how she could be charging more by conducting multiple procedures, spending less time with each client, and suggesting costly implants more often. He did not really come right out and say all that, but it was very clear from how Mary described it that he was angry with her for not seeing the clinic as a money making business. He started asking her to "learn from some of the other dentists and how they have helped clients benefit from implants".

Mary told me implants were the "real money maker for the clinic" and she realized she was being seen as "a drag on their bottom line". Over the course of six months, this tense exchange between her manager and Mary continued. He started to ask her many personal questions about her dating life, her family, and how she spent her free time. Mary told me she felt he was "just trying to build a personal relationship" and that he "told me he has a personal style and considers all the dentists like family".

I felt he was being very manipulative, inappropriate, and creepy. But, Mary did not seem to see anything wrong. I asked her if she felt he was stepping over any limits and she said she "hadn't noticed anything". So, in the counter-transference, I felt scared for her and thought she was being naïve and making herself into a bendable toy for his bidding. I started to also feel irritated by the degree of blindness she showed in most of her relationships. But, I felt less cross when I thought about how she must have to go along with whatever mother says or wants to avoid severe consequences. As a result, I pondered how she allows or even orchestrates her boyfriends, bosses, and possibly her analyst to be another object that she depends on but eventually feels trapped by, controlled by, punished by, and abandoned by but she then tries to turn the tables and do the trapping, controlling, punishing, and rejecting herself.

Over the months, Mary became aware that the manager seemed to now be telling her off more openly, telling her she was not pulling her weight in the clinic, and that she was "a great disappointment and letdown to him on a personal level". Mary told me she thought she "might be fired if she didn't start selling lots more implants. I now realize this clinic is not about helping the customer, it is about selling the most expensive procedure we can as often as we can. And, since I don't believe in that and I don't do that, I am seen as a giant liability".

As she elaborated on these thoughts and feelings over the weeks, Mary became full of intense and contrary phantasies. She thought she should "stop being so much of a problem and start realizing that every job is not perfect. I do have to sell what makes money and in exchange I get a paycheck. I can't be so idealistic". Mary also said, "I am worried they will fire me and also sue me or somehow ruin my life going forward. I hear they could spy on me and if I ever say bad things about them they would make sure to ruin my career and tarnish my name".

These persecutory fears of retribution for her expression of opinion, difference, or separation were part of the paranoid conflicts Mary struggled with internally. I interpreted this to be a fear of separation from her mother, from me, from boyfriends, and from others in which she was convinced we would retaliate in dire ways. Mary could only barely consider this as a state of mind. She told me she felt this "to be true".

Mary also said, "I don't need them. I will find something that is better and suits me and is exactly what I want. I feel I can find something where I am helping people without taking advantage of them and where the management is only thinking of what people want and need and how to help them. I am going to find a new job that is all about the importance of service to those in need and if I have to take a pay cut that is fine. I also will no longer work all these ridiculous hours and never have time off. I plan on only working part time and spend my free time with friends, developing hobbies, and volunteering. I am going to start a wonderful new life!"

This ultra-positive stance went on for several weeks and developed into almost a manic idealism of what she could find. I interpreted it as a way she wanted to have an ideal loving mother connection with work instead of this current turncoat persecutory mother rejection with work. I also commented on how by relating in this naïve and idealistic manner with me and not stopping to have to face the anxiety and uncertainty of finding a new job, she positioned me into the stern or lecturing parent who had to remind her of the realities of the market place and how every job has its corporate money making side and she would have to find a way to fit into that.

With these interpretations and our ongoing exploration, Mary settled into a more realistic job search and started to put together a few interviews with companies that obviously were out to make a profit but also seemed genuinely geared towards customer service. In the end, she was recruited to go back to her old job at the non-profit dentistry school where she made far less money but had better hours and was able to work with a staff of dentists dedicated to helping those who needed care but were unable to afford regular clinics. And, they asked Mary to teach some classes, which she felt honored to and was excited about. The new job seemed like a thought out decision that might work out well.

Discussion

Steiner (2011b) has described how patients hang onto their defenses and avoid progress because they are reluctant to give up the illusion of protection those defenses provide. Mary felt comfortable with the control and power she found when her family seemed to need her and see her as smart and knowledgeable. When they relied on her, Mary seemed to quickly see that dependence as a way to turn the tables and be the leader and feel powerful. It also seemed to be a way of finally feeling valuable and to put her mother in her place by showing off that she was the leader now. However, since dependence, separation, and difference had such painful, aggressive, and frightening meanings to Mary, she quickly fell prey to such situations, quickly fled from them, or quickly tried to master them in passive or controlling ways that were intense and stormy.

Steiner (2011a) has pointed out that a patient's defenses are much harder to understand, unravel, and work with when they form a pathological organization, which in turn creates psychic retreats that the patient can turn to and lodge themselves within. While sheltered from their dreaded objects, the ego also is unable to clearly see their objects anymore so the initial paranoid or depressive distortion remains unmodified regardless of actual external changes. Mary remained in a passive, naïve, and persecutory state much of the time until she would switch roles and become controlling, very black or white, and either fuse or detach in a dramatic way.

Feldman (2009) has written about how no matter how we may try, driven by our counter-transference anxiety based enactments, to reassure, suggest, or force the patient to feel better, they may ultimately choose to feel in control, familiar and superior when up against a persecutory object by continuing with their ancient and time honored method of relating to their objects. This lets them maintain a climate of resentment, hostility, and omnipotence, which is felt to be more preferable and comfortable than facing the grief, anxiety, loss, dependence, and envy that lies underneath their armored walls.

For Mary, it was comfortable and familiar to be a naïve victim who was passive and under someone's thumb. But, this time worn position was also one of power, control, arrogance, and superiority. She was able to feel better than her manager and her company, she was able to devalue me and throw me away just as she felt her mother always threatened and did. She was able to enter as the smartest and most important when her family faced a health crisis. By not changing her victim↔tormentor roles and her idealizing↔abandoning/dismissing roles, Mary could stay in charge and not have to face a new way of living, relating, and feeling.

Many borderline or psychotic patients come into treatment with the common experience of chaotic childhoods and the subsequent chaotic internal feelings that leave them feeling fragmented, empty, and unbearably anxious. This was the case in both case reports. In thinking more about the nature of these patients' lives, their transference methods of relating to me, and the counter-transference they bring out, my sense is that in the paranoid-schizoid position their ego's anger, fragmenting loss, and emotional hunger bombard their good part-objects. These hostile feelings and actions occur when the ego feels threatened with separation from the ideal part-object.

If these part objects are not plentiful, cohesive, and able to withstand the ego's aggression, then they simultaneously perish and then return as bad objects seeking revenge. This is when the patient feels captured, pressured, and controlled and needs to sever the connection with the object or begin controlling it and attacking back. Possessing, feeling possessed, retreating, and feeling abandoned are all parts of an awful vicious cycle created by pathological projective identification.

This is the intrapsychic experience of loss and separation in the paranoid-schizoid experience (Klein 1946). Projective identification brings out the worst aspects of dependence and independence, need and self-direction. The hope of the depressive position (Klein 1935, 1940) shifts to dread and security turns into danger and loss. While feeling powerful in being able to refuse the help of the object, the ego is left to suffer feelings of abandonment and despair. If this grandiose stance is lifted, the fear becomes a phantasized punishment or retribution from the object or an abusive fusion and unending slavish dependence.

Speaking from a Kleinian perspective, Salzberger-Wittenberg (1970) notes how when patients reveal a deep unconscious demand to have the object be as they wish, ideal and always available, it is not just a power play based on greed or envy, but also a defense against catastrophic anxieties of abandonment and of a terrifying inner void. Klein (1963) shows how the feeling of being left alone is a phantasy of being left without the object but also of being left instead with terror, self-hatred, persecutory dread, helplessness, and the eternal unknown.

For my patients A and B, they were always demanding the guarantee of love and reassurance but always dreading the loss and robbery of that and the appearance of hatred and abandonment in exchange. For my patient Mary, she had experienced her mother in that way and felt a victim to that with her job, with boyfriends, and with me her analyst. But then, in her mind, Mary grabbed the power, turned the tables, and was that way with her family, her job, and her analyst.

The loss of the ideal object, the desired or demanded good object crushed by projective attacks, leaves the ego exposed to the worst of persecutory anxieties. From the Kleinian perspective, these include the phantasies of starvation, complete abandonment, no way of understanding or being understood, and the horror of internal fragmentation.

For Mary, this came out in her fears that, if she did not give up her career to move back and care for her mother, she would end up sick, alone, and a homeless invalid. In our exploration, we discovered this to be her awful punishment, her mother's dreadful revenge for Mary's not doing her bidding. Even when she was able to separate herself from her mother in her mind, Mary still was convinced it was only "a matter of time" before she would fall prey to some dire illness, be completely dependent and helpless, and have no one to help her or save her. To counter this awful fear, Mary at times became omnipotent and needed no one. That is how she ended her treatment as well. Also, Mary was worried about being fired from her job and never finding another one, leaving her alone and financially broken. During this time, she called for "emergency" sessions and looked forward to her time with me. As soon as she found a new job she quit her old one, she discarded me and her boss, feeling completely independent and confident in a manic and powerful manner.

Loss of and rejection from the much needed good object bring on feelings both of terror and of rage. A primitive and pathological cycle can begin in which the infant projects its desires and unhappiness into the object. If that object is already unavailable or is somehow unable to process those hostile projections, the infant feels rejected and subject to the fears of annihilation. The infant rages even more in desperation and frustration, ready to tear, eat, and swallow the object's valuable supplies. The ego phantasizes this increased hunger to have the potential to either destroy the object or cause the object to retaliate. Thus, the ego is again in a state of loss and persecution. In a vicious oral cycle, the ego feels the needed nutrient object is not only taken away leaving the ego starving, but the good object becomes spoiled food that attacks and poisons. Feelings of rage, abandonment, and betrayal flood the ego.

179

While these patients have usually suffered external trauma, neglect, and loss in their childhoods, my clinical focus is on the deeply imbedded and self-perpetuating nature of intra-psychic loss (Waska 2002). The lack of forgiveness, repair, restitution, or understanding in this dark internal world leaves the ego in perpetual danger and despair. This was certainly the internal perspective of both B and of Mary. In this paranoid-schizoid experience of primitive loss, desperately sought after idealized good objects turn into abandoning, attacking, bad objects. Loss of the good object brings with it annihilation of the self. This was the internal experience for A when B was not being his expected or demanded object.

Pathological reliance on projective identification, splitting, masochism, and manic defenses rigidify a cycle of idealization, greed, envy, loss, and persecution. If the analyst can focus on these elements in the transference and focus on the ongoing phantasies of idealization, oral aggression, loss, persecution, then these pathological cycles can gradually change. Loss can shift into mourning and fragmentation can transform into integration.

Each patient, regardless of diagnosis, engages the analyst in a specific manner, interpersonally and intra-psychically. This pattern of relating, the transference, is guided by the patient's unique set of internal object relations and his or her particular way of dealing with anxiety. Projective identification is, therefore, a defensive mechanism that colors each transference/counter-transference situation in a one-of-a-kind way.

The search for the specific meaning behind the patient's unconscious communications seems to be at the heart of the psychoanalytic process. Interpretations that are guided by the information transmitted in the process of projective identification can be more in-tune with the patient's internal world. This therapeutic process is very difficult and arduous to consolidate when the patient blocks any efforts towards analytic contact from the beginning and experiences analytic contact as a threat to either their pathological state of dependency or their pathological state of independence.

In redefining Bion's (1962a) concept of containment, Steiner (2011a) states that when the analyst can accept the patient's projections, refrain from excessive reaction or enactment, and come to a sufficient understanding of them to be able to make provisional interpretations regarding their meaning or communication motive, the patient can feel safer and less anxious.

However, some patients are so emotionally combative, defensive, and convinced that they face a wall of dismissal and rejection that they see their object as never wanting or willing to take in their projection. Some patients refuse the analyst entrance into their minds and then feel ignored or unloved. These rigid and extreme reactions to new, different, or healthier relationships make the process Steiner is describing impossible from the beginning.

If the patient allows the analyst to partake in their projections and the analyst is able and will to take them on, a process of initial containment can potentially take place. However, Steiner (2011a) notes, this does not facilitate a true therapeutic separation and disengagement with the phantasies that constitute the projective process.

The second level of containment is when the patient can separate from those projections by withdrawing them from the object of the analyst or other and begin the healing but painful process of mourning the loss of those phantasy states and accept the reality of self and other. Rather than just feeling understood, guided, or saved by the analyst, the patient must realize they are responsible for their own choices in life and must find their way day to day without the constant internal or external reassurance of the object.

True mourning involves the grief of accepting the deep dependence on the object that exists and then to give that up and face the uncertainty of individuation and the unknown aspects of life as a separate and independent entity who joins with others but still is different and unique and ultimately on their own.

In both clinical reports, with A and B as well as Mary, the patients were unable to face this second stage of containment, this transformational grief, mourning, and separation. Instead, they clung to omnipotent possession and manic independence. The analyst was unable to help them move past their rigid pathological organizations that formed a rigid defensive zone of superiority, blame, persecution, and panic. Their intense conflicts around dependence and independence as well as nurturing versus abandonment were created and maintained by a pathological cycle of projective identification that involved a constant quest for control and certainty in an internal world of total chaos and endless uncertainty.

12

CAPTURED AND ABSORBED INTO THE FAMILIAR

During the course of psychoanalytic treatment, some patients will attempt to transform the analytic process into something less than analytic and more of an acting out of desired, feared, and familiar object relational phantasies. Specifically, they kidnap the analyst's interpretive function and convert it into friendly advice, authoritarian dictates, soothing reassurance, loving encouragement, stern disapproval, and other exaggerated one dimensional role images. Even when the analyst tries to interpret this element of transference, the patient may quickly absorb this into the non-analytic relationship they envision, hope, or fear is going on.

In addition, the analyst may unwittingly act out this particular deactivation of analytic process and unconsciously begin to enjoy being part of a fatherly, friendly, loving, or adversarial role that allows them to feel powerful, in control, adored, feared, or needed. The patient's unconscious manipulations and idealization can trigger this type of enactment. The patient strokes the analyst into feeling good while using them as part of a conversion of the psychoanalytic procedure into something much more familiar and safe that they can maneuver, shape, and steer.

Examples of this include when the analyst might interpret how a patient is being very passive in some capacity and instead of exploring, reflecting, or considering this message the patient takes it as advice to be more active or as a criticism to stop being so passive. Then, they apologize and feel guilty. Or, the analyst might wonder if the patient's drinking could possibly be a defense against loss and sorrow and the patient immediately hears that curiosity or concern as a shaming judgment. Then, in fear and retaliation, they never mention drinking again but continue to drink behind the analyst's back. So, they use the analytic method and the analyst's interpretations as a vehicle for stylized acting out of specific object relational phantasies and conflicts.

These are common situations in every treatment but some patients use this way of relating throughout the treatment and try to absorb the analyst into a non-analytic process of interactive enactment. This difficult clinical problem is based in projective identification cycles of aggressive control and helpless despair as well as not wanting to allow the analyst access to the patient's mind due to a sense of being intruded upon and trespassed on. These phantasies, through projective identification, can also emerge in reverse. In that aspect of transference phantasy, the patient ends up with a sense of not being allowed into the safety or guidance of the analyst and instead feels controlled and dominated by the analyst. The variations are endless but center on the automatic distortion of the analytic method into a crude concrete version of the patient's familiar internal life and inner conflicts.

Case material: Luke

Luke was a patient who tried to take over the analytic situation by converting it into a concrete enactment of desired pathological non-analytic relating through his masochistic passivity. This seemingly helpless stance hid a more active, controlling, and subsuming transference that dragged the analyst into a particular form of acting out.

Luke came into treatment for help with his chronic depression and "a lack of self-confidence". He lives with his girlfriend, a high powered executive who travels a great deal for business. Luke and his girlfriend had just moved to the city where I practice ten months earlier. He took care of most of the housework and paperwork for the two of them and called himself the "house wife". Listening to the manner in which he said this, I interpreted it as a way of telling me of his resentment and desire to be more of a person with an identity and purpose. But, I said he was also reluctant to be the one who came out and said it and had me say it instead. Luke said, "Sometimes I do feel that way about revealing my feelings but I also am ok with the whole thing since she makes the money that pays our bills". So, I thought Luke was envious and angry, but also guilty and uncertain about having these more direct, active, and aggressive feelings. Also, he enjoyed being taken care of by me and by his girlfriend.

Luke was taking some classes at the local college in the hope of becoming a computer programmer. When not in school or taking care of the couple's home, Luke was training for a running marathon. He enjoyed this and felt of substance and purpose but also told me he "wished my girlfriend would be there for the events and take more interest in what I am doing. But, I understand she has no say over her business schedule so I am ok with that".

Again, I interpreted that Luke allowed himself to share some of his more difficult feelings with me but then felt uncomfortable and guilty about it so he tried to take it back. This dynamic was common in his treatment but what was much more sinister, difficult to track, and elusive to interpret was the way Luke took what I had to say and turned it into something else. He projected a rigid and familiar set of phantasy elements into me and then absorbed the new me into his internal world. Luke eliminated my analytic interest and curiosity, subsuming and converting our relationship into something he desired, feared, and was familiar with from archaic object relational experiences.

When I say archaic, I mean ancient internal visions of self and other. It is true that Luke grew up with an intimidating alcoholic father who dominated the home and allowed for no one to express themselves let alone disagree or develop themselves as an individual. However, my approach is to work with the internal state that emerges over and over in the transference and in the current internal phantasy conflict state being presented in the office. Actual childhood experiences are always distorted, exaggerated, rebuilt, transformed, or altered by the ongoing fear and desire based projective identification cycles that are often over utilized in relational situations that involve conflicts around love, hate, and knowledge. These internal struggles color history. Therefore, memory and historical experience is never static. So, we try to understand the patient's current version of history through transference and unconscious phantasy derivative.

The way Luke described his current life to me sounded lonely and like he always felt on hold until his girlfriend announced their next activity. However, he never actually said this to me. Also, Luke told me he was always having arguments with his girlfriend because she "wants to have sex but I am not in the mood". From his description, I assumed he did not want to have sex with her out of anger or hurt but he also never said this to me or to her.

When I brought up that he seemed to be hiding this more aggressive and hurt side from me, he seemed to take what I said about his defensive, passive transference and convert it into a vision of me giving him advice on how to better his sexual relationship with his girlfriend. So, in the next session, Luke said, "I thought about what you said and I think you are right. I should be more open minded to her advances. So, last night, I went ahead and said sure to her request. We had a good time".

I felt surprised and hijacked, taken for a ride by how Luke took my analytic comments and changed me into this advisory, parental, guiding person who had allegedly counseled him on building a better sexual relationship. I interpreted this and Luke said, "Guess I didn't hear what you said right. But, it still helped. I felt like you were advising me what to do and it worked". I felt like he unconsciously had taken over my analytic status and replaced it with a non-analytic version of an object he seemed to hope for. However, as this system of transference continued, I wondered if I was also being turned into yet another girlfriend figure who told him what to do and ran the show as the dominant and smart one of the pair.

In other words, in the transference, Luke was commanding over me and twisting me into someone who commanded him. If I attempted to interpret this, he would again absorb it, kidnap me into this system, and tell me, "Oh, I see. You are right. I need to do that differently". He fought off reflections or realizations of his inner feelings and conflicts by assigning me the supportive and suggestive leader role. He forced me to be his mentor leader with parental advice. I had no choice in this transference dynamic. He would not allow me to be otherwise.

In the transference, some of our more difficult patients attempt to psychologically kidnap the analyst and replace them with an agent of their core phantasies and object relational desires, conflicts, and fears. The technical approach to such impasses is complicated and difficult. The patient's strategy of seeming to go along with the analytic process while secretly, unconsciously, replacing it with their own desired version of a longed for or dreaded bond makes it easy for the analyst to lose their footing, become frustrated, or simply proceed blindly into an ongoing enactment.

The patient can covertly be manipulating the analyst interpersonally and intrapsychically to be a specific way, having their object as they expect, desire, or dread. The analyst can be involved in this mutual enactment for quite some time. Once the analyst begins to notice the patient converting them into these non-analytic modes of being, it is helpful to begin making analytic observations (Waska 2012). These are consistent verbal observations of exactly *how* the patient is using the analyst, where the patient is locating the analyst in their phantasy world, and the ways the patient seems to need to relate to the analyst.

In other words, this is a clinical observation of the transference, a verbal offering to the patient of exactly how, not why, they are coloring and shaping the transference. This is especially helpful with more difficult to reach borderline and narcissistic patients but also the more troubled and fragile depressive patients. Only later is it helpful to interpret the *why* of the transference. Once the *how* is clarified and explored, understanding the *why* of the transference is more useful and easier to discover.

Betty Joseph (1985, 1997) makes the same point in describing her work in the here-and-now transference situation. When the patient is attempting to subsume us into their internal world and kidnap or convert what we say to better act out their internal desires and to better solidify their internal defenses, we first begin by confronting and observing what we see. Then, we try to bring the patient into a mutual exploration of how they are actively attempting to shift the analytic process into something archaic and familiar, more in line with unconscious desires or fears based in core conflicts around love, hate, and the urge to learn or know.

During our work in the first year of psychoanalysis, on the couch, Luke attempted to enlist me into several different modes of relating in which he tried to convert the more analytic moments of our work into something more concrete and transference based. I would take my stance as his analyst and make my interpretation and then Luke would kidnap, subsume, and convert my input into his version of the object. In the process, he made us into a very static, one dimensional set of objects wedded to each other in predictable, lifeless ways that were never questioned or examined, but simply adhered to blindly.

As Grotstein (2009) notes, the practice of psychoanalysis involves the focus on the derivative function of the patient's reports, his interactions with others,

CAPTURED AND ABSORBED INTO THE FAMILIAR

and the nature of his interpersonal activities with the analyst as all being projective identifications of internal objects and of conflicts with the analyst and mixed feelings about unconscious objects.

So, with Luke, it was important for me to notice how he repeatedly tried to make me be his teacher, his judge, his coach, his wife, and his parent. No matter what I said, he tended to quickly subsume it into his pathological organization (Spillius 1988) with his familiar cast of internal characters. Bion's (1962b) ideas regarding the interpersonal aspects of projective identification, the idea of projective identification as the foundation of most transference states (Waska 2010a, 2010b, 2010c), and the concept of projective identification as the first line of defense against psychic loss (Waska 2002, 2010d) difference, or separation all form the theoretical base of my clinical approach. Taking theory into the clinical realm, I find interpreting the how and the why of the patient's phantasy conflicts in the here and now combined with linkage to original infantile experiences to be the best approach with such patients.

In doing so, the main thrust of the analyst's observation and interpretation remains focused on the patient's efforts to disrupt the establishment of analytic contact (Waska 2007) and instead implanting a new version of the analyst, a clone of desired, dreaded, and known objects. So, over and over, I interpreted Luke's transference efforts to turn me or transform me from interested analyst into the disapproving authority who wants him to do things my way. Repeatedly, he tried to turn me into a very one dimensional version of rigid objects in his phantasy life.

So, when Luke took an elective course in poetry and told me about his writing assignments each week, it was usually with a self-deprecating and devaluing tone. I interpreted that Luke was quick to transform me into a disinterested or even a disapproving parent object when he brought up something he might be proud of, the accomplishment of his poetry. Even when I expressed interest in hearing what he was doing or wanted to know about the topic of the poems he was writing, Luke merely responded with something disparaging.

While it was Luke who was putting his poetry down, I thought that in the transference he was doing that to quickly be in alignment with what he assumed to be a bored or irritated object. He was being agreeable so as to not cause a fuss with me, but in phantasy, he had taken my neutral or even positive support or curiosity and absorbed it into a predictable and familiar dynamic similar to how he felt his relationship with his girlfriend to be.

I interpreted this capture and reconstitution of my identity into his prefabricated model of who I was supposed to be. I also interpreted how he seemed anxious and unwilling to allow me to freely be myself in his mind. Luke was able to take this in for periods of time and it seemed to help him relax and feel more secure. But, he would then suddenly tell me he would "work on it so I don't do that". I then interpreted that he was hearing me as an unhappy, punitive teacher and he was now trying to keep me happy and do things my way.

Overall, this moment-to-moment focus on the transference in which I interpreted the nature of how he was relating to his object of the analyst was helpful. Over time, we were able to understand that Luke wanted someone to be with instead of feeling so alone and neglected. So, he avoided independence and any success with his life. Also, he wanted to be guided and directed as a way of feeling loved. So, he avoided any autonomous action. And, Luke was sure that all his objects were selfish and prone to anger and rejection if he did not do it their way. So, he both wanted to silently rebel but also went along with whatever he thought I, as his rigid or demanding parent, might want so as to not cause trouble or not hurt my feelings.

Indeed, Luke often was sacrificing his desires and needs to please what he imagined I needed or desired from him. Bit by bit, this dedicated focus on his transference style of absorbing me into a very restrictive and conservative phantasy system was helpful and Luke gradually made changes and found a broader personal freedom.

This way of working very close to the interpersonal, interactional, and intra-psychic elements of the total transference situation (Joseph 1985) and staying in touch with the complete counter-transference (Waska 2011a, 2011b) is the theme most recognized in the work of Betty Joseph and her followers (Hargreaves and Varchevker 2004). While the inclusion of genetic links and interpretation of the past in the present is also of great technical value, more in line with the valuable work of Segal (1981), the focus of the present as sum total of the past is of greater help to patients such as Luke.

Interpretations, when accurate, introduce the patients to new ways of thinking and of experiencing themselves, their objects, and the world at large. We introduce our patients to the unknown and the unfamiliar. This can be frightening in a persecutory sense and bring on great anxiety, grief, or guilt (Waska 2006). Therefore, most patients will try to avoid these new windows into their inner world. Defensively, the patients I am describing in this chapter dive deeper into their psychic retreats (Steiner 1993) by capturing the analytic tone and the interpretive message to make it into something they own, control, and know.

Steiner (2011a) has written about the analyst being excluded from the patient's phantasy and being treated as an outside observer. Quite the opposite, the patients I am examining try their best to quickly include or absorb and subsume the analyst and the analytic process into their familiar phantasy and then see the analyst as a known and familiar internal aspect of their object relational world, even if dreaded and feared. They do not allow for any difference, any separation, or any newness and unknown elements in the clinical moment.

Thus, the analytic interpretations are absorbed into their pathological psychic system. This is the attributive version of projective identification

(Britton 1998) followed by an absorption and the appropriation aspect of projective identification. Luke projected his familiar, dreaded, and desired outline of his objects onto me and in the process canceled out and erased the reality of who I was and my analytic function. Then, he absorbed this replacement back into his well-known internal world where he could easily relate, retaliate, or retreat from that object.

During the start of a recent session, Luke told me he was "worried about whether I was getting paid properly by the insurance company". First, we spent about ten minutes sorting out the actual aspects he was confused about with the insurance payment process. But, then I interpreted that he was worried about taking up too much of me without giving enough back. He partly agreed. Then, Luke went on to talk about how a friend of his had heard about how he was writing poetry for his class and asked him to write a poem for a special event she was orchestrating where there would be various readings and art exhibitions. Luke was quick to talk it all down, telling me he was sure this was simply because they were neighbors and casual friends and that she "was just being polite". He went on to tell me how she was an alcoholic and was always "going on about something grandiose and nonsensical".

The way Luke was talking so negatively about his poetry made me feel like he was presenting himself in a way that would not cause any trouble if I did not like his poetry. In other words, he was adjusting to the role he had assigned me as an object who was disinterested or unhappy with his poetry.

I made this interpretation and added that he was scared to be himself, feel proud of his poetry, and openly share his excitement about this opportunity. I said he might feel he would be causing trouble with me and we might not be on the same page. He was careful to not ruffle me and cause conflict so he kept himself at zero to please me as an object who would resent him having value or feeling confident and wanting more air space.

This was a clinical interpretation of the death instinct in which a person kills off any life inside of them or life between them and the object as a way of preserving the peace and keeping the connection alive. This is a defensive use of the death instinct in the projective identification phantasy (Waska 2004).

In response, Luke said, "Do you think it would be good for me to feel more valuable? I will try and be more confident if that will help. I don't want to give her a poem for the show but I will if you want me to". So, he had replaced me and my analytic interpretation with a parenting object who wanted him to only live life a certain way. Luke was quick to then bow down to that object and be a loyal empty vessel to carry out my bidding. He had absorbed me and captured my analytic attempts in this rigid projective system where we now operated in a very concrete and limited fashion.

I went on to interpret this to which Luke said, "I guess I should stop that". I interpreted that this response was the same thing, a rapid giving in to whatever I wanted and a denial and erasing of my more analytic curiosity and invitation for him to reflect with me about the way he might really want to relate to me. When I kept to this path of inquiry, Luke slowly was able to allow himself to look beyond the selected and mandated transference and told me, "I am uncomfortable showing off or feeling proud. I feel guilty and selfish. I think I am showing off for something that I didn't really do or don't deserve. I feel like a fraud that way".

I said, "So, to keep yourself safe from being called too greedy or a show off liar, you make me into someone who is disapproving of you and someone who doesn't really believe in you and then we can both feel comfortable putting you down instead of relating in a risky way about your talents, your anger, your joy, or your achievements".

Luke said, "I want someone on my side. I always feel lonely when my girlfriend is away. I wish she would be more supportive of my stuff and be interested. But, I think I have to just let her run the show because I never get much of a message from her that she cares". I said, "Well, you seem to ignore or dash my message of caring when I put it out there so perhaps that might happen with her too". Luke said, "That is something I never thought of but I can see how I might set that up without really knowing it. But, I guess that means I will have to speak out more and tell her what I want. I will try that soon, Doc".

I said, "The way you said that last part, it seems to be partly you being yourself, putting yourself out there, and sharing your ideas with me and partly you trying to please me and paint me as someone who needs you to do it my way". Luke said, "You are certainly on top of your game today! I get it. I have to do these things for myself and then they count".

I said, "Exactly. When you do it for me it doesn't ever count and you end up feeling more and more empty. The other thing that you just brought up is how alone you feel when you express yourself and define yourself as a separate person with ideas and feelings. I think you start to feel alone and abandoned. You don't like becoming your own person since it feels like we are abandoning you. If you sacrifice yourself and cater to me and your girlfriend, you feel like you have that connection and aren't alone. But to do that you have to make me into this selfish, demanding parent who always wants it my way and never notices you for your special self".

Luke replied, "I want to find a way to be myself and not feel so empty and alone all the time". This was another significant moment in the progress Luke was making in his analytic journey, slowly allowing himself and others to be who they are without having to confine, control, or censor them.

Case material: Joe

Joe was a patient who seemed to use me to make psychological test runs in practicing what it might be like to stand up to his objects and to demand more from them. To use me in this manner, Joe had to rely on extensive projective identification dynamics in the transference and often pulled me into a particular way of interacting with him.

During the two years Joe has been seeing me, twice a week on the analytic couch, we have made a great deal of progress. Over the course of his psychoanalysis, we have discovered several core conflict themes (Clarkin, Yeomans, and Kerberg 1999, 2006; Luborsky 1984) and have made headway on most of them. He seems to have taken his childhood experiences with his mother, distorted and expanded by projective identification processes and the contributing and resulting wishes and fears, and used them as a rigid object relational vehicle for experiencing and relating to most of his objects, but particularly with women.

Markman (2010) has pointed out how Michael Feldman and Betty Joseph are contemporary Kleinians who really lead the way in emphasizing the importance of monitoring just how the analyst is being affected, pressured, and used by the patient in a variety of unconscious ways. Feldman (2009) has studied the many ways the patient has us represent particular objects or aspects of particular objects as well as the way the patient's unconscious actions propel the projective identification process that creates these rigid transference profiles.

Feldman (2009) elaborates on how the patient's projective identifications can be a difficult counter-transference challenge and how the analyst can feel a temptation to reject, deny, or fight against the type of object they are being assigned. I would expand this notion to include a variation of Gill's (1979) ideas about the resistance of the patient to consider or acknowledge the transference as well as the reluctance or resistance to give up or resolve the transference.

So, I think that especially in cases where the patient's reliance on projective identification is intense or rigid, the pressure on the analyst to become a certain type of object and to hold certain feelings, act certain ways, or think in certain manners creates an equal set of resistances in the counter-transference experience. In other words, the analyst may resist or deny the counter-transference pleasure or power they feel being involved in certain enactments. Even if they are able to notice and acknowledge to themselves their role in these acting out dynamics, they may be reluctant to give it up, using therapeutic justifications to feel ok about keeping the status quo.

With Joe, he would relate to me and interact with me in ways that pulled me to confront him about his intellectual justifications that hide his deeper emotional feelings, often aggressive, that he felt very anxious and guilty about. During the course of Joe's psychoanalytic treatment, he repeatedly invited me, pressured me, and corralled me into a very narrow way of being with him. By his actions in the transference of repeatedly presenting me with countless tales of how unstable, volatile, and nasty his girlfriend was and how horrible she treated him, I was led into a counter-transference mode of either becoming the assertive, manly spokesperson for all his hidden rage and resentment or I became the stern parental authority, the father who tells him he is not being a man and how he needs to step up and be more assertive.

As mentioned, I ended up at times in the counter-transference version of Gill's (1979) concept of transference resistance. I did not want to admit to myself that I felt gratified wielding my power in these ways. When I realized it, I found myself justifying it and reluctant to give it up. However, the more I worked on myself in this capacity I was able to move through this tempting stance Luke placed me in and started to interpret it to him and continued to face my own counter-transference involvement.

But, initially, the extent of Joe's projective identification dynamics has made it easy to slip into these counter-transference enactments. It is also easy to not acknowledge them and to stick with the gratifying, righteous, or powerful side effects of this role in which I can tell him what to do or to place judgment on his girlfriend. To give that up, I had to feel batted around by his fluctuating loyalties to someone he feels sorry for or by his repressed, guilt ridden, and denied feelings of anger and outrage. Also, to give up my counter-transference role I had to feel powerless and unable to control either one of them. These are exactly the states of mind Joe faces much of the time so here I am infused with them through his projections and then become reluctant to face them.

However, when I am willing and able to notice these transference↔ counter-transference acting out moments, I have then been able to reflect on them enough to gradually interpret them to the benefit of the treatment. As a result, bit by bit, Joe has been able to re-own his unwanted projected feelings and thoughts and to brave the confrontation with his girlfriend both in mind and in reality. In doing so, or in trying to do so, Joe has begun to face his deep depressive anxieties about hurting his objects or possibly destroying his girlfriend. This anxiety matched a traumatic childhood history in which he feared destroying or abandoning his fragile mother or causing her to become angry and seek revenge. His mother had been institutionalized after losing her first child in a boating accident. We have talked about his phantasy of nursing, healing, and watching over his invalid, broken mother, trying to resurrect her into a whole and healthy object and putting his life on hold until that golden day.

In examining my counter-transference and in working with Joe's transference, I have been able to interpret Joe's need for me to be the assertive, direct man who can express anger that might hurt the object but to go ahead and say what needs to be said. However, when I do, he immediately feels guilty and scared to identify with me so he rejects me as something bad and opposite of him and he takes the stand of an accepting, forgiving, and understanding object always ready to take his troubled and troubling object back. Then, he has to convince me to back off and give the object a chance.

Recently, Joe had a moment of significant progress in being able to tolerate and face the reality of his fragile and easily provoked internal objects. He told me that this recent conflict with his girlfriend and the anxiety he feels telling me all about it is "very much like when my mother would love me unconditionally one moment and then, without warning, hate me. It was a red hot hatred. She despised me. I felt so bad. But, I had to ignore it. I tried my best to figure out what she needed from me because I felt I had to always watch over her and take care of her. She was so fragile and so weak". I said, "You wanted her love but dreaded her hate. You tried to forgive her and tried to save her, rescue her, and justify her behavior. But, I imagine you also grew to hate her back sometimes".

Joe replied, "I couldn't have those kinds of feelings. She was too weak. I had to take care of her". I said, "Just as you have a hard time dealing with your aggressive or assertive feelings with me or your girlfriend. It feels overwhelming to have a mix of love and hate". He said, "Very hard, just impossible".

Joe was envious of his girlfriend's ability to be so aggressive and direct. Through projective identification, he tried to get me to be aggressive and direct towards her. Then, he could absorb this and make it his own without having to bear the risk or the guilt. But, he quickly began to feel overwhelmed by the guilt of having hurt his fragile mother/girlfriend object and in touch with how he lost her love and found hate in its place (Feldman and Paola 1994).

This combative and defensive strategy of projective identification to avoid hate, guilt, and lost love left Joe continuously in a state of anxiety, desperate justification, and denial to avoid unbearable guilt (Safa-Gerard 1998). In fact, he tried to bring up self-blaming examples of how he was bad and how he felt guilty to distract us from anger at others and instead to be angry at himself for being less than perfect. He would make up elaborate stories of how he was suddenly aware of his prejudice against blacks as a way to get us to focus on him and judge him but also to become distracted from his real hate and guilt at his girlfriend and at his mother. Now, instead, we were to "place close attention to these basic cultural defects that I have developed in this society that is so imbalanced. I hope I can try to find some ways of reaching a better sense of diversity and acceptance of others". He was more comfortable situating his hatred towards himself in a logical and intellectualized way with a superior sounding solution in which he became properly understanding and diverse.

During a recent series of sessions, Joe was more open and stark about his view of his girlfriend as well as his internal relationship with his mother. I had routinely interpreted that he seemed to view me, his girlfriend, and his mother as objects that he needed to please, control, and keep happy to avoid us becoming hurt, rejecting, or broken. So, he kept his more intense, competitive, or aggressive feelings hidden. In response, Joe told me he "doesn't so much love my girlfriend but really wants to find a way to cure her of her mental problems". I said, "You don't want to focus on being here with me and having me help you with your mental problems. Maybe that feels too dependent or vulnerable. You would rather be at her bedside".

Joe said, "It sounds extreme but I like the idea that I could be the one who will always administer to her, watch over her, and find a way to cure her of all those awful feelings that leave her so sad and angry. I feel very sorry for her". I said, "You want to keep eternal watch at your mother's bedside and cure those you love of all our pain and poison".

Joe said, "Yes. I want that and that is my job. I don't want to stop that. I get something out of it and I give them something too". I said, "It is a difficult job since you are always on call for the crisis and the near death. You have to endure all the drama and make us all happy and healthy all the time. Eventually, you grow angry and want to quit your job and leave us to suffer. But, then you feel very guilty and run back to save us".

Joe said, "I do that. I know I can't save everyone but I like the idea and I want to keep trying". I said, "Instead of finding someone to love, you have to be with someone who is always sick and troubled. You have to live in the graveyard instead of celebrating life with a partner". Joe replied, "I know, but I know that place so well and I am comfortable there".

In the next session, Joe came in and told me that he was thinking of quitting his treatment because "you were too harsh and what you said didn't feel right. You seemed to be putting my girlfriend down and said things about me that are not true". I asked him for details. He said, "You told me that I saw my girlfriend as a sick person and all I wanted to do was to cure her of her mental problems. I felt offended but I felt I had to go along with what you said and so I did. But, later when I thought about it, I didn't like it or agree with it".

We spend the rest of the session and some of the next one discussing these persecutory feelings and his very rigid vision of betrayal in the transference. Again, I was deemed a very specific type of object and felt that no matter what I said or did I would not be able to clear the air. I noticed myself feeling scared that I would never be forgiven.

But, we did manage to talk about it and some of this immediate capture and transformation of my identity into someone so judgmental and controlling was reduced. However, this projective identification phantasy was difficult to work with and ever shifting. Just when we seemed to be speaking the same language, Joe would turn on me in this way and hear me in a certain persecutory manner. Or, he would deposit his aggression into me in a way that left him so scared, guilty, or anxious that I was taking away his phantasy of caretaker and he would have to give up his bedside, graveyard career of helping others. Then, in his mind, he would have to start being an equal to someone who he could express all of his feelings to and have them do the same without anyone perishing or returning for punishment. This was a very uncomfortable shift towards the life instinct and a shift away from an ancient pathological bond he was reluctant to give up.

All these recent revelations show Joe to be operating in a primitive sadistic and depressive mode, trying to avoid grief and mourning by constantly substituting his fallen objects with the next best thing. Here, we have a transference in which the analyst is forced to be a certain type of object and no matter what we say or do, the patient hears us as the familiar, desired, or designated object they demand.

Joe's dynamics are consistent with individuals who are psychologically without. Their inner worlds are without any stable, soothing object that they can trust and attach to. Due to various unconscious conflicts and the excessive use of projective identification, they ignore or discard the objects they do have to rely on and choose to find a substitute that they can control, shape, and use for their immediate and rigidly defined gratification. We become what they want and lose who we are as they continue to feel empty from taking in only what they imagine will fulfill their exact demands for their molded object. We and our patient's objects end up like Frankenstein's monster, a creature created by and for the crazy professor who alone in his lab tries to piece together something from multiple tragedy and unfixable loss.

Overall, these are patients who are overwhelmed with conflicts regarding envy, hurt, emotional hunger, rage, despair, and chronic experiences of loss. Some of these are rooted in actual childhood trauma and others are the result of unconscious projective identification cycles around issues of love, hate, and knowledge. These patients tend to try to capture love rather than find it, earn it, develop it, or provide it. Instead of cultivating a mutual, equal, reciprocal love, they attempt to capture love, avoiding a resurfacing of painful envy, dependency, shame, loss, guilt, mourning, and sorrow.

Of course, a captured love or a kidnapped love is no love at all. The captured love or Frankenstein love engineered in the laboratory of unconscious conflict is a monster, a prisoner, a puppet, and a political player in a dark psychological drama with no ending in sight. We try to step in and provide insight or assistance to such individuals, letting them know we can tell they are without and that we can see how they try to obtain or capture an object to sustain, regain, or gratify themselves. When we interpret that this strategy is really unsustainable and bound to leave them even more empty and envious and guilty or paranoid, their reaction is to deny, retaliate, or double their efforts at capturing us and putting us on the strings of their puppet show. We can easily fall into this sadomasochistic show and provide them with temporary pleasure and power, but if we can regain our analytic balance, there is a chance, albeit a slight one, that we can help them risk a new way of living, a new way of relating. We can help such patients to not take prisoners and instead to allow others to take a look inside them. As a result, they too can find a healthy way into their objects and end up sharing and growing instead of taking and feeling invaded. Loss is no longer the principal presence in the patient's life, guilt does not define the nature of interactions, and control over self and other is no longer a life or death issue.

Conclusion

When a patient acts helpless or talks about their overwhelming sense of personal helplessness and lack of agency, or if the analyst is seen as not providing enough or not understanding fully, it is often a combination of both a controlling, dominating, and devaluing of the analyst with a desperate, hopeless, and weakened state of mind failure that pulls the analyst to manically prove, convince, or argue that all is well and improving or to feel beaten down and hopeless or weak (Feldman 2011). The two cases presented show a great deal of effort put upon the analyst to be a certain way or the analyst will be seen as useless, misunderstanding, or ignoring the patient's interests. This leaves the analyst frustrated, ready to debate, and engage in a power struggle or to forfeit the abstract and align himself with the patient's concrete transference belief about themselves and their objects.

The ways these patients manage to convert, subsume, and absorb our analytic abilities into their own rigid, non-symbolic system are varied but all are elements of provocative projective identification (Joseph 1987) effort in which words, tone, attitude, action, silence, and manner of relating converge to bait the analyst to join them in becoming a specific object. This means they must abandon reflection and the mourning and loss involved in facing the reality of one's own strengths and shortcomings and the less than ideal nature of the object. Instead of accepting this difficult yet rewarding task, these patients tend to lure the analyst into mutual defensive stances or psychological distractions, and to replace the analytic procedure with caricatured role plays of phantasy relations.

Spillius (1988) has described the evocative nature of projective identification. The patients I have described provoke and evoke particular sets of responses in the analyst in order to avoid facing the loss of certain control, desire, safety, and power. They avoid the grief, persecution, and guilt that can emerge when allowing for a separate, different, and unknown object into their minds. Therefore, they use excessive projective identification dynamics to pull the analyst into their premade, preset, and already known image of what their object is or should be. They resist the interpretations and the working through of these transference states and cling to what they have defined as known about self and other.

As Mason (2011) has noted, projective identification is a combination of expulsion and acquisition. The patient tries to rid themselves of the painful reality of loss, envy, guilt, and helplessness and in turn seeks to transform the object into something that can be owned, controlled, and known. Both depressive (Klein 1935, 1940) and paranoid (Klein 1946) anxieties are at play. This clinical situation creates specific difficulties for the analyst in interpreting and in avoiding enactments.

13

THE GIVE AND TAKE IN
PROJECTIVE IDENTIFICATION

As Melanie Klein discovered, the infant as well as the adult patient are constantly struggling to find balance within various object relational phantasies of loving, appreciative, and understanding objects as well as greedy, cruel, and unavailable objects. These objects are created through a mix of actual experiences with external figures that are then internalized and filtered with the ego's own spectrum of distortions based on conflicts regarding love, hatred, and knowledge. In other words, projections of one's own desires for love, one's own cruel superego demands, and the search for answers to one's endless curiosity about the nature of the object are all shaping and coloring the ego's experience of the other. So, current Kleinian thinking (Spillius 1992) understands projective identification to play an enormous part in early development as well as the individual's view of self and other throughout the life cycle. With our more challenging patients, we find they overuse splitting and projective identification to manage, defend, and take pathological control over their object relational world (Daniel 1992).

Case material: Fran

Fran was twenty-two years old when she was arrested for drunk driving. By age twenty-three, she had been in several fights and numerous near fatal situations that were all the result of her black out drinking. Fran went into a spiral of depression after her boyfriend broke up with her, ended up quitting her job, and moving back home with her parents. Her father was very concerned and "forced her to call up a therapist". So, I began seeing her once and sometimes twice a week.

Based on her history and the way she came to me "because of her father", I immediately made the interpretation that Fran might feel pushed by her father to see a man whom she did not know or trust. And, I said that she is probably not sure if she was in my office for herself, for me, or for her father. Here, I made a minor interpretation of the transference due to my assessment of her anxiety level and probable phantasy state, a technical approach of the Kleinian school (Etchegoyen 1991).

Fran agreed and said she "knew she had some issues and should work on them but did not like feeling that her father was making the decision". I replied, "In some ways, you may have turned over the decision to him by not taking care of yourself. It sounds like you have been living life on the edge for a while". Fran said, "Yes. I know I have gotten into trouble with drinking. After I drink too much, I always black out. Then, anything can happen. But, now I have decided to monitor my drinking and be more careful".

I noticed myself in the counter-transference wanting to make a parental like comment about how just "being more careful" did not sound like enough and maybe even naïve or stupid. I said nothing but kept this feeling aside as possible information about how she might be starting to utilize me in the transference. This was in line with the Kleinian approach to understanding counter-transference as often being colored by the projective identification aspects of the patient's transference dynamics.

I found myself climbing into the shape of a sarcastic, short tempered, or critical authority and losing my grip on my regular state of mind, a more neutral, curious, and investigative way of thinking. Here, I felt something was not necessarily taken out of me, but replaced without asking. Fran's passive and provocative way seemed to push that more flexible and smooth place in me aside and invade me with this more rigid and rough edged state.

Rosenfeld (1971), Segal (1974), Joseph (1985, 1987), and Sandler (1976) are a few of the Kleinians who have pointed to how the patient brings what starts as an unconscious phantasy to life with the analyst through the interpersonal domain of the transference, repeating various object relational conflicts of the past and behaving in ways that get the analyst to feel or think in ways that the patient either cannot express or contain or does not want to express or contain.

Therefore, in the counter-transference, the analyst may slowly or suddenly experience aspects of the patient's mind that unless understood can bring the analyst to participate in enactments that parallel the patient's acting out. While not always avoidable, these counter-transference moments are part of the "complete counter-transference" situation and can provide enormous and useful information to the analyst about the patient's struggle (Waska 2010a, 2010b, 2010c, 2011a, 2011b) that can eventually be gathered into helpful interpretations (O'Shaughnessy 1989).

When we talked about her drinking history, I noticed that Fran was defensive and tried to justify it. She said she "was just having fun". Again, I noticed that her way of presenting herself and this self-destructive history evoked a response of, "What do you mean fun? The next thing that happened that night was you woke up in the hospital!" So, in the counter-transference, I contained these urges to chastise her and wondered about this unsolicited transaction or unannounced exchange that was taking place between us. She seemed to want either a judgment or a tolerance from me and in order to get that she inserted this authoritarian or less than tolerating mindset that I had to navigate. To put herself at the mercy of the court and see how I might vote against her or with her, she had to transform herself into a handcuffed prisoner on the witness box. This was done with aggression and interpersonal force so that I ended up feeling on the witness box as well. If I failed the test we would both have to pay.

When I noticed this critical parent and provocative kid bond that Fran seemed to want with me, I made that interpretation. Fran seemed somewhat interested and told me, "That is what it feels like with my father". Again, I was using the concept of how projective identification is a universal component of most treatment situations (Spillius 1992) and therefore creates complicated but ultimately valuable counter-transference experiences that can be utilized to assist the patient in understanding what they need from or fear from the object as well as what they desire but fear from themselves.

I said, "So, maybe you hate being told what to do but there might be something inviting or comfortable about this way of being with me or men in general". Fran said, "I don't like the idea that I am looking for that but I do know my ex-boyfriend really gets on my nerves for doing that to me as well!"

Over time, I noticed this same provocative stance about her drinking came up when she told me things like, "I know I easily get into trouble with drinking, but I wanted to have some fun", "I didn't care what happened that weekend", or "I haven't gotten drunk in months so I don't think going out to the club with my friends was any big deal".

I felt Fran was lighting a fire for me to rush in and give her a lecture or scolding. I made this interpretation, saying I found it important to notice how she handed off any responsibility or thinking about consequences to me, so she looked like a dumb teen and I had to be a responsible adult.

Here, I was interpreting the projective identification exchange or sometimes one-way street projective process Fran seemed to favor. There was a random psychic kidnap and ransom dynamic she facilitated in which I was forced to hold an aspect of her but if I intervened or reacted, there were consequences. She immediately denied any association to the projective elements and quickly took on the identity of the opposite, which was mostly the persecuted victim misunderstood by me.

Fran said she "could see what I meant" and "did feel like she had lots of people in her life telling her what to do and she was sick of it because she knew she was messing up more than anyone else did". I asked her what she meant and Fran said, "I am really unhappy with myself and my life in just about every category so I don't need anyone to tell me off". I said, "You are very angry with yourself so I would just be an echo of that". She nodded yes. Here, we were getting to the root of the projective identification based transference in which Fran was overwhelmed by her own defiance and crucial enforcement of a phantasy of "what should be", as commanded by those she relied on.

Another way this transference emerged was when Fran left me a message saying she could not make the next appointment. She did not ask for another time and just left it up in the air. I called her back and left a message offering her a couple of alternative times. After not hearing back from her, I left another message. After I left a third message, I also called her father's phone number. I was aware that this would probably cause some type of problem and also realized I was probably stepping into the invitation to act out with her that was initiated by her not returning my calls. The insurance company that was covering most of her treatment had left me the father's number initially so I used that as my justification to call. Her father passed on my message to her and she called me back immediately. We rescheduled.

When we met, she seemed agitated but said nothing. I asked her if something was bothering her that she was not saying. Fran said she was upset about my calling her father. She said, "I feel like now both of you are making me be here". I said, "I have become another annoying pushy father in your life?" She said, "That is what it feels like!"

I said that I thought her not returning my calls was a sign of her feelings about me and that she might have been fighting back or resisting me as another pushy father in her life. She said "that could be". I added that by not returning my calls, she left me with the choice of either ignoring her and filling in the time that could be hers with someone else, to which she might feel rejected, or I would have to pursue her through her father to which she obviously felt controlled. So, I interpreted that she was putting me in a no-win situation with her and leaving herself in a no-win relationship with me. Fran said, "If you hadn't called me back and then filled my time, I would have thought you were just being the ass I thought you might be". I said, "So, you have very strong ideas about who I might be to you and you would quickly confirm them". She nodded.

Here, I think Fran was demonstrating her conflicts between the life and death instincts and the struggle between the desire to search out the object and find union versus the aim to avoid the object or destroy any contact with it, including differences or need (Etchegoyen 1991; Segal 1993, 1997b).

This was a particular transference state that seemed to be dominated by her use of projective identification in which Fran constantly tried to cultivate particular states of mind in me. She seemed to want to not trade but simply and forcefully replace certain tolerant and curious aspects of my mind with more rigid and dictatorial ways. These were parts of her own mind she was rejecting as they were so severe and persecutory. However, in attempting to propagate my mind with them instead, she was not noticing or able to utilize the more gentle and forgiving aspects of me that were there to begin with, ready for her taking. So, she only made room for a one-way street in our relationship or a boomerang effect in which I would return all her unwanted mental toxins with a vengeance. This was also the essential makeup of various enactments that occurred throughout the treatment.

Some of these formidable transference and counter-transference states came out during a recent analytic session. Fran came into my office and asked me, "How are you?" This was said in a manner that seemed genuine and slightly worried. I noted this to myself as a way she seemed worried about her object and as a result she was checking in on my well-being. Fran sat down and began to tell me in a very fast manner that "everything was just about the same and nothing much to report since last time. Everything is ok. I have just been working and doing my thing. So, that is about it".

I felt Fran had rapidly dumped a controlled summary of herself onto me and now was done but also was now anxious about what to do next and what else was required of her. I made this interpretation and she said, "Well, I just wanted to report everything and bring you up to speed with what has been going on". I said, "Actually, you haven't let me know anything about what you are feeling or thinking. So, this summary or dump-and-run that you did seems to be a way of not having to share much with me but also a way to meet your obligations to me".

Fran said, "I do feel like I am supposed to come in with some kind of report for you. It makes me think of my father. He always wants to know what I have been doing and how I am improving. I know he cares but it is really annoying sometimes". I said, "So, you have decided you have two annoying fathers?" Fran replied, "I guess so. I don't want anyone to tell me I am being stupid". I said, "Are you one of those people?" Here, I was interpreting the projection of her harsh superego to which Fran said, "I am furious with myself sometimes and I can't bear that over my head". I said, "So, maybe it is easier to hear it from me and your father than the harshest critic of them all, you!" Fran nodded yes and began to cry.

Then, Fran went back to her quick summary and again presented a nervous delivery of "the latest" and a review of "since I have seen you last". I interpreted that with her asking how I am at the beginning and her nervous summary of the latest, it seemed to show that she is worried about how I am feeling towards her and if I am happy or unhappy. I interpreted that she seems to want to please me and make sure I am not unhappy with her. Fran said, "That is so weird! I was talking with my friends over the weekend and that is what they said too. They said I seem to always be trying to make everyone ok and make sure everyone likes me. I hated to hear that. But, I think it is true. I worry what other people are thinking about me and what my reputation is".

Here, it seemed like Fran was describing not so much any anxiety over trying to assist or please a needy or hurt object out of guilt or concern. Rather, it was more of a narcissistic desire to gain status. So, this was not so much a depressive anxiety but more of a paranoid-schizoid conflict regarding narcissistic phantasies of power, depletion, and disgrace. It was about the agony of the self not the concern for the other.

After a few moments of talking about wanting others to like her and have everyone be "ok", Fran mentioned she had celebrated her birthday over the weekend. She said she had gotten together with friends and went out to celebrate and then sat around and talked all night. Here, I noticed she said nothing about whether she had drank or not, setting up a certain type of transference in which I now had to be the parent who asked about whether she had been a good girl or not.

I waited and listened, gathering more before information before making any interpretation. I was also noting the shifts and variations Fran made from one state of mind to the next. As I listened, she went back to talking about pleasing others.

Fran said, "It is funny you are bringing up how I want to take care of you because that is just what my friends said. One of my best friends said I am always trying to make everyone ok and doing whatever it takes to please everyone".

Fran talked about that for a while and then turned to telling me about how the next day she got a message from her ex-boyfriend saying he hoped she had been careful about drinking on her birthday. Fran said she was furious that he was "in my business and judging me that way. Who the hell is he that he thinks he can tell me I am screwing up! I am not a little kid and he is not my parent!"

I said, "From what I hear, he sounds like he was used to your destructive drinking patterns so he was worried you might fall off the wagon on your birthday and was just trying to be supportive. But, you hear it as very critical and attacking. I noticed you never told me that you went out drinking on your birthday. Maybe you are worried I will be just like him and come down on you as well?"

Fran said, "That is exactly right. I made a point of not mentioning it since I figure you will just tell me I am stupid for drinking at all". In the counter-transference, I felt like saying, "It's true! You are stupid for drinking even one beer!" Here, I was aware that my inquisitive and empathic function was replaced with a much harsher judgmental mindset, set into place by Fran's pseudo naïve, provocative way of presenting herself. She was not taking ownership of her actions and then attacking others for being concerned about them.

Trying to use my feelings as information that could be contained and translated, I said, "Well, you make it very black and white between us very fast. So, right now I have to either say nothing to prove I am not a judgmental father sticking my nose in your business or I could ask you questions about how and why you choose to drink when you know you have a problem with it and risk you seeing me as just one more person against you. There isn't much middle ground for us".

Here, I was interpreting the splitting and projective identification Fran was employing in the transference. I was pointing out how I was now controlled and only given two choices, both being proof of my betrayal. My normal feeling of having many ways of being and many ways of relating had been shrunken down and restricted to this very limited and useless set of two. It was as if Fran had replaced my more inclusive and holistic mindset with the more stripped down barren view she held of herself and of others.

She replied, "Well, I did think about my drinking and made sure to pace myself and be careful. I had two or three drinks at the bar and then another four or five over the course of about five or six hours. So, I thought I was pretty responsible about it. All my friends were completely drunk but I wasn't". In the counter-transference, I again noticed myself wanting to lecture Fran and tell her that even if she paced herself, she was still drinking and even one or two drinks was a stupid risk for someone with her drinking history. I noticed how this judgment got in the way of my considering that she indeed was making progress by even considering her action. But now I, like her, only focused on how bad she was. Again, projective identification seemed to rule the transference and control and infect the counter-transference. By gradually noticing these feelings and phantasies in myself, I was able to provide her with some useful interpretations of her own cruel focus on the negative and her elimination of the positive.

Next in the session, Fran shifted to telling me about going on a date with someone she had just met. She explained that she normally only goes out on one or two dates with men and ends up having sex with them but never enters into a long term relationship. I asked her why she avoids getting close to men, whether it be with me on an emotional level in the transference or with other men on a romantic level. So, I was asking why she had to keep her distance from any man in her life. I assumed her critical view of herself and of others would make a close connection very painful or persecutory.

Fran told me, "I just have casual hookups with men because I don't picture anyone really wanting to be with me. I don't think they would honestly want to spend time with me like that". I said, "That sounds very sad. Why wouldn't we want to be with you except in that more cold, distant, or callous way?" Here, I used the word "we" to make the transference interpretation complete. I find that with some patients who externalize much of their conflicts, it is helpful to not only make direct transference interpretations as well as extra-transference interpretations, but to combine them to highlight the object's universal presence in their mind and the global nature of the patient's projections. The patient is often describing their overall internal phantasy conflicts between self and other, with the object taking on the persona of either the external person or the analyst in each and every setting. So, this type of total transference interpretation keeps the focus on the internal dynamics instead of using the external as a defensive shelter.

Fran responded, "I don't think anyone would want me. I don't feel attractive at all. I see myself as fat and unattractive. I am definitely not desirable. I am so sick of how I look. I have tried to change my diet and monitor what I eat, but I never lose any weight. I need to go to the gym but I just don't feel like it. It is all too boring so I don't want to do it. I hate the gym. I don't have the motivation at all".

The entitled, dismissive way Fran was presenting herself to me at this point about the gym and the overall narcissistic manner she was relating to me created a certain experience in the counter-transference. Once again, I felt shrunken down to a singular, judgmental way of viewing her that seemed to be a match for her "above it all" way of dismissing something she does not like, whether it be the gym or coming to see me. As a result, I noticed myself wanting to scold Fran, to lecture her, and to criticize her. I wanted to say, "Hey! You are being lazy. It doesn't matter if you like the gym or not. If you want to lose weight and not be fat, you should be going to the gym regularly!" This urge was very similar to the counter-transference urges I had about wanting to lecture her on her drinking.

I felt like Fran had ejected this harsh and demanding voice from her own mindset and enlisted me to take ownership of it. With it, she felt tormented by her own persecutory superego. Without it, she felt like a spoiled child demanding their way and acting entitled to whatever she pleased. But, now she was facing an angry, withholding, or rejecting parent. This is often one of the core conflicts with thin-skinned and even thick-skinned narcissistic patients (Rosenfeld 1987; Bateman 1998; Britton 2004). Also, even though it seemed her sad self-loathing was being defended against by the narcissistic defiance, it was more than just a defense. For Fran, this narcissistic mindset was a core aspect of her personality and therefore needed to be worked with as both defensive and offensive in nature.

So, I interpreted, "It seems by the way you are talking about feeling fat and unhappy but then saying you don't want to go to the gym and don't want to be bothered with exercising, you set me up to be your critical parent who will lecture you and tell you off for being so spoiled and stubborn". Fran said, "I see what you mean but that is how I feel. I just don't want to do it. I don't feel like it and if I don't like something I hardly ever do it". Here, she seemed to be increasing the level of provocative interaction with me, pulling me even harder into being that judgmental parent. So, I now switched to interpreting the more defensive aspect of her narcissism. I interpreted, "Since you don't really tell me why you are so unhappy, the focus becomes what you should do and what you are not doing. But, in the meantime, we are losing focus on what is really going on inside of you".

Fran said, "Why should I tell you how I really feel? You are just going to tell me what to do and I don't like that. I feel like the minute I open my mouth, everyone does that. So, I just keep everything to myself. My father, my friends, my boyfriends, and you all seem to have some kind of opinion about what I should be doing and I just want to do what I want and be left alone". Here, she ignored my interest in her feelings and cast me as a persecutory object telling her what to do.

Again, reflecting on what sort of mindset she seemed to allow or prevent in me and in herself, I interpreted, "It seems you won't allow for any difference between us. Either I go along with whatever you say or do or I am putting you down. I don't get to have an opinion without it feeling hurtful". Fran said, "I guess I just want my way sometimes". I said, "But then you only have yourself to be with. No one else is allowed unless they are a mirror of you. I have to agree with you or I am saying you are bad". Fran blurted out, "I have to be that way! If I don't then I feel terrible. I KNOW I am fucking up! I tell myself that all day long. So, of course I don't want to hear that from anyone else and I don't want to focus on it. I am telling myself off all day so I certainly don't need anyone else to join in with that!" Fran was crying at this point.

I said, "You are constantly attacking yourself like a terrible critical parent, so you naturally expect me to do the same. If I am curious about your decisions or your thoughts, you are sure I must be coming down on you. You are so ready to hear it that way because you already are yelling at yourself. You won't allow any room for me to be otherwise. I don't get a chance to be different from you and maybe see things less angry or less critical than you". Fran was quiet for a bit and then said, "Maybe. I do get so worked up I feel like everyone is using me as a punching bag. I hate myself and I am sick of hearing everyone tell me how I need to be. I think you are like that too. But, maybe you have a point. I don't know. I will think about it".

Here, I was interpreting the difficulty Fran had when she felt out of touch with the ideal object or when she felt she failed to become or maintain herself as the ideal self. Instead of realizing, allowing, and mourning this lack of perfection in herself or others, Fran tried to fend off this grief in paranoid or narcissistic ways. This usually fell apart rather quickly and she was left with a sense that she was a bad person and as a result of projection, surrounded by bad and disappointing objects. So, for her the container function of the object was unavailable and what she needed contained was overwhelming to the self and by projection to the object (Bion 1962b).

Part of this problem was Fran's not tolerating any differences between herself and the object, elements characteristic of libidinal and destructive narcissistic patients struggling with the life and death instincts (Rosenfeld 1987). We had to be in agreement at all times and in agreement with her ideas but not ever with my interpretations. There could not be any separation, need, or difference. I had to go along with whatever she said or I was against Fran and she felt the same about me in reverse.

Only having met with Fran for a few months, we are making a bit of progress. Fran is more able to access, tolerate, own, and work on her own cruel judgment and demand of perfection. She relies less on pathological projective identification mechanisms. As Rosenfeld (1971) has noted, projective identification is sometimes for communication but often with borderline and narcissistic patients, it is used to evacuate something that is felt too burdensome or unbearable. Likewise, it can be used to rob the object of something that felt missing, lacking, or is targeted through envy.

With Fran, she affected me through her splitting process in which she used me as part of her unconscious relational bond with an idealized parental object who should go along with everything she did or said and never question what she did or said. But, her fragile narcissistic state would break down and internally her forced to be understanding and supportive object would suddenly rebel, betray, and criticize her. Fran initiated and maintained this particular transference mode by her provocative statements, her anxiety around pleasing me, and her narcissistic attacks when I do not deliver exactly what she wants. By addressing these pathological aspects of her projective process, we were able to work our way through some of it some of the time. This allowed us to find a more healthy communicative aspect of her unconscious manner of relating to me and gradually utilize that information to see what was really troubling her so much (Feldman 1992). However, the intensity of Fran's narcissistic transference and the brittle and modest treatment we have at this point make for a very rocky and turbulent climate.

Given the nature of Fran's conflicts and the combative way she related and reacted to her objects, I would not be surprised if the treatment either continued with a high degree of turbulence and chaos for months before slowly settling down or Fran could easily decide I was so against her or not providing her with the emotional echo she demanded that she might abruptly terminate at any moment.

Work with desperate and difficult borderline and narcissistic patients involves ongoing agony for both parties and often ends poorly. Eternal uncertainty, constant doubt and dread, and jarring and sudden failure are all part of the experience for both patient and analyst in these hard to reach cases. This is the nature of the internal landscape when we encounter pathological issues between the life and death instincts (Segal 1993) and the unpredictable struggles in the realm of narcissism and primitive paranoid phantasies of love and hate (Segal 1997a). We must try to provide the best therapeutic envelope within which these patients can emotionally thaw out over time but sometimes we are not given that time. However, as illustrated with Fran, whatever level of encounter we have, we must see what we can offer, how that is taken, what we are given in return, and what we can learn from either a mutual exchange or a pathological extract and insert process.

Case material: Z

Z was a young woman from Brazil who was significantly overweight and spoke with a thick accent. She could understand me with no problem but I noticed that she spoke in a broken manner that over time was to lead to numerous transference and counter-transference issues. Z presented herself in a very polite and meek manner and was quick to see me as an authority with great knowledge. I have seen her for four years, twice a week, in psychoanalytic treatment. Z came to see me as the result of her numerous failed attempts to have a successful romantic relationship. In addition, she suffered from a severe depressive state and long standing anxiety. Z always ended up dating judgmental, controlling men who were unavailable emotionally and often cheated on her. She would be very naïve and never questioned anything, even when obvious red flags came up. And, Z often blamed herself during these rocky relationships as well as after they ended.

Z was an example of someone who has been deeply affected by early family circumstances combined in damaging ways with the patient's own unconscious phantasies and conflicts about those external circumstances. In examining the early oedipal conflicts of the child (Klein 1928, 1945), Melanie Klein discovered certain crisis states that can occur. Elaborating on Klein's findings, Britton (1992) has noted how when the child or young adult feels they have done damage to their object in phantasy, they make an effort to repair and restore the object.

However, if those efforts fail for some reason, the damage is denied with manic omnipotence. If this effort also fails, the patient resorts to more pathologically compulsive actions to make amends. My own view of this has to do with a breakdown of normal depressive anxieties when the object is unstable, weak, or prone to cycles of both collapse and furious retaliation. When this is the case, the young child can become so afraid of hurting the object that they become passive and inert to protect the object. This same neutral and formless defense is used if the object appears prone to revenge when hurt, creating a more persecutory or paranoid (Klein 1946) phantasy. So, for some patients, normal reparation is felt to be too dangerous and the initial healthy urge to push against the object and the healthy trust in an object being resilient and able to heal seems gone. Emotionally playing possum is the identification with a dead or injured object in an effort to not further drain or hurt the object with one's own liveliness or strength. It is also a defense against a possible attack. To pretend to be emotionally dead is also a way to avoid being killed.

This was the case with Z. Her early upbringing with her mother and father was very traumatic. Her father was an angry man prone to intense and stormy moods. He was "always on the edge, ready to tell me off. I had to go along with whatever he said or did to avoid a crisis. I tried to be very quiet and fade into the background". Z's mother was a chronically depressed woman who spent most of Z's upbringing in bed or crying in the kitchen. During her analysis, we have examined how Z was always wary of ever expressing her own self, especially any differences, strong opinions, or needs, in front of her father and now with me and other men. With her mother, Z remembers feeling she was too fragile to weather any conflict or difference from Z, so Z kept her own identity under wraps. We have understood this as her way of protecting her mother and not showing off. If her mother was too weak to have her own life, Z felt she should not make her feel worse by having her own. This fear of harming the object by being a fully functioning and expressive person seemed sadly confirmed when her mother killed herself the week after Z graduated high school at the top of her class.

Throughout the analytic treatment, there has been an ongoing pattern in the transference that fuels a continuous counter-transference experience. In how she relates to me and how she conducts her life, Z seems to have no common sense. Combined with a very passive way of talking to me, this intrapsychic and interpersonal dynamic pulls me to be the forceful "doer", making obvious suggestions and filling in the blanks Z leaves in what she says and how she seems to not think about things. Here, I believe she is vacating her mind, creating emptiness by projecting common sense and knowledge out of herself to prevent conflict or difference. She is left quiet, vacant, and lifeless. I am boosted up and filled up as the guide to common sense and knowledge.

When Z puts me in command through this controlling projective process, she must then follow my commands. This leaves her grateful, guided, and protected, but also controlled, belittled, and resentful. This transference pattern of evacuation of knowledge and bestowing superior power and strength to her object emerged through her specific use or misuse of the English language. As mentioned, she was from Brazil and had a fairly strong accent. When she spoke to me, Z tended to leave out many details from whatever story she relayed. This enlisted me to constantly ask for more, as if I was a demanding, impatient parent with a withholding little kid who had to be prompted for more information every step of the way.

In addition, Z tended to use incorrect tenses and misuse common phrases or metaphors. I would end up correcting her, stopping her in the middle of her story to point out her misuse of the language. Reflecting on how I had shifted from analyst to language tutor, I said, "I notice we often slip into a situation where I am conducting a Proper English 101 class and you are my failing student who needs special tutoring. This is interesting since you are a very smart person with a successful career that depends on your careful knowledge of the facts. Also, you have lived here most of your life. So, I think this is not an issue of language problems but something emotional or psychological".

Z would reply, "I know! I agree! But, my boyfriends have always said the same thing. They always correct me. At work, I can carefully review whatever I say because I submit most of my reports online through email. But, in person, this happens all the time!" When I examined the details in most of Z's verbal "mistakes", there were definitely some problems she had with North American metaphors and slang. But, when asked, she almost always knew and understood the proper tense of words and the full meaning of what she normally left out or said backwards. In other words, Z had the knowledge and verbal skill but something else got in the way.

Over time, we discovered two elements that created this transference phenomenon. First, Z said she "thought those problems might happen when she felt anxious. When I asked her for specifics about when and why she felt anxious with me, the second element, the real underlying reason, came out. It seemed that whenever Z was ready to express herself more directly, openly, or boldly, she became anxious. As we explored this, I interpreted that she was worried about how she might impact me and what my reaction might be so she decided to eliminate the problem altogether by stripping her communication of any possible offensive or overly expressive elements. She only told me the bare bones basics, so safe and basic that what little was left did not really make much sense.

In addition, I interpreted that this was also the way she related in general. In other words, not just with language but with many other aspects of her life, Z had stripped herself down to a faint, non-expressive shell that did not make much of an impression. She was very safe but hardly recognizable except for the impression the object made on her now putty-like personality.

So, over the course of many months, in countless similar situations, I worked through my feelings, thoughts, and conflicts within the complete counter-transference (Waska 2007, 2010a, 2010b, 2010c, 2011a, 2011b). Specifically, I tried to take account of everything that I said, felt, and thought as well as the overall pattern of how I related to Z as all a part of a counter-transference state that emerged out of my patient's transference process. I was operating under the technical direction that her transference was primarily shaped by her use of projective identification (Joseph 1987) and as such generated ongoing intrapsychic and interpersonal invitations for me to understand, punish, defend, assist, or control her.

As a result, there is an inevitable acting out that occurs in which the analyst will slip into various enactments and step into a variety of acting out patterns with the patient. If the analyst can avoid the more destructive aspects of this and slowly can come to unpack the deeper meanings and motivations of the patient's projective push-and-pull, then the counter-transference can serve as a clarifying instrument instead of a series of confusing actions and reactions (Steiner 2000, 2006).

As I worked with and through the complete counter-transference, I began to notice that many of the ways I corrected Z and the ways I filled in the blanks for her were parental in nature, often with an aggressive tone or domineering manner. For her part, she acted the role of a timid young girl who wanted help and guidance but also feared the older, stern authority. This was similar to the dynamic that occurred with my other patient, Fran. However, this was not as intense, aggressive, or primitive. The phantasy behind it was different and more depressive than paranoid-schizoid.

In the counter-transference with Z, I found myself identifying with her lack of self-definition and when she presented vague stories with no real punch line or point, my own anxiety pushed me to want to make a point and to demonstrate my aliveness or my common sense. I felt compelled to strike out and state my opinion rather than float hopelessly in the darkness.

Other times, in the counter-transference, I was frustrated and worried about my object being such an empty void; I wanted my patient Z to provide me with more sure footing. I reacted to that anxiety, the very anxiety Z must have felt growing up, by trying to control Z, fix her, and make her better by giving her proper language skills. I was filling in the blanks for her and pointing out how she might go about dealing with some situation she claimed to be clueless about. I was trying to fill her up with my knowledge and make her a complete object I could count on. I was trying to save Z from being her sad crumpled depressed mother with nothing to offer and I was trying to talk some sense into a useless unavailable father.

Klein (1935) and later Steiner (1992) have noted that after trying to own and later identify with the precious object, the ego will later try to control or deny the moments in which its much needed object is separate, gone, missing or even seemingly dead. Eventually, in optimal development, the ego must gradually let go of the object and accept the object as flawed, failing, and never under one's full control. The permanence and perfection of the object is brought to the painful light of reality in normal depressive functioning, bringing in a new sense of loyalty, love, and gratitude that emerges from the sadness and anxiety of separateness and dependency.

I think part of the complete counter-transference is allowing the patient to be less than what we hope for and letting the patient suffer in their own self-made pathological solutions to their internal conflicts without imposing a fix out of our own anxiety. As analysts, we must endure the plight of the patient to some degree throughout the length of the treatment. Certain moments can be more painful than others.

With Z, I had to realize and accept that it was not my job to fill in the blanks and that she had to find a way to fill in her own blanks without me forcing knowledge into her. I had to have faith that she might slowly learn about her own feelings and allow herself to express them. I could help her in that but I had to allow her to suffer and struggle as part of that assistance. This was my counter-transference loss, pain, and lack of control in the depressive position (Klein 1935, 1940).

Joseph (1978) has explained how many of the more difficult to reach patients such as Z have buried their thoughts and feelings in others, through projective identification. Therefore, the analysis becomes a stage for action rather than thought and the analyst must take up the task to reclaim the lost or aborted thoughts and feelings and find a way to reintroduce them to the patient. The analyst helps the patient to reclaim, or perhaps to claim for the first time in their lives, these formerly unbearable aspects of themselves.

Z put her more expressive thoughts and more direct feelings into me and took inaction and mis-action as her road to self-protection and protection of the object. As Britton (1992) has noted, some patients cannot traverse the depressive position because of the conflicts between love and hate. When the hazards of knowledge about the self and the object emerge in the oedipal phase of development, some individuals do not want to risk the damage they may bring to their objects from this delicate and possibly dangerous mix of love, hate, and knowledge (Klein 1928, 1945).

For Z, to know the truth about her parents was to face all their flaws, weaknesses, and inability to choose her over their emotional problems. This brought on a phantasy of her own identity, her mind, and her thoughts as weapons that could disrupt any remaining shred of relationship for good. So, she elected to sacrifice herself to protect the other and to allow the object to live and speak in her place. The fragile balance and difficulties regarding separateness and difference that come out of love, hate, and knowledge were too much and could bring about disaster for Z and her objects. So, she found a way to eliminate these risks and herself in the process. Her lack of language skills was symptomatic of her lack of a self. I had to fill in the blanks because she made herself a blank.

It is a sign of real progress that more and more Z can come into a session and actually tell me what she thinks and feels about a topic, about herself, or about me, whether it is positive or negative. And the fallout of this new relational bravery is much less and much more survivable than before. Z has started to take ownership of herself and allows herself a say in her own life.

SUMMARY

This book has used extensive case reports to illustrate the complex nature of clinical practice in the field of modern psychoanalysis, practiced from a Modern Kleinian Therapy perspective. The author has taken the reader deep into the moment-to-moment and day-to-day reality of the contemporary psychoanalyst as he meets with a variety of patients both eager for help and unconsciously reluctant to change.

In particular, this book highlights the more turbulent and chaotic cases of individuals and couples who seek help but rapidly construct a very brittle and slippery transference environment in which numerous object relational conflicts are played out. These are the more difficult cases that often end abruptly and often barely get off the ground before collapsing. These are the patients struggling with more primitive and disturbing internal dilemmas that feel irresolvable or dangerous to try to change. This results in therapeutic standoffs and impasses as well as a variety of acting out patterns by the patient that easily draws the analyst into parallel enactments.

Throughout the book, the author used extensive and detailed case material to examine the importance of noticing, understanding, and making use of the counter-transference feelings and thoughts that are so common with the more volatile patient in the borderline and narcissistic spectrum as well as the more primitive neurotic patient. When not examined, these counter-transference feelings bring about cycles of enactment that parallel archaic acting out phantasies and behaviors in the patient. In the course of a psychoanalytic treatment there are always many clinical situations that create counter-transference pulls or invitations to participate in enactments of various degrees. In these projective identification based transferences, the patient is often successful in drawing the analyst into archaic object relational patterns of acting out. During these moments, the analyst must struggle to find a way to stay therapeutically balanced. The urge to rush to judgment with punitive, seductive, rejecting, controlling, or manipulative comments rationalized as interpretations must be managed. If these unavoidable counter-transference enactments are managed and studied, they can provide useful information about the patient's internal struggles and can show the way to making more helpful and more therapeutic interpretations. This counter-transference information can be utilized to make therapeutic interpretations and gradually help the patient face their unwanted aspects of self and other.

When trying to establish analytic contact with a patient, the patient often will make efforts to prevent, destabilize, or pervert that effort. The anxiety, aggression, love, or guilt that may be behind those resistive reactions can be better understood by closely monitoring one's own counter-transference anxieties, aggression, caring, or guilt as it appears in relation to the patient. By tracing the nature and course of his own feelings and thoughts in relationship to the patient, the analyst can regain firm footing in the analytic process and then offer the patient better insight into their warded off emotional crisis.

In each chapter, the author provided a great deal of detailed clinical material to illustrate the very complex dynamics that unfold when working with the more confusing and closed off patient, often in the pre-depressive or paranoid state of mind. In addition, the case reports show the often limiting and less than ideal clinical situations that the contemporary analyst must contend with. Often, we see very troubled and disturbed patients only once a week because of managed care restrictions, financial hardships, and the limits of family and employment. In these settings, some patients are seen on the analytic couch and others are seen sitting up. The level of pathology ranges from very fragmented borderline or narcissistic profiles to entrenched neurotic issues. Instead of trying to create various artificial distinctions between psychoanalysis and psychotherapy based on frequency of visits or use of couch, the author has demonstrated the benefits of practicing low frequency psychoanalysis from a Kleinian perspective, based on exploration of the transference and phantasy conflicts as the defining criteria.

This new clinical approach is Modern Kleinian Therapy, a therapeutic endeavor to reach troubled and troubling individuals who otherwise rarely find their way to healthy, sustaining attachment or reciprocal whole object relational harmony. Indeed, these patients usually experience the self and object as endangered, dangerous, out of reach, evil, and unknowable. They experience growth and change as desired but equally feared and avoided. These emotionally combative and near psychological collapse patients come to us and ask for but resist our help. Unfortunately, these same "last resort" and "final attempt" type cases are delivered to us with external restrictions of time and money, forcing us to work in low frequency hardship situations that often end abruptly and prematurely. Modern Kleinian Therapy is a model of effective psychoanalytic work that is constructed to offer relief and solution to deep, chronic internal conflicts under these less than optimal conditions by establishing and maintaining analytic contact and beginning to unravel, modify, and heal these turbulent and torn minds.

While some patients are unable or unwilling to step into the difficult and uncharted explorations that psychoanalytic work entails, the author has demonstrated how the effort to establish analytic contact with each individual can pay off and provide valuable support, containment, and growth for most patients under most circumstances. This is the essence of Modern Kleinian Therapy. The patient may display great resistance to the challenge of psychoanalytic treatment. They may subtly invite the analyst, through projective identification processes, to succumb to counter-transference despair and the idea that one must give up the psychoanalytic quest and settle for something less valuable or complex because of frequency, diagnosis, or length of treatment limitations. But, if the analyst maintains their faith in the process and keeps a hold of the hope of help and change regardless of how daunting the task may seem, we can offer the patient an opportunity for respite from their emotional nightmares and a chance to choose something more safe, secure, and pleasing. This is the goal and gift of Modern Kleinian Therapy.

In illustrating the Modern Kleinian Therapy method, the author has examined how the contemporary psychoanalyst is forced by a myriad of circumstances to treat many cases that involve low frequency, severe and chronic psychiatric issues, and involved and complicated transference states that often result in impasses or a sudden collapse of the entire treatment situation. The author has shown how even with couples, the fundamental technical elements of Kleinian technique can be helpful in establishing some degree of analytic contact even with these more troubled and turbulent patients.

Throughout this book, the reader has been introduced to a rich mixture of theory and clinical exploration within the moment-to-moment therapeutic situation by the use of a wealth of detailed verbatim case material. Every chapter has included a great deal of actual "he said, she said" clinical data that engages the reader to the material and brings the theory alive.

This book shows the therapeutic power the modern Kleinian approach can have with patients throughout the diagnostic spectrum. By attending to the interpersonal, transactional, and intrapsychic levels of transference and phantasy with consistent here-and-now and in-the-moment interpretation, the Kleinian method can be therapeutically successful with neurotic, borderline, narcissistic, or psychotic patients, whether being seen as individuals, couples, or families and at varied frequencies and duration. This volume shows that by making the goal of psychoanalytic treatment the gradual establishment of analyst contact, a broader range of patients can be helped and understood.

In conclusion, this collection of clinical tales is unique in providing the reader with a close up view of exactly how the Modern Kleinian analyst works with their most challenging cases and how even when these cases abort prematurely, there still can be a modest degree of psychological assistance provided if the technical goal of analytic contact is pursued at all times. Equally, the consistent effort to find and establish analytic contact can restore and energize treatments that seem to be stalled in some chaotic or fragmented manner. This means the Kleinian analyst is always mindful of the details regarding the total transference, the complete counter-transference, and the ever evolving unconscious and interpersonal threads of projective identification as they unfold in the moment-to-moment therapeutic exchange.

BIBLIOGRAPHY

Aguayo, J (2011) 'The Role of the Patient's Remembered History and Unconscious Past in the Evolution of Betty Joseph's 'Here and Now' Clinical Technique (1959–1989). *International Journal of Psychoanalysis*, 92: 1117–1136.

Ahumada, J (2004) 'Musings on Neville Symington's Clinical Presentation'. *International Journal of Psychoanalysis*, 85(2): 262–264.

Anderson, M (1999) 'The Pressure Toward Enactment and the Hatred of Reality'. *Journal of the American Psychoanalytic Association*, 47: 503–518.

Aronson, M and Scharfman, M (1992) *Psychotherapy: The Analytic Approach.* Jason Aronson, Northvale, NJ.

Arundale, J (2011) 'Here and Now Interpretations'. In J Arundale and D Bellman (Eds), *Transference and Countertransference: A Unifying Focus of Psychoanalysis* (pp. 27–43). Karnac, London.

Barugel, N (1984) 'El Papel de la Identificacion con el Objeto Atacado en el Desarrollo del Yo, Volume 6, Simposio de la Asociacion Psicoanalitica de Buenos Aires'. *Actas*, 120–133.

Bateman, A (1998) 'Thick- and Thin-Skinned Organizations and Enactment in Borderline and Narcissistic Disorders'. *International Journal of Psychoanalysis*, 79: 13–25.

Bion, W (1959) 'Attacks on Linking'. *International Journal of Psycho-Analysis*, 40: 308–315.

Bion, W (1962a) 'A Theory of Thinking'. *International Journal of Psycho-Analysis*, 43: 306–310.

Bion, W (1962b) *Learning from Experience* (p. 128). Heinemann, London.

Bion, W. (1963) *Elements of Psycho-analysis*. Basic Books, New York; Heinemann, London.

Blass, R (2011) 'On the Immediacy of Unconscious Truth'. *International Journal of Psychoanalysis*, 92: 1137–1157.

Britton, R. (1989) 'The Missing Link: Parental Sexuality in the Oedipus Complex'. In R Britton, M Feldman, E O'Shaughnessy, *The Oedipus Complex Today: Clinical Implications* (pp. 83–101). Karnac, London.

Britton, R (1992) 'The Oedipus Situation and the Depressive Position'. In R Anderson (Ed.), *Clinical Lectures on Klein and Bion* (pp. 34–45). Routledge, London.

Britton, R (1998) *Belief and Imagination: Explorations in Psychoanalysis*. Routledge, London.

Britton, R (2004) 'Narcissistic Disorders in Clinical Practice'. *Journal of Analytical Psychology*, 49(4): 477–490.

Britton, R (2008) 'Narcissism in Narcissistic Disorders'. In J Steiner (Ed.), *Rosenfeld in Retrospect* (pp. 22–34). Routledge, London.

Brown, L (1987) 'Borderline Personality Organization and the Transition to the Depressive Position'. In J Grotstein, M Solomon, J Lang (Eds), *The Borderline Patient: Emerging Concepts in Diagnosis, Psychodynamics, and Treatment, Volume 1*. Analytic Press, London.

Caper, R (1997) 'A Mind of One's Own'. *International Journal of Psychoanalysis*, 78: 265–278.

Caper, R (1998) *A Mind of One's Own*. Routledge, London.

Carey, F (2002) 'Singular Attention: Some Once-a-Week Therapies'. In B Bishop, A Foster, J Klein, and V O'Connell (Eds), *Challenges to Practice, Volume 1* (pp. 43–59). Karnac, London.

Cartwright, D (2010) *Containing States of Mind: Exploring Bion's Container Model in Psychoanalytic Psychotherapy*. Routledge, London.

Cherry, S, Cabaniss, D, Forand, N, Haywood, D, and Roose, S (2004) 'Psychoanalytic Practice in the Early Postgraduate Years'. *Journal of the American Psychoanalytic Association*, 52(3): 851–871.

Chessick, R (1994) 'What Brings About Change in Psychoanalytic Treatment?'. *Psychoanalytic Review*, 81(2): 279–300.

Clarkin, J, Yeomans, F, and Kernberg, O (1999) *Psychotherapy for Borderline Personality*. Wiley Press, New York.

Clarkin, J, Yeomans, F, and Kernberg, O (2006) *Psychotherapy for Borderline Personality: Focusing on Object Relations*. American Psychiatric Publishing, Washington, DC.

Cooper, S (2010) *A Disturbance in the Field: Essays in Transference–Countertransference Engagement*. Taylor & Francis, New York.

Daniel, P (1992) 'Child Analysis and the Concept of Unconscious Phantasy'. In R Anderson (Ed.), *New Library of Psychoanalysis, Volume 14: Clinical Lectures on Klein and Bion* (pp. 14–23). Routledge, London.

De Forster, Z (2006) 'Psychoanalytical Psychotherapy for/with Couples: Theoretical Basis and Clinical Utility'. *International Journal of Psychoanalysis*, 87(1): 255–257.

Dicks, H (1967) *Marital Tensions: Clinical Studies toward a Psychological Theory of Interaction*. Routledge, London.

Eizirik, C (2010) 'Panel Report: Analytic Practice: Convergences and Divergences'. *International Journal of Psychoanalysis*, 91: 371–375.

Etchegoyen, R (1991) *The Fundamentals of Psychoanalytic Technique*. Karnac, London.

Feldman, M (1992) 'Splitting and Projective Identification'. In R Anderson (Ed.), *Clinical Lectures on Klein and Bion* (pp. 74–88). Routledge, London.

Feldman, M (1994) 'Projective Identification in Phantasy and Enactment'. *Journal of the American Psychoanalytic Association*, 56: 431–453.

Feldman, M (2004) 'Supporting Psychic Change: Betty Joseph'. In E Hargreaves and A Varchevker (Eds), *In Pursuit of Psychic Change: The Betty Joseph Workshop* (pp. 20–37). Brunner-Routledge, London.

Feldman, M (2009) *Doubt, Conviction, and the Analytic Process*. Routledge, London.

Feldman, M (2011) "A Day with Michael Feldman", Weekend Conference at San Francisco Center for Psychoanalysis, 12 November.

Feldman, M and Paola, H (1994) 'An Investigation into the Psychoanalytic Concept of Envy'. *International Journal of Psycho-Analysis*, 75: 217–234.

Feldman, M and Spillius, E (1989) *The New Library of Psychoanalysis, Volume 9: Psychic Equilibrium and Psychic Change: Selected Papers of Betty Joseph*, Eds M Feldman and E Bott Spillius. Tavistock/Routledge, London and New York.

Friedman, L (2008) 'Is there Life After Enactment? The Idea of a Patient's Proper Work'. *Journal of the American Psychoanalytic Association*, 56: 431–453.

Gill, M (1979) 'The Analysis of the Transference'. *Journal of the American Psychoanalytic Association*, 27: 263–288.

Gill, M (1994) *Psychoanalysis in Transition: A Personal View*. Analytic Press, New York.

Gold, S (1983) 'Projective Identification: The Container and Reverie as Concepts in Applied Psychoanalysis'. *British Journal of Medical Psychology*, 56: 279–285.

Grotstein, J (1985) *Yearbook of Psychoanalysis and Psychotherapy, Volume 1: A Proposed Revision of the Psychoanalytic Concept of the Death Instinct*, Ed. R J Langs (pp. 209–326). Lawrence Erlbaum Associates, Hillsdale, NJ.

Grotstein, J (2009) *But at the Same Time on Another Level: Psychoanalytic Theory and Technique in the Kleinian/Bionian Mode, Volume 1*. Karnac, London.

Hargreaves, E and Varchevker, A (2004) *In Pursuit of Psychic Change: The Betty Joseph Workshop*. Routledge, London.

Hinshelwood, R (2004) Contrasting Clinical Techniques: A British Kleinian, Contemporary Freudian and Latin American Kleinian Discuss Clinical Material'. *International Journal of Psychoanalysis*, 85(5): 1257–1260.

Joseph, B (1978) 'Different Types of Anxiety and Their Handling in the Analytic Situation'. *International Journal of Psycho-Analysis*, 59: 223–227.

Joseph, B (1983) 'On Understanding and not Understanding: Some Technical Issues'. *International Journal of Psycho-Analysis*, 64: 291–298.

Joseph, B (1982) 'Addiction to Near-Death'. *International Journal of Psycho-Analysis*, 63: 449–456.

Joseph, B (1985) 'Transference: The Total Situation'. *International Journal of Psycho-Analysis*, 66: 447–454.

Joseph, B (1987) 'Projective Identification: Clinical Aspects'. In J Sandler (Ed.), *Projection, Identification, Projective Identification* (pp. 65–76). International Universities Press, Madison, CT.

Joseph, B (1988) 'Object Relations in Clinical Practice'. *Psychoanalytic Quarterly*, 57: 626–642.

Joseph, B (1989) *Psychic Equilibrium and Psychic Change: Selected Papers of Betty Joseph*, Eds M Feldman and E Bott Spillius. The New Library of Psychoanalysis, Tavistock/Routledge, London and New York.

Joseph, B (1997) 'The Pursuit of Insight and Psychic Change', Conference on Psychic Structure and Psychic Change, University College, London.

Joseph, B (2000) 'Agreeableness as Obstacle'. *International Journal of Psychoanalysis*, 81(4): 641–649.

Joseph, B (2003) 'Ethics and Enactment'. *Psychoana Eur*, 57: 147–153.

Kernberg, O (1992) 'Psychopathic, Paranoid and Depressive Transferences'. *International Journal of Psycho-Analysis*, 73: 13–28.

Kernberg, O (2011) 'Limitations to the Capacity to Love'. *International Journal of Psychoanalysis*, 92: 1501–1515.

Klein, M (1928) 'Early Stages of the Oedipus Conflict'. *International Journal of Psycho-Analysis*, 9: 167–180.

Klein, M (1931) 'A Contribution to the Theory of Intellectual Inhibition'. *International Journal of Psycho-Analysis*, 12: 206–218.

Klein, M (1935) 'A Contribution to the Psychogenesis of Manic-Depressive States'. In *The Writings of Melanie Klein, Volume 1: Love, Guilt, and Reparation and Other Works 1921–1945* (1975, pp. 262–289). Free Press, London.

Klein, M (1940) 'Mourning and its Relation to Manic-Depressive States'. *International Journal of Psycho-Analysis*, 21: 125–153.

Klein, M (1945) 'The Oedipus Complex in the Light of Early Anxieties'. In *The Writings of Melanie Klein, Volume 1: Love, Guilt, and Reparation and Other Works 1921–1945* (1975, pp. 370–419). Hogarth Press, London.

Klein, M (1946) 'Notes on Some Schizoid Mechanisms'. *International Journal of Psycho-Analysis*, 27: 99–110.

Klein, M (1952a) 'The Origins of Transference'. *International Journal of Psycho-Analysis*, 33: 433–438.

Klein, M (1952b) 'Some Theoretical Conclusions Regarding the Emotional Life of the Infant'. In M Masud and R Khan (Eds), *The International Psycho-Analytical Library, Volume 104: Envy and Gratitude and Other Works 1946–1963* (1975, pp. 61–93). The Hogarth Press and Institute of Psycho-Analysis, London.

Klein, M (1957) *The Writings of Melanie Klein, Volume 3: Envy and Gratitude*. Hogarth Press, London, 1975.

Klein, M (1963) *On the Sense of Loneliness, in Our Adult World and Its Roots in Infancy and Other Essays*. Heinemann, London.

Luborsky, L (1984) *Principles of Psychoanalytic Psychotherapy: A Manual for Supportive Expressive Treatment*. Basic Books, New York.

Markman, H (2010) 'In this Room at This Time'. *Fort Da*, 16(2): 9–21.

Mason, A (2011) 'Projective Identification'. In E Spillius and E O'Shaughnessy (Eds), *Projective Identification: The Fate of a Concept*. Routledge, London.

Newman, K (1988) 'Counter-Transference: Its Role in Facilitating the Use of the Object'. *Annuals of Psychoanalysis*, 16: 251–285.

Ogden, T (1991) 'Analyzing the Matrix of Transference'. *International Journal of Psycho-Analysis*, 72: 593–605.

O'Shaughnessy, E (1989) 'Enclaves and Excursions'. *International Journal of Psycho-Analysis*, 73: 603–611.

O'Shaughnessy, E (1992) 'Clinical Experiences of Projective Identification'. In *New Library of Psychoanalysis, Volume 14: Clinical Lectures on Klein and Bion* (pp. 59–73). Routledge, London.

Perlow, M (1995) *Understanding Mental Objects*. New Library of Psychoanalysis, Routledge, London and New York.

Pick, I (1992) 'The Emergence of Early Object Relations in the Psychoanalytic Setting'. In R Anderson (Ed.), *Clinical Lectures on Klein and Bion* (pp. 24–33). Routledge, London.

Racker, H (1957) 'The Meanings and Uses of Countertransference'. *Psychoanalytic Quarterly*, 26: 303–357.

Rather, L (2001) 'Collaborating with the Unconscious Other: The Analysand's Capacity for Creative Thinking'. *International Journal of Psychoanalysis*, 82(3): 515–531.

Rosenfeld, H (1971) 'A Clinical Approach to the Psychoanalytic Theory of the Life and Death Instincts: An Investigation into the Aggressive Aspects of Narcissism'. *International Journal of Psycho-Analysis*, 52: 169–178.

Rosenfeld, H (1975) 'Negative Therapeutic Reaction'. In P Giovacchini (Ed.), *Tactics and Techniques in Psychoanalytic Psychotherapy, Volume 2*. Jason Aronson, New York.

Rosenfeld, H (1979) 'Difficulties in the Psychoanalysis of Borderline Patients'. In J LeBoit and A Capponi (Eds), *Advances in Psychotherapy of the Borderline Patient* (pp. 203–204). Jason Aronson, New York.

Rosenfeld, H (1983) 'Primitive Object Relations and Mechanisms'. *International Journal of Psycho-Analysis*, 64: 261–267.

Rosenfeld, H (1987) *New Library of Psychoanalysis, Volume 1: Impasse and Interpretation: Therapeutic and Anti-therapeutic Factors in the Psychoanalytic Treatment of Psychotic, Borderline, and Neurotic Patients*. Tavistock, London.

Rosenfeld, H (1990) 'Contributions to the Psychopathology of Psychotic States: The Importance of Projective Identification in the Ego Structure and the Object Relations of the Psychotic

Patient'. In E. Bott Spillius (Ed.), *Melanie Klein Today, Volume 1: Mainly Theory*. Routledge, London.

Roth, P (2001) 'Mapping the Landscape: Levels of Transference Interpretation'. *International Journal of Psychoanalysis*, 82(3): 533–543.

Rusbridger, R (2004) 'Elements of the Oedipus complex: A Kleinian Account'. *International Journal of Psychoanalysis*, 85(3): 731–747.

Safa-Gerard, D (1998) 'Bearable and Unbearable Guilt: A Kleinian Perspective'. *Psychoanalytic Quarterly*, 67: 351–378.

Salzberger-Wittenberg, I (1970) *Psychoanalytic Insight and Relationships: A Kleinian Approach*. Routledge, London.

Sandler, J (1976) 'Countertransference and Role-Responsiveness'. *International Review of Psycho-Analysis*, 3: 43–47.

Sandler, J (1984) 'On Interpretation and Holding'. *Scandinavian Psychoanalytic Review*, 7: 161–176.

Schafer, R (1994) 'The Contemporary Kleinians of London'. *Psychoanalytic Quarterly*, 63: 409–432.

Schafer, R (1995) 'Aloneness in the Countertransference'. *Psychoanalytic Quarterly*, 64: 496–516.

Schafer, R (1997) *The Contemporary Kleinians of London*. International Universities Press, Madison, CT.

Searles, H (1986) *My Work with Borderline Patients*. Jason Aronson. New York.

Segal, H (1962) 'The Curative Factors in Psychoanalysis'. In *The Work of Hanna Segal* (pp. 69–80). Jason Aronson, New York.

Segal, H (1974) *An Introduction to the Work of Melanie Klein*. Basic Books, New York.

Segal, H (1975) 'A Psychoanalytic Approach to the Treatment of Schizophrenia'. In M Lader (Ed.), *Studies in Schizophrenia*. Headly, Ashford.

Segal, H (1977a) 'Counter-transference'. *International Journal of Psycho-Analysis*, 6: 31–37.

Segal, H (1977b) 'Psychoanalytic Dialogue: Kleinian Theory Today'. *Journal of the American Psychoanalytic Association*, 25: 363–370.

Segal, H (1981) *The Work of Hanna Segal: A Kleinian Approach to Clinical Practice*. Jason Aronson, New York.

Segal, H (1993) 'On the Clinical Usefulness of the Concept of Death Instinct'. *International Journal of Psycho-Analysis*, 74: 55–61.

Segal, H (1997a) 'Some Implications of Melanie Klein's Work: Emergence from Narcissism'. In J Steiner (Ed.), *Psychoanalysis, Literature, and War* (pp. 75–85). Routledge, London.

Segal, H (1997b) *Psychoanalysis, Literature, and War: Papers 1972–95*, Ed. J Steiner. Routledge, London.

Segal, H and Britton, R (1981) 'Interpretation and Primitive Psychic Processes: A Kleinian View'. *Psychoanalytic Inquiry*, 1(2): 267–277.

Spillius, E (1983) 'Some Developments from the Work of Melanie Klein'. *International Journal of Psycho-Analysis*, 64: 321–332.

Spillius, E (1988) *Melanie Klein Today. Developments in Theory and Practice*. Ed. E Bott Spillius. The New Library of Psychoanalysis, General Ed. D Tuckett. Routledge, London and New York.

Spillius, E (1992) 'Clinical Experiences of Projective Identification'. In R Anderson (Ed.), *Clinical Lectures on Klein and Bion* (pp. 59–73). Routledge, London.

Spillius, E (1993) 'Varieties of Envious Experiences'. *International Journal of Psycho-Analysis*, 74: 1199–1212.

Spillius, E (1994) 'Developments in Kleinian Thought: Overview and Personal View'. *Psychoanalytic Inquiry*, *14*(3): 324–364.

Spillius, E (2007) *Encounters with Melanie Klein: Selected Papers of Elizabeth Spillius*, Eds P Roth and R Rusbridger. New Library of Psychoanalysis, Routledge, London.

Spivak, A (2011) 'The Interpretive Act'. In M Diamond and C Christian (Eds), *The Second Century of Psychoanalysis*. Karnac, London.

Steiner, J (1979) 'The Border Between the Paranoid-Schizoid and the Depressive Positions in the Borderline Patient'. *British Journal of Medical Psychology*, *52*: 285–391.

Steiner, J (1984) 'Some Reflections on the Analysis of Transference: A Kleinian View'. *Psychoanalytic Inquiry*, *4*(3): 443–463.

Steiner, J (1987) 'The Interplay Between Pathological Organizations and the Paranoid-Schizoid and Depressive Positions'. *International Journal of Psycho-Analysis*, *68*: 69–80.

Steiner, R (1989) 'Review of *Some Observations on Projection, Identification, Projective Identification*: Edited by Joseph Sandler. London: Karnac Books. 1988'. *International Journal of Psycho-Analysis*, *70*: 727–735.

Steiner, J (1990) 'Pathological Organizations as Obstacles to Mourning: The Role of Unbearable Guilt'. *International Journal of Psycho-Analysis*, *71*: 87–94.

Steiner, J (1992) 'The Equilibrium Between the Paranoid and the Depressive Position'. In R Anderson (Ed.), *Clinical Lectures on Klein and Bion* (pp. 46–58). Routledge, London.

Steiner, J (1993) *New Library of Psychoanalysis, Volume 19: Psychic Retreats: Pathological Organizations in Psychotic, Neurotic, and Borderline Patients*. Routledge, London and New York.

Steiner, J (1994) 'Patient-Centered and Analyst-Centered Interpretations: Some Implications of Containment and Countertransference'. *Psychoanalytic Inquiry*, *14*(3): 406–422.

Steiner, J (1996) 'The Aim of Psychoanalysis in Theory and in Practice'. *International Journal of Psychoanalysis*, *77*: 1073–1083.

Steiner, J (2000) 'Containment, Enactment and Communication'. *International Journal of Psychoanalysis*, *81*(2): 245–255.

Steiner, J (2001) 'Response'. *International Journal of Psychoanalysis*, *82*(1): 173–174.

Steiner, J (2004) 'Gaze, Dominance and Humiliation in the Schreber Case'. *International Journal of Psychoanalysis*, *85*(2): 269–284.

Steiner, J (2006) 'Interpretive Enactments and the Analytic Setting'. *International Journal of Psychoanalysis*, *87*(2): 315–320.

Steiner, J (2008) 'The Repetition Compulsion, Envy, and the Death Instinct'. In P Roth and A Lemma (Eds), *Envy and Gratitude Revisited*. Karnac, London.

Steiner, J (2011a) *Seeing and Being Seen: Emerging from a Psychic Retreat*. Routledge, London.

Steiner, J (2011b) 'The Impostor Revisited'. *Psychoanalytic Quarterly*, LXXX(4): 1061–1071.

Sweet, A (2010) 'Paranoia and Psychotic Process: Some Clinical Applications of Projective Identification in Psychoanalytic Psychotherapy'. *American Journal of Psychotherapy*, *64*(4): 339–358.

Waddell, M (2002) *Inside Lives: Psychoanalysis and the Growth of the Personality*. Karnac, London.

Waska, R (2002) *Primitive Experiences of Loss: Working with the Paranoid-Schizoid Patient*. Karnac, London.

Waska, R (2004) *Projective Identification: The Kleinian Interpretation*. Brunner/Routledge, London.

Waska, R (2005) *Real People, Real Problems, Real Solutions: The Kleinian Approach to Difficult Patients*. Brunner/Routledge, London.

Waska, R (2006) *The Danger of Change: The Kleinian Approach with Patients who Experience Progress as Trauma*. Brunner/Routledge, London.

Waska, R (2007) *The Concept of Analytic Contact: A Kleinian Approach to Reaching the Hard to Reach Patient*. Brunner/Routledge, London.

Waska, R (2010a) *Treating Severe Depressive and Persecutory Anxieties States: Using Analytic Contact to Transform the Unbearable*. Karnac, London.

Waska, R (2010b) *Love, Hate, and Knowledge: The Kleinian Method of Analytic Contact and the Future of Psychoanalysis*. Karnac, London.

Waska, R (2010c) *The Modern Kleinian Approach to Psychoanalysis: Clinical Illustrations*. Jason Aronson, New York.

Waska, R (2010d) *Selected Theoretical and Clinical Issues in Psychoanalytic Psychotherapy: A Modern Kleinian Approach to Analytic Contact*. Novoscience, New York.

Waska, R (2011a) *Moments of Uncertainty in Psychoanalytic Practice: Interpreting Within the Matrix of Projective Identification, Counter-Transference, and Enactment*. Columbia University Press, in press.

Waska, R (2011b) *The Total Transference and the Complete Counter-Transference: The Kleinian Psychoanalytic Approach With More Disturbed Patients*. Jason Aronson, in press.

Waska, R (2012) *Success and Failure in Psychoanalysis: Klein in the Trenches*. Rodopi Press, in press.

Williams, P (2010) *Invasive Objects: Minds Under Siege*. Routledge, New York.

Winnicott, D (1968) 'Playing: Its Theoretical Status in the Clinical Situation'. *International Journal of Psycho-Analysis*, 49: 591–599.

Winnicott, D (1974) 'Fear of Breakdown'. *International Review of Psycho-Analysis*, 1: 103–107.

Zavattini, G (1988) 'The Other One of Me, That is My Other Half: Reflections on Projective Identification'. *Rivista di Psicoanalisi*, 34(2): 348–374.

INDEX

projective identification 195, 204;
Y's case 14
Etchegoyen, R. 104, 165, 167

fathers: Abbott's case 87, 94, 95; Dennis's
case 39–40, 41–2, 43, 48; Fran's case
196, 198, 199, 200; F's case 156–7;
Larry's case 148; Luke's case 184; Tom's
case 141; Z's case 206; *see also* parental
object
fear 56
Feldman, Michael 8, 32–3, 37, 48, 115,
178, 190
forgiveness 52, 125, 134, 180
free association 148
Freud, Sigmund 50, 149, 166, 167
Friedman, L. 116
fusion 42, 47, 106, 170

Gill, Merton 8, 115, 190, 191
"give & take" cycle 6
God 18
good object 47–8, 56–7, 64, 72, 165–6,
171, 178, 179–80; *see also* ideal object;
object relations
grandiosity 8–9, 14, 135
grief 5, 72, 125, 139, 170, 181; avoidance
of 195; depressive position 159; Joe's
case 194; new ways of thinking 187
Grotstein, J. 2, 38, 185–6
guilt 7, 25, 34–5, 167, 194; Abbott's case
90; analyst's own 70, 71, 79; avoidance
of 195; counter-transference 82; couples
treatment 52, 101, 102, 103, 106;
depressive resistance to 86; F's case 156,
158, 159, 166, 168; Joe's case 191, 192;
Larry's case 147; Luke's case 183, 189;
new ways of thinking 187; ownership of
anger 96; parental pressure 173;
persecutory 150, 155; resistance 212;
superego 165; termination of therapy
138

hate 23, 56, 140; analytic contact 113;
conflicts around 1, 48, 84, 149, 152,
184, 196, 209; counter-transference
seductions 82; couples treatment 101;
F's case 165; infantile experiences 81;
Joe's case 192; phantasies 68, 205;
projective identification cycles 194; Z's
case 210
helplessness 28, 96, 122, 145, 159, 165,
179, 195

Hinshelwood, R. 168
hopelessness 39, 96, 145, 156, 159,
195
hostility 103, 171, 178; *see also*
aggression

ideal object 13, 15, 57, 163, 179, 180,
204; *see also* good object
ideal self 14
individuation 5, 47, 100, 181
infantile experiences 81
inferiority, sense of 26, 136
insecurities 27, 28, 29
internal objects 6, 65–6, 160, 165, 171,
186; *see also* object relations
interpretation 48, 50, 152, 165, 180, 213;
Abbott's case 90, 91, 95; classic Kleinian
method 166; counter-transference 69,
85, 102; couples treatment 60–1, 66, 67,
101, 110, 120, 125, 127–8, 134, 136–7;
Dan's case 32–3; Dennis's case 42;
embedded enactments 116–17, 120,
131; emphasis on 23–4; Fran's case 198;
Larry's case 147; new ways of thinking
187; of the past 37, 49; total transference
202; transference anxiety 95
intrapsychic conflict 50, 100–1, 114, 115

jealousy 27–8, 52, 79, 85
Joseph, Betty 21, 48–9, 66–7, 68, 115,
171, 190; compliance 75; primitive
defenses 153; projective identification
42, 48, 167, 209; transference 65, 185,
187; unconscious phantasy 197

Kernberg, O. 8, 143
Klein, Melanie 1, 50, 167, 209;
abandonment 179; child development
105; couples treatment 100; death
instinct 149; infantile phantasies 81,
196; internal objects 165; oedipal
conflicts 206; transference 143;
unconscious processes 166
Kleinians of London 8, 37, 48
knowledge 23, 68, 106, 137, 152; analyst's
attempt to introduce 116; analytic
contact 113; conflicts around 1, 48, 84,
134, 149, 184, 196, 209; counter-
transference seductions 82; couples
treatment 101; evacuation of 207; F's
case 165; infantile experiences 81; of
patient's internal world 168; projective
identification cycles 194; Z's case 210

Made in the USA
Columbia, SC
31 October 2020